Making It Work

Other Books by Alan Weiss

The Innovation Formula: How Organizations Turn Change into Opportunity (with Michel Robert) 1988

Managing for Peak Performance: A Guide to the Power (and Pitfalls) of Personal Style 1989

Monographs

The Revolution around Us: Human Resource Development in the 80s 1983

Surviving and Succeeding in the Political Organization 1978

MAKING IT WORK

Turning Strategy into Action
Throughout Your Organization

Alan Weiss

HarperBusiness
A Division of HarperCollinsPublishers

International Standard Book Number: 0-88730-412-5

Library of Congress Catalog Card Number: 90-4851

Printed in the United States of America

Library of Congress Cataloging-in-Publication Data

Weiss, Alan, 1946–
    Making it work: Turning strategy into action throughout your organization/ Alan Weiss
        p.   cm.
    Includes bibliographical references and index.
    ISBN 0-88730-412-5
    1. Strategic planning. 2. Organization. I. Title
    HD30.28.W38   1990
    658.4′012—dc20   90-4851
                                                                                          CIP

90 91 92 93 CR/HC 9 8 7 6 5 4 3 2 1

For Danielle and Jason, the world's greatest kids

Contents

Acknowledgments

My sincere gratitude to the clients of Summit Consulting Group, Inc. for their sharing and openness. Particular thanks to Art Strohmer and his colleagues at Merck—small wonder it's America's Most Admired Company for so many years in a row. Thanks also to Susan Siegel and Keith Darcy at Marine Midland Bank, Jim Coakley at GTE, Michel Robert at Decision Processes International, Ron Gartner at Mercedes-Benz, and my editors at Harper & Row, who have been wonderful partners through three books.

My deep appreciation goes to Maria, for her companionship, tolerance, and keen sense of taste, and to L. T. Weiss for his unerring editorial assistance.

Introduction

I've been observing large and small organizations for two decades. And despite changing times, changing mores, and changing personnel, there has been a perverse kind of reverse alchemy that seems to grip a great many senior managers. They seem to have found the secret for turning gold into lead—turning excellent strategies into woefully incompetent performances. But unlike the alchemists of old, who labored over cauldrons of strange mixtures while uttering even stranger incantations, we can identify the ingredients of the modern, unfortunate reverse alchemy.

For many years I was in a position to observe at close hand an international management training firm which provided its clients with a unique, practical approach to strategy formulation. Its clients included the likes of Dow Chemical, a federal reserve bank, Dow Corning, and Fuji Photo. Yet the organization itself rarely achieved its growth goals, suffered high levels of turnover and discontent, and was eventually sold while in serious financial straits.

I tried to understand what had gone wrong. During the final 15 years of its independent existence, the firm had spent massive amounts of time and energy on its *own* strategy. The very people helping Kawasaki Steel formulate its strategy were formulating their own. I know of no organization that has spent as much—in quality *and* quantity—in trying to create its future. Conservatively, the strategy was consistently sound; liberally, it was occasionally brilliant; but continually, it failed. And the more it failed, the more the firm tried to fix the formulation process.

In working with over 300 organizations on five continents, I've discovered that the failure of strategies is most often—yes, *most* often—not the result of poorly conceived strategies but rather the result of poor implementation. Or, to be more precise, it is the result of a weak connection between the strategic vision—the "what" the organization is to become—and the implementation—the "how" of the organization's approach to attain that vision.

Scores of books that hit the shelves proclaim the best methods for formulating a strategy—matrices and models, formulas and theorems, old hat and new wave. And there are high-priced consultants, esoteric courses, and fad-of-the-month clubs as well. Surprisingly a great deal of this advice is actually quite useful. There are many methods for setting strategy just as there is a multitude of organizational settings requiring distinctive approaches.

But all of these approaches share the purity of the formulation process; that is, they are challenging cerebral exercises, general-staff-type intellectualizing far removed from the mud, bullets, and enemies of the front.

Strategy formulation devoid of planning for its implementation is like learning all the chess openings but never playing a game or conceptualizing the great American novel but never sitting down at a keyboard.

No responsible executive has the right to engage in strategy formulation unless he or she also engages in the planning of strategy implementation and *actively participates* in that implementation. The best organizations—and I've worked with Merck, Johnson & Johnson, Hewlett-Packard, *The New York Times*, Citibank, Caterpillar Tractor, Mercedes-Benz, and scores of others—have excellent strategies *and* excellent implementation capabilities. I've found that there are clear techniques, traits, and processes that these organizations consciously or unconsciously apply to realize their vision. Similarly, I've worked with other firms—and they are in the hundreds—which are sublimely unaware of these techniques, choose not to utilize them or, worst of all, *think* they're using them but are not. ("Of course we communicate our strategy—every member of the executive committee receives a three-ring binder." "We've always prepared to form an alliance, as long as we get the better of it.")

Organizations—and I've found that this applies to public and private, large and small, the multinational giant and the local PTA—will inevitably shoot themselves in their feet unless they have sound strategies. But a fine strategy without a practical implementation plan will simply result in a shot in the same foot with a silver bullet. It's no less painful, and the blood quickly overwhelms the elegance. And what we're seeing today with unnerving frequency is the elegant strategy getting mugged in the streets of organizational reality. Or, in a perverse twist of ancient alchemy, modern executives are unwittingly allowing golden strategies to turn into lead and making their organizations often sluggish and sometimes poisoned.

It's time that executives and all organizational leaders took their best-laid plans and led the way to making them work—in fact and not just on paper. That kind of pragmatic strategy implementation is underway today in progressive organizations all over the world. The techniques that can make it happen are discussed in the following pages. The volition to apply them lies with you.

East Greenwich, RI
December 1989

Making It Work

1

The What, Why, and How of Strategy: The Fat Lady Sometimes Sings First

Once upon a time a pet food company was engaged in a highly competitive battle for the huge dog food market. Its top executives adapted a careful strategy, one that had worked countless times before, the development of a feeding regimen based on a dog's age and relative activity. The premise was that the food would meet the varying nutrition requirements of the dog as it progressed from frantic puppyhood through active adolescence to mature middle age and quiet later years. If a customer accepted the idea at the outset, then a brand loyalty could be expected for the duration of the dog's life.

The company, we'll call it Rover, Inc., launched its new approach to "lifetime canine nutrition" with great fanfare, using innovative techniques in its promotion, packaging, and dealer incentives. However, after a brief sales surge, Rover executives were horrified to see their market share *decline* by 15 percent, with no plateau in sight. Rover's president, a crusty no-nonsense type who was perennially named "one of America's toughest," convened a meeting to find out, naturally, who was to blame for this fiasco.

"All right," he bellowed, "who blew it?"

Drenched in perspiration, the marketing vice president rose unsteadily to his feet. "I can only assure you," he stuttered, "that we used customer surveys and field tests of buyers that were unprecedented in their sophistication and scope. Our techniques were exactly congruent with our strategy."

With that, the president's glare turned to the vice president of sales. She responded gamely. "We provided imaginative packaging displays and rebate offers and trained the field force in the types of questions in issues the new nutrition strategy called for. There was nothing more we could have done to support this product."

Feeling the water sloshing at his feet, the vice president of research and development rose unsteadily. "Now wait a minute. We adhered to our strategy perfectly. We were able to place unprecedented combinations of nutrients and supplements into our formula. No one is even close to us on this."

1

"Well, if everything followed the strategy so precisely," screamed the president of Rover, Inc., "then why isn't the stuff selling?"

A hand appeared in the air in the rear of the room. It belonged to a lowly management trainee who had been invited to attend a "crisis" meeting as part of his development. Acknowledged in a room in which no one else wanted the floor, he said, "I think I know what the problem is, sir."

"You do! Well, what is it!?"

"The dogs," reported the trainee matter-of-factly, "just don't like the stuff."*

For the past several years my colleagues and I have worked with organizations of all sizes, shapes, and intents in the area of successful *implementation* of strategy. It is our belief that most organizations develop potentially effective strategies and that all organizations are capable of developing such strategies. Matrices, models, and maps abound, all with the intent of assisting top management in setting, establishing, and formulating strategy. Often, simple and plain common sense provides the best template of all in creating an effective strategy. But if the executive team feels it isn't quite up to the job, there is a plethora of consulting firms, extension programs, and business school professors who are anxiously waiting for the chance to help. (Although we don't question the wisdom of getting an occasional outsider's view of corporate strategy, we wonder just what the shareholders are paying top management for if the job doesn't include being capable of establishing and implementing a strategy without outside help.)

There are two elements in successful strategy. Pure and simple, they are

1. What do we want to achieve?
2. How do we intend to do it?

The problem is the connection between points 1 and 2. There are very few sources, and certainly even fewer maps and matrices, that explain how to proceed from establishing *what* the organization's future should look like to *how* to implement that unique vision. On the assumption that a straight line is still the shortest route between any two points, let's try to make it as simple as possible. In figure 1.1 are the only combinations of the four basic relationships between the *what* and the *how* that can exist.[1]

The basic relationships are as follows:

Category 1. These are organizations that establish clear strategies and implement them well; that is, they are strong in both the *what* and the *how* dimensions. It is simple to cite such organizations. At this writing, they

---

*I'm not sure of the origin of this story, which I've embellished here, but I'm of the belief that it might have begun with Russell Ackoff of Wharton—professor, author, and master storyteller.
[1]See *Top Management Strategy: What It Is and How It Works*, by Benjamin B. Tregoe and John W. Zimmerman, Simon and Schuster, New York, 1980, pages 20–22, and *The Strategist CEO: How Visionary Executives Build Organizations*, by Michel Robert, Quorum, Westport, Conn., 1988, pages 22–24, for elaborations of this model.

What to do

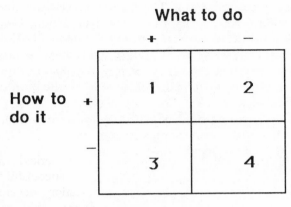

Figure 1.1

include Merck & Co., Johnson & Johnson, American Airlines, Honda, Citibank, and Boeing. The question to be answered, of course, is exactly how they consistently achieve category 1—how *do* they translate their strategies into operating realities?

Category 2. These organizations operate well enough but don't have coherent strategies. They are lulled into a false sense of well-being by short-term profits and operating efficiencies, but they are vulnerable to abrupt changes in their markets and unexpected events in the environment. They generally lack resiliency. American car manufacturers suffered when a combination of the fuel crisis, intensified foreign competition, and heightened customer awareness of such issues as safety created turbulence in an industry accustomed to dictating preferences to the buyer. Organizations in category 2 aren't implementing any strategies—they are simply trying to do as well as or better than they did yesterday.

Category 3. This is a category of organizations that have well-defined and carefully thought-out strategies but have not demonstrated the ability to successfully implement those strategies. In the high-tech field, for example, it's common to encounter an organization with the clear vision to establish itself as the "leader in microchip miniaturization and capacity" but which doesn't have the foggiest idea of how to go about doing it, *even though its technology, expertise, and capitalization may be more than sufficient for the task.* People Express, Laker Airways, Coleco toys, and Federal Express's Zap Mail are examples of the right destination but the wrong road to get there.

Category 4. This category belongs to those whom the American philosopher George Santayana might have had in mind when he defined fanatics as "those who lose sight of their goals and consequently redouble their efforts." These are the organizations—Braniff Airlines, Penn Central when it was still in the railroad business, Wickes prior to Chapter 11—that have no cogent idea of where they should be going and also don't have the capacity to implement well. The difference between category 2 and category 4 organizations is that the former have in place systems, procedures, cultures, and values that provide for successful implementation of *whatever* is desired (or left to default). A category 4 organization probably couldn't successfully implement even an excellent strategy, much less a vague or uncertain one. (Organizations often flirt with this category—Chrysler paid a visit, as have the City of New York, Sears, and others.)

The benefit of a strong strategy is readily apparent: a direction and a vision are established to lead the organization toward, one hopes, its continuing destiny. But the benefits of strong implementation of strategy can be subtle. Aside from creating an expeditious route to that destiny, the stronger an organization's ability to implement strategy, the more that organization can tolerate a vague and imperfect strategy. "Self-correcting" mechanisms will be in place to hone, refine, and clarify the strategy as the organization seeks to implement it. But if the implementation abilities are not strong, these self-correctors will not function, and the organization will struggle with a rudder that seems unable to hold a true course.

Sears, the giant retailer, is one example of this phenomenon. Sears has in place a value system, management, and operating procedures that stand it in good stead, even though its direction has wavered. At one point, Sears seemed unable to determine whether it was competing with upscale stores like Bonwit and Bloomingdale's or with major discounters like K-Mart. The result confused shoppers and affected profits. The store's newest strategy is its "one low price" policy, introduced with great publicity and at great volume. Whether the new strategy will get the organization out of its doldrums remains to be seen at this writing, but it is clear that the strength of Sears' ability to *implement* a strategy was of tremendous importance during both the confusing period of uncertain competitors and the transition to a new approach to the market. Sears could be identified as a category 2 organization seeking to move back to category 1 and kept stable and maneuverable throughout the process by its implementation ability. However, there are signs that it is losing its touch at implementation and that category 4 may be beckoning. The new strategy may be too little, too late:

> Coherent the strategy is. But where has it been during a decade of decline? The biggest stumbling block: bureaucratic infighting. Setting up Brand Central was just one turf battle. Another broke out during development of a new store format for urban markets. . . . [Sears'] efforts to rework its structure have created tremendous internal turmoil. Sources say buyers are preoccupied with who will lose their jobs. Says one former buyer who still consults for Sears: "It's very difficult to carry on a business conversation down there."[2]

Before venturing any further, it's probably a good time to establish a definition of what strategy *is*, so that we're all speaking about the same

---

[2]"The Big Store's Big Trauma," by Brian Bremner and Michael Oneal, *Business Week*, July 10, 1989, page 55.

thing. There is no magic definition of strategy, and in sessions we run with executives we typically get the following list when we ask them to define the term:

- A plan to achieve the organization's goals
- A process to reach predetermined objectives
- The method to reach goals
- The ends the organization seeks to reach
- The means to the organization's ends
- Our mission
- Whatever we determine it is

So, is strategy a means, a mission, an end, a plan, a process, a method, or something that is defined by top management situationally? What is the relationship between strategy and planning? And how do you sort out conversations that include:

- "We need a marketing strategy."
- "What is our strategy to respond to the competition's offer?"
- "We need to plan our strategy."
- "We need a strategy to create our plan."
- "What's our pricing strategy?"

Our subject is strategy implementation, so we'll bow to the experts on strategy formulation to establish a definition. Here are three that we find to be succinct, useful, and reflected in the realities of organizational life:

> [Strategy comprises] those policies and key decisions adopted by management that have *major* impacts on financial performance. These policies and decisions usually involve significant resource commitments and are not easily reversible.[3]

> The framework which guides those choices that determine the nature and direction of an organization.[4]

> Our approach. . . [is] to identify the *key* factors that dictate the. . .*direction* of an organization together with the *process* that the CEO. . .uses to set direction.[5]

The first definition is useful for our purposes because it emphasizes the significance and notes the irreversibility of the endeavor. That is not to say that strategy is inflexible; it is to liken strategy to a supertanker whose course you wish to change. No matter how hard the helmsman leans on the wheel, the ship requires miles to change its course. (I once worked in a firm in which the CEO was advised by his president that something couldn't be done because the recently revised strategy prohibited it. The CEO looked at the strategy document for a moment, then crossed out the offending paragraph with his pen and told the president, "There, now we can do it.")

---

[3]*The PIMS Principles: Linking Strategy to Performance,* by Robert D. Buzzell and Bradley T. Gale, Free Press, New York, 1987.
[4]Tregoe and Zimmerman, *Top Management Strategy,* page 17.
[5]Robert, *The Strategist CEO,* page 20.

The second definition is useful because it is crystal clear, it is simple, and it connects strategy with guiding choices—effective implementation. And the third definition includes the idea of process and content, of what's to be done and how it's to be done. Perhaps an effective synthesis for our purposes would be: "Strategy is a process by which significant decisions that establish the nature and direction of the organization are made and which establishes the policies and beliefs that will help the organization to achieve those ends."

Here is a quick test to determine if you and your colleagues agree on what your organization's strategy is *and* whether or not it's being effectively implemented. You can take the test yourself, or you can ask your colleagues (peers and/or subordinates) to complete it as well and compare notes.

Strategic Clarity Test

1. Everyone in a key management position would cite the same strategy. □ yes □ no

2. The strategy could be expressed and understood in two or three sentences. □ yes □ no

3. The strategy guides day-to-day operating decisions. □ yes □ no

4. The strategy is the basis for the organization's planning procedures. □ yes □ no

5. All employees are aware of the organization's basic business goals. □ yes □ no

6. The implicit and explicit beliefs of the organization support the organization's direction. □ yes □ no

7. The strategy is the guiding factor in times of crisis or marketplace surprise. □ yes □ no

8. Key decisions are made by using the strategy as a test bed. □ yes □ no

9. Strategy is a *proactive* process, not a reaction to the marketplace. □ yes □ no

10. There are formal meetings to set, debate, refine, and monitor strategy. □ yes □ no

Strategy Implementation Test

1. Top executives lead the way in exemplifying values and direction. □ yes □ no

2. There is ongoing effort to involve all employees in working toward long-term goals. □ yes □ no

3. Communications reflect strategic beliefs, direction, and progress. □ yes □ no

4. Innovation within the strategic framework is encouraged and supported. ☐ yes ☐ no

5. Orientation, training, and development are based on the strategy. ☐ yes ☐ no

6. Accountability for achieving strategy is assessed at all management levels. ☐ yes ☐ no

7. Progress toward long-term goals is continually assessed. ☐ yes ☐ no

8. The organization acts consistently in good times and bad. ☐ yes ☐ no

9. Bureaucracy is discouraged; empowerment is encouraged. ☐ yes ☐ no

10. The organization's strategy has consistently been fulfilled. ☐ yes ☐ no

Scoring

On each test, add up the yes and no responses. On the clarity test, here are some guidelines:

9–10 yeses: Your organization gets an A+. Your strategy is probably clear and well defined, and it is used as a framework for the daily operations of the endeavor.

7–8 yeses: Not bad, but room for improvement. There is probably an operating strategy, but it may get shunted aside or ignored in crisis, with personnel changes, or from inertia.

5–6 yeses: At best there is a mist which sometimes clears momentarily to reveal your direction. Strategy is left for "special occasions" and does not help in really running the organization.

0–4 yeses: Your organization is in a hand-to-mouth situation, is purely reacting to its environment, and does not seriously attempt to develop a strategic view.

In the clarity test, questions 1, 6, 8, and 9 may be the most important, since they deal with consistency and the integrity of the process. So, no matter what your overall score, these areas constitute fundamental aspects to improve and reinforce.

In the implementation test, here are the guidelines:

9–10 yeses: Your organization is highly effective at implementing its chosen strategy, and it will tend to exploit excellent strategies and mitigate damage from poor (or absent) strategies.

7–8 yeses: Your organization implements strategy well as a general rule, but it may have some minor problems with given departments or personalities.

5-6 yeses: Implementation is rather poor, and the organization is probably in the habit of asking "What went wrong—we seemed
to be very clear on what was to be done." (See Rover, Inc.,
above.)

0-4 yeses: There isn't the slightest deliberate relationship between the
organization's strategy and what the organization actually
does. No one seems to understand that, and no one really
cares.

In this test, all ten questions are vitally important, with number 1 perhaps
first among equals.

If you took the tests individually, you should now have your personal
assessment of the organization's current ability to generate a strategy and
to "make it happen." If you took the tests with your colleagues, your comparing of notes will tell you how accurate your perceptions are. (Strong
inconsistencies among the responses must lower the scoring for everyone
in the clarity test!)

Given the test results, let's take one more look at our matrix of the four
categories, figure 1.2.

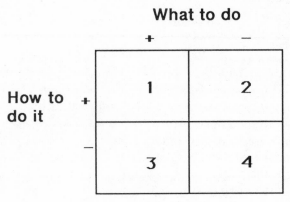

Figure 1.2

The combined scoring from the tests could be applied to your organization's location in the matrix in this manner:

Clarity Test	Implementation Test	Matrix Area
9–10	9–10	1
9–10	0–8	3
0–8	9–10	2
0–8	0–8	4

These comparisons might seem rather harsh. For instance, isn't there a
qualitative difference between an organization scoring 7 and one scoring

0 on either test? Assuming that the pursuit of excellence is the goal, the answer is no, not really. We don't pretend that the test is an infallible scientific assessment of your strategic profile and direction, but we have found that it tends to reflect the organizational environment as determined by the best possible source: the individual working within that environment. And if you and your colleagues achieved a consensus in your responses, the results are even more reliable. The only place an organization should be, on a long-term basis, is in category 1. Category 4 is often an obvious fiasco, but categories 2 and 3 can easily camouflage the poor direction and/or inefficiencies that may be undermining organizational success.

We'll conclude this chapter with the key factors which, our experience tells us, determine the success of strategy implementation. They are the eight keys which unlock the door to let strategy into the organization.

The Key Linkages to Strategy Implementation

Inertia: Stopping the Irresistible Force.

Every organization is in motion. It is actively competing for more market share, defending itself against competitors, pursuing specific quality and service standards, or simply wandering down the road without apparent rhyme or reason. In the better organizations, the motion is determined and encouraged by management. In the best organizations, the motion is carefully orchestrated to support the values and vision of the organization's strategy. Unfortunately, in many organizations the motion is random and is determined by external (and often extraneous) forces such as local managers, unions, competitors, and economic conditions.

To implement a strategy, especially a "new" or changed strategy, the motion must be adjusted to be in concert with the direction of the business. This might be the most fundamental aspect of successful strategic implementation, but it's also the most overlooked and neglected. Management at all levels, but with the cue from the top, must engender the following:

The strategy must be popularized so that every employee can not only be a part of it but can clearly *see* his or her part in it. Simplicity and clarity are the keys. Here, for example, are three clear missions:

Eat the Cat
Beat Benz
Follow the Customer

The first is the guiding vision of Komatsu, and it's very clear that surpassing Caterpillar is the message that all employees and managers are to bear in mind in every activity in which they are engaged. With such clarity, Komatsu has been successful in developing into a worldwide competitor in the heavy-equipment market and has enjoyed substantial success in Caterpillar's backyard. (And this competition has forged a changed Caterpillar organization: highly innovative, lighter on its feet, and once again profitable.)

"Beat Benz" is the rallying cry of Toyota. Not content with its tremendous U.S. market success, Toyota employs the typical Japanese trait of continually seeking to improve quality. So it chose the king of the hill and is pursuing that competitor in terms of its greatest strength: quality. (For its part, Mercedes bills itself as "engineered like no other car in the world.") How successful can such public manifestations of vision be? At this writing, Honda's Acura has dethroned Mercedes as highest-rated marque in customer satisfaction and has repeated for a second year.

"Follow the Customer" is the motto of McDonald's. The growth of the chain has been guided by management's clear direction that the outlets must follow the buyer, not attempt to attract the buyer to set locations. The organization even modified architecture and arches to adhere to that direction, and we now have the luxury of being able to visit a McDonald's on a crowded New York City street, in an enclosed shopping mall in virtually any state, or in dozens of foreign countries. (During my last visit to Singapore it was proudly pointed out that the McDonald's on Orchard Street held the single-day record for volume.) This consistent, clear direction has determined the nature and scope of the distribution system and has made McDonald's synonymous with fast food.

Of course, a catchphrase or a buzz word is merely an indicator of an organization's efforts to keep its direction clear, crisp, and visible. Komatsu, Toyota, McDonald's, and similarly successful organizations "push" the vision continually, every day and in every way, and reinforce it with symbolic behavior, shared values, and rewards—the appropriate "culture." Here are some other examples of organizations attempting to do the same thing. They were chosen at random from a single issue of *Business Week:*

"Uncommon problems. Uncommon solutions." (DuPont)
"Building businesses into leaders." (ITT)
"Mack quality: depend on it." (Mack Trucks)
"Your business can take off in all directions."
   (South Carolina Development Board)
"We put our reputation on the line every day." (First Chicago)
"Excellence in communications." (Alltel)
"No excuses. Nothing but performance."
   (Arkwright Mutual Insurance)

These might be aimed purely at the public and potential customers, but the best organizations are consistent in conveying such messages to the employees as well. Finally, inertia can only be overcome—the motion can only be influenced—if the implementation of strategy is itself a *strategy separate from the business strategy.* A well-defined, carefully thought out business direction does not automatically translate itself into successful implementation. In fact, the former may well be easier to accomplish than the latter. Implementing a strategy is a separate, discreet undertaking that requires focus, planning, and commitment from the top.

Ownership: Painting Everyone into the Picture.

A critical mass of people must be "enlisted" to support the strategy. This is a question not just of numbers, but also of key positions. (Try to foster customer service when your customer service managers feel alienated or mistreated.) Deliberate programs are required to create this critical mass. For example:

- Spread accountability. Create local responsibility and trust people at all levels to "do the right thing."
- Provide visible, tangible rewards for those whose actions with the customer, service, and/or product best support the strategy.
- Create rewards (and punishments) for top management, so that the implementation of strategy will be managed by those who can best influence the direction.

There must be techniques for involving people from all over the organization in the strategic direction and its underpinnings. These are the people who will adhere to or depart from the strategy every day and whose activities can't be constantly monitored for compliance. They must want to support the strategy intrinsically—because the organization has made it reasonable, logical, practical, and rewarding to do so. Strategies "happen" because thousands of employees (or scores or hundreds in smaller organizations) are naturally supporting and reinforcing it every day, without direct supervision or influence. (One of my clients is fond of pointing out that his profitability is not determined on a daily basis by those around him on the executive floor of headquarters. "Every day, the decisions of our middle managers make us or break us," he says. "*They* are where the action is.")

"Empowerment"—unfortunately, too trendy a term—simply means providing for the ability of people to influence their work in a productive, significant manner. Empowered employees can support and nurture a strategic direction; powerless employees can only stand by and watch what happens. If the critical mass is watching and not doing, the strategy is in trouble from neglect if not from misdirection.

How far down the organization can such empowerment go? The answer is, how far do you want to go? A couple of years ago I took my family to Disneyland. My kids were impressed with the rides and attractions, and my wife was impressed with the family atmosphere and general *bonhomie*. But my consultant's eye was impressed by something else: the incredibly sincere positive attitude that every employee manifested. I kept looking for an exception—someone having a bad day dealing with a line-jumper or a food vendor being hassled.

Finally, after a particularly well-attended parade down Main Street, I noticed the street sweepers cleaning up in the wake of the festivities. The crowd had dispersed, leaving the inevitable litter on the ground, and the sweepers, dressed as ice cream vendors and other characters, meticulously cleaned up the trash. As one worked nearby, I asked him, "What's it like to be a street sweeper in Disneyland?" His expression changed instantly to a much more serious demeanor. Had I at last turned up an unhappy employee?

"I'm not a sweeper," he informed me. "I'm part of the act. I'm in the show."

I was thunderstruck. Small wonder that the Disney parks are always immaculate! The sweepers see their role as "part of the show," not as street cleaners. The Disney management has successfully painted everyone into its picture of the organization and its direction. Are your employees part of your show?

Institutionalization: Do You Have It under Your Skin?

The direction—the motion we've talked about—must be self-perpetuating and self-reinforcing. A top priority of the executives who have formulated the strategy must be to establish, implement, and monitor programs and activities that enhance the right direction. And any existing programs championed by top management have to be reviewed for their consistency with the new strategy and changed if necessary.

In the progression of figure 1.3, what is normally the hardest and what is the easiest thing to change?

Figure 1.3

Values often must be changed or altered to support a strategy, but *that is usually the wrong place to start.* It is generally easiest to change behaviors, because they are most susceptible to rewards, punishments, and external influences. Consequently, if you want an employee to treat customers with more care and patience, you build such emphasis areas into performance reviews and the reward system and you provide some clear way to measure progress (my bank places customer questionnaires at each teller's window). Eventually, you will have influenced behavior in the direction you need to take. If you're consistent, and if top management provides exemplars, attitudes will then modify. ("I thought it would be extra work to explain new products, but it's actually a nice break from the routine and the customers are quite appreciative.") Finally, even strongly held values will be subject to modification ("My job responsibilities involve helping the customer get the best service possible") and employees will define their jobs in terms of the end product or objective and not in terms of the activity or task. There is a fundamental difference between an employee who says "My job is to be at my desk by nine and answer the customer-service phones" and one who says "My job is to convince all customers that we will provide them the finest service they can get anywhere." The first person is innovative about how to stretch the coffee break; the second is innovative about how to get a customer an out-of-stock product. The efforts are usually identical, but the impacts on the organization are worlds apart!

All—that is, every single aspect—of training, development, and, for new employees, orientation must include the message of the strategy. Not just some training or select programs on goals. *Every* formal employee development activity should have the form and substance of strategy deliberately and consistently built into it. That is what institutionalization is all about. If you scratch the organizational skin, the strategy is underneath. It's not a Band-Aid that's placed on top.

Innovation: What if We Do Put the Cart before the Horse?

I have never seen an organization consistently involve people in the implementation of strategy when the freedom to fail and the tolerance of risk taking were not intrinsic elements. Since strategy is a direction, the motion needed to achieve it must be some type of forward motion. Conservatism, defensiveness, fear, and protection serve only to circle the wagons. The defensive posture may be temporarily successful in warding off an attack *but no organization has ever achieved long-term success, let alone dominance in a market, in a defensive posture.* You see, when the wagons are in a circle, the only possible motion is circular.

There must be a commitment to continuous improvement. The very nature of the work requires constant examination. Are the employees engaged in truly value added activities in terms of the customer, product, and service? The issue of empowerment discussed above is highly relevant here also. The more employees can determine their own approaches and design their own jobs, the more effectively a strategy will be implemented. (Roy Walters & Associates, a New Jersey firm, is particularly successful at helping clients develop self-directed work teams that can effectively implement strategies that they call "transformational"—totally different approaches to the work.)[6]

---

[6]See "Work Teams Can Rev Up Paper Pushers Too," *Business Week,* Nov. 28, 1988, page 64.

Many firms *think* they foster innovation, but they don't—they foster problem solving. Now, problem solving is a noble activity and is needed in every organization, but not at the expense of innovation. The difference is shown in figure 1.4.

Problem Solving

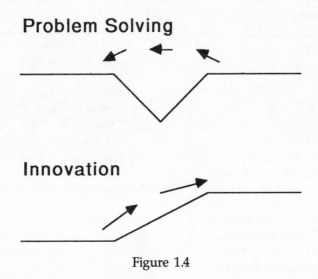

Innovation

Figure 1.4

In problem solving, something (or some person or some process) goes wrong and you fix it. Good organizations do this all the time. However, the best result of effective problem solving is that *you are as good as you used to be!* You've restored the performance to the way it was before, acceptable to be sure, but no better than that. In innovation, *you are setting new standards,* and that is the hallmark of leading organizations. You simply cannot implement a strategy successfully—be it a new direction or an affirmation of an existing course—if the organization is intent on retaining the *status quo* and fixing things that go wrong. Successful strategy implementation requires that people are looking to *improve* performance constantly—by small, incremental changes that create dramatic results.[7]

Here is a quick test: Look at figure 1.4 and estimate the ratio of your management time spent on problem solving to that spent on innovation. In our work with hundreds of organizations, *the ratio is 90–10!* That's right, 90 percent of management time devoted to problem solving and 10 percent to innovation. I don't know what the proper ratio for your oganization and your strategy is, but I can tell you it can't be 90–10! If 90 percent of the time your organization is trying to achieve past levels of performance and only 10 percent of the time trying to establish new levels of performance, the chances are that your strategy won't be realized. As a rule, the more significant the changes in your strategy are, the more innovation

[7]See *The Innovation Formula: How Organizations Turn Change into Opportunity,* by Michel Robert and Alan Weiss, Harper & Row, New York, 1988, page 12.

must be stimulated. But even in relatively unchanging organizations, the changes in the outside environment require that more and more time be spent on innovative approaches if strategy is to be successful.

Feedback: Knowing When to Hold and When to Fold.

Strategy is not set and left to fend for itself, like a water sprinkler deposited on the front lawn, nor will "automatic" monitors keep it up to date. Even a timer on the sprinkler will fail to allow for rain (how many lawns have you seen being watered during a downpour!) or for changed conditions: different landscaping, a barbecue, or a water shortage. The organization's strategy must be monitored and evaluated continuously, and the best way to do that is *not* by checking on various activities, but by checking on the *outputs.* Here's an example of the differences:

Activities	Outputs
Meetings of executives	Customer feedback on service
Periodic strategy sessions	Employee feedback on customer usage
Communication on what the strategy is supposed to be	Communication on how the strategy is actually working
Surveys gathering strategic inputs	Surveys gathering strategic consequences
Fitting into models and matrices	Assessing competitive market share

I once worked with an organization that implemented "face-to-face" meetings with its work force in an effort to secure feedback directly from the people on the firing line. The concept was excellent, but the execution was poor (this would be a category 3 in figure 1.1). The managers asked to conduct the meetings were not given any training in or preparation for running them, told what to expect, or told what to do with any feedback. The result could have been seen in anyone's crystal ball: The sessions were held as lectures, with the manager informing his or her troops about the latest company developments in line with the company strategy. At the conclusion came the deeply revelatory "Any questions?" and that was that.

In an attempt at a quick fix, the organization made those sessions part of every manager's emphasis areas for evaluation, with the intention of rewarding the correct behavior. However, the measure was based on *how many* of the sessions were held, not *how effective* the sessions were, so legions of people were marched into meetings to listen to their managers do their level best to meet their quantitative feedback requirements!

The real fix, of course, would have involved training managers in why the sessions were being run, how to run them, and what to do with the feedback. The *activity* was the meeting, but the real *output* desired was feedback from the employees about how well strategy was working. This quantitative vs. qualitative, form vs. substance conflict is encountered again and again when organizations aren't absolutely clear on their feedback requirements.

Blaise Pascal once said that "evil is never done so thoroughly nor so well as when done with good intentions." The same holds true for management. The purpose of strategy is to provide a guide to achieve a future vision. Midcourse corrections and adjustments are a part of any good strategy, but they can be effectively accomplished only when someone bothers to consult the lookouts and ask what they see. Here is my favorite story about disregarding feedback.

It was a dark and stormy night. The huge naval ship plowed its way through tremendous waves as it sailed down the coast. There was no moon. The fog was total. The rain came down in bucketsful.

Suddenly, a light was spotted in the distance on a collision course. So a message was sent to the oncoming ship. "We are on a collision course. Change your heading 10° north."

A return message was received. It said, "Change *your* heading 10° south."

So a second message was sent. "This is Rear Admiral Johnson. We are on a collision course. Change your heading 10° north."

And the immediate reply was, "This is Seaman Fourth Class Jones. Change *your* heading 10° south."

Naturally, a third message was promptly sent. "I am standing on the bridge of the largest capital ship in the navy, and every gun and missile is pointed directly at you. We are on a collision course. Change your heading 10° north."

The final reply was, "I am standing in a lighthouse. Change *your* heading. . ."

To implement strategy successfully, we not only have to set up feedback channels but also be willing to listen to them and be flexible in our responsiveness to them. Our survey work has consistently shown that both employees and customers are willing to provide specific feedback to management. It is incumbent on management to understand what it should be looking for and the best way to determine it. And this gathering of information needs to be done every day, not at special events or as a special project given to human resources or to an outside consultant. At best, either one should be demonstrating to management how to obtain feedback as a daily part of the job, not doing it for management.

I was intrigued by a client-sponsored awards dinner during which an informal poll showed that nearly half the 200 attendees did not recognize the vice president of operations. "Oh, so that's him," said one manager when the VP was pointed out, "I always wondered if he might be wandering around in my department. But he can't be—I've never seen that guy before."

Exemplars: "Don't Do What I Do, Do What I Say."

There are two ironclad rules in organizations that absolutely guide behavior. They are extremely simple, yet they are almost always disregarded.

Rule 1: Perception *is* reality.

Rule 2: People believe what they see, not what they hear or read.

Here are some brief examples from client observations of the rules being ignored:

Example 1.   A utility client develops a strategy that includes providing the highest levels of customer service. The organization initiates service campaigns, puts up posters, and publishes, in the house organ, frequent reminders of the need for top-level service. Yet customer complaints remain at current, unacceptable levels, as do complaints to the Public Utilities Commission, which the organization wishes to reduce at all cost. Customer service supervisors are reprimanded for poor compliance to the new policy and threatened with poor performance reviews. A visit to the 35-person customer service unit reveals:

- Torn carpeting patched with duct tape
- Red walls surrounding the area
- Rules enforced regarding punctuality and absence that are clearly unenforced in units that can be seen across the halls
- No personal visits from any manager above the immediate supervisors
- Too many supervisors and coordinators and not enough representatives

The customer service representatives weren't rebellious, in fact, they actually felt better when they were performing in such a way that complaints were minimized. They *heard* the company's campaign, and *read* the reminders. But what they *saw* was an organization paying lip service to customer service (even though the strategy was sincere in its intent, the execution was inadequate) with poor working conditions, lack of attention, and a "low man on the totem pole" status (this last phrase had become a department slogan more powerful than any of the company campaigns).

When the discordancies were discussed with the senior vice president for administration—who sits on the committee which sets strategy—his response was classic: "What can you expect from those people? They give me the dregs to work in customer service—who else would want to work in that job? There's no sense sending good money after bad."

Example 2.   A family-owned, moderate-size retailer of home products devised a strategy to transform itself into an employee-owned, participatively managed concern. The owner had superb reasons for doing so, and he and his president, who was not part of the current ownership, devised plans to increase employee involvement, commitment, and appreciation of ownership so that actual transfer of ownership would be attractive and informed.

Yet several months after the steps were initiated (pushing decision making downward, allowing for local responsibility in buying, rotational assignments among stores), there seemed to be no appreciable difference in employee morale, involvement, or regard for top management. We traveled to every store and quickly found out why. One morning at 8 A.M. at a distribution warehouse, several of the drivers took me to a window.

"You see that gray sedan beyond the gate?" they asked.

"Yes, I do. The driver looks like. . ."

"That's right, it's Rick (the president). He's there at least three times a week. The company can't reconcile inventory and sales in this operation, and he suspects that some of us are stealing the stuff or allowing contractors to come in and take it. That's why we just put in our time, collect our checks, and get out of here at the end of the day."

Example 3. The head of the sales department was upset that his people weren't "holding up their end of the bargain." The strategy of the corporation—after it was acquired by a larger competitor—included a commitment to the highest levels of ethics and integrity with both customers and colleagues. Guidelines were published to specify what constituted unethical behavior and emphasize that ethics were more important than monthly sales quotas. For example, one guideline explained that it was inappropriate to send materials to a customer before they were actually requested on the order simply to improve the current month's numbers.

"I *know*," said the vice president, "that there is still arm-twisting of customers to take more than they need, that sales projections aren't done according to legitimate prospects, and that there is even cheating on expense reports. We might have to clean house totally."

The enemy, of course, was "us." It seemed that the vice president was famous throughout the department for purchasing first-class air tickets (which was his right) and then trading them in for coach class and pocketing the difference. He was also observed sending his boss sales reports that did not match the cumulative total of the reports turned into him; his reports were always more optimistic. And his behavior hadn't changed one whit after the acquisition, although he "supported" new policies enthusiastically.

Exemplars are the people in any organization to whom others look for standards of conduct. It is their lead that is followed, especially when policy and procedure aren't applicable. In fact, one quick, revealing diagnostic question we ask when assessing value systems is, "What do you do in the absence of guidelines and procedures?" In the organizations with the poorest exemplars, the answers are invariably "I give it to my boss. . . let her worry about it," or "I do what I have to in order to protect myself" (even if it means a disservice to the customer). From our best clients, those with excellent exemplars, we generally hear "I use my judgment—I'll be supported," or "I try to work out something reasonable between the customer and the company." These people have seen examples of such behaviors from those they respect and from those in positions of visibility. The best response we've ever heard is from Merck & Co., the pharmaceutical giant voted "America's Most Admired Company" in the annual *Fortune* poll of CEOs and executives for four years in a row. Throughout Merck, thousands of middle managers ask themselves this question when confronted with a decision for which policy and procedure are lacking: "What's the right thing to do?" Since every organization faces such decisions every day, management's response to them is the key to adhering to or departing from strategic goals.

So, successful implementation of strategy is dependent on the existence of exemplars in formal and informal positions of visibility and leadership whose actions people *see* and use as models of their own behavior. Without exemplars *whose actions are in concert with the organization's strategy*, implementation will receive superficial commitment at best. As one manager said when diagnosing why his organization wasn't responsive to the strategic direction, "Who ever heard of moving in *any* direction when the first question we all ask is 'How can I cover my rear end?' "

Consistency under Pressure: "Captain, We're between a Rock and a Hard Place."

No organization can expect its strategy to sail along in calm, untroubled waters. The 50s were probably the last decade when that was possible, and organizational America, at least, enjoyed the simple times so much that it's doubtful that many organizations were engaged in creating strategies at all. It's hardly a strategic masterpiece to say, "We're the only show in town, so let's tell the customer what is needed, then we'll produce it and tack on our profit margin." So we happily purchased obsolescing, poorly made automobiles, patiently stood in long lines during the bank's few open hours, and ate packaged foods that grandmother might not have been proud to call her own.

Today, of course, change is the norm, and the competitive global realities have provided consumers with unprecedented choices for their discretionary funds. Yet even the most agile of strategies in the most flexible of companies sometimes isn't spry enough to leap unscathed through a crisis. A vital aspect for any successful strategy's implementation is that consistency is maintained even in the face of crisis. In fact, a crisis can be the crucible that strengthens a strategy when employees (and customers) see that the organization, as expressed in its demeanor, has been consistent in its adherence to its values and beliefs.[8]

---

[8]For a discussion of crisis management and the *how* of dealing with it, see *Crisis Management: Planning for the Inevitable*, by Steven Fink, AMACOM, New York, 1986. For organizing for crisis management, see *Crisis Management: A Team Approach*, by Robert F. Littlejohn, American Management Association Management Briefing, New York, 1983.

Here are some organizations which experienced crises covered by the news media. Which fared well in the eyes of the consumer, and which suffered?

Audi	Exxon
Union Carbide	Kraft Foods
Johnson & Johnson	Merck

In the famous Audi case of "unexplained, sudden acceleration," the company took the position that its cars were blameless and that, in effect, ignorance and mistakes by the drivers were the causes. Subsequent government testing seems to support the company's claim.[9] Yet it was the organization's response, and its perceived *attitude*, that caused it problems. When the buyers of your top-of-the-line product believe you are telling them that they don't know how to drive and that their own ignorance caused the problem, no amount of testing, science, or fact will overcome the perception that the organization doesn't care about its customers. Audi's strategy and its market share couldn't possibly persevere in that kind of environment. Astonishingly, Audi didn't learn from Ford's earlier debacle with the Pinto and its tendency to catch fire when involved in rear-end collisions. Ford took a beating which harmed its products and reputation for years.

Union Carbide's reaction to the Bhopal disaster and Exxon's to the Valdez oil spill were similarly marred by immediate refusals to accept responsibility and what was perceived as executive stonewalling. Will Exxon ever recover from an event which became the butt of jokes of every comedian in the hemisphere, not because of the accident itself or the tragic despoliation of the environment, but rather because of the organization's perceived arrogance? This is a classic example of a top exemplar: CEO Lawrence G. Rawl not only refused to visit the site but could not be found for some time after the accident! What responsibility, integrity, and candor signals did *that* send to customers and employees?

Contrast Valdez to an explosion in a Merck manufacturing plant in Puerto Rico. Two lives were lost in the disaster, which was attributed to human error. CEO Roy Vagelos, en route back from a trip to Australia, immediately altered his plans and went to the Puerto Rico site. After one day of page 1 coverage, the tragedy was placed in perspective, the company did everything it could to comfort the families of the killed and injured, and an inquiry was launched to ensure that such a tragedy wouldn't happen again at any Merck site. Small wonder that Merck people ask "What's the right thing to do?" in areas of ambiguity.

Of course, the supreme example of effective crisis management and consistency to beliefs is the Johnson & Johnson reaction to the Tylenol tampering crisis. CEO James Burke became *the chief company spokesperson*, fully accessible to the press. Although in no way responsible for the tampering, J&J voluntarily removed all Tylenol from shelves, publicly reassured

---

[9]See "Sudden Acceleration Probe of Audis Finds No Defect," by staff reporter, *The Wall Street Journal*, July 14, 1989, page C8.

their customers, and suffered a temporary market loss, because their reputation was more important than their current market share. (One client executive once told me that he was warned by a subordinate that imposing further quality standards and testing could cost his company a billion dollars. He replied, "Just how much do you think our reputation is worth?")

Finally, on a lighter note but equally important for our purposes, because these kinds of crises are much more common, there is Kraft Foods running a sweepstakes promotion in which it is expected that very few people will win the first prize—a van worth $17,000. Somewhere in the process of printing the matching tickets (no one will say where) a mistake is made that creates hundreds of winners of the van alone. Kraft immediately stonewalls, then declares the contest void, then says that winners can send in their tickets if they choose to but the tickets may not be honored, and then offers each winner $250 and the chance to enter a drawing to win the van.

Of no small significance is the fact that contract law would probably support Kraft's position, but here is a manufacturer of foods that we bring into our homes. We trust the company to use the highest-quality standards, to advertise honestly, and to stand behind its products. Yet its top management says to the public (and its employees) that there are times when commitments shouldn't be honored. Boycotts have been threatened, and Kraft's reputation is beginning to look like its Swiss cheese. Consider this: 200 vans at, let's say, $14,000 (Kraft's actual cost) come to $2,800,000. And many of the winners would probably settle for a cash substitution of less than $14,000. What Kraft has said to anyone who cares to listen is "We have our price."[10]

The ability of the captain and crew to hold the ship's course even in unfavorable winds and in uncharted waters will determine how ultimately successful the ship will be in arriving at its chosen destination. It's awfully hard for the crew to climb the masts in the storm, though, when the officers can be seen huddling under shelter or moving personal belongings into the lifeboats.

Training and Development: Don't Catch a Fish for Me—Teach Me How to Fish.

The final key to the successful implementation of strategy is by no means the least important one, though it is generally perceived to be the poor cousin of most organizations. No strategy can be implemented if the organization isn't constantly training and developing its people to do the kinds of things that the strategy call for, and not those things which have simply "always been done anyway."

---

[10]"How Kraft Could Have Prevented the Big Goof," by Robert S. Abramson, *Boardroom Reports,* Aug. 15, 1989, page 10.

Ironically, training and development are often the first things that are cut in hard times, seldom receive top executive attention (though they get lots of lip service and annual report space), and are generally considered as perquisites and not requisites by many line managers. ("Do the job I'm looking for and we'll send you to the widget convention in Amelia Island this year." "You don't have time to go to some fool training program on planning—we're overwhelmed with work here!") Can you imagine the athletic team whose management calls a press conference after a mediocre or, worse, losing season, and proclaims:

"Well, we're unhappy with our results from last year, and after reviewing the organization, we in top management have determined that we will reduce practice time, cut back on coaches, and reduce the budget by 15 percent. That should make things better."

The fans, of course, would riot, and management would be lucky to find a comfortable rail on which to be ridden out of town. Yet top management does exactly that kind of thing every day, with nary a peep from the shareholders or boards of directors. It's ludicrous on the face of it, but so was Audi's response and so was trying to get the lighthouse to change its course.

Also, a fundamental difference between training and development is often not understood. *Training* (I prefer education) is the development of skills and the transfer of knowledge that enables someone to perform the current job, today, to acceptable standards. *Development* constitutes the activities, including skills and knowledge acquisition and experiences, that prepare someone to do *tomorrow's* jobs at anticipated standards. Training is present, development is future; and although they often augment and support each other, they are separate undertakings. If all you're providing is training, you'll never be ahead of the game, because tomorrow will constantly catch you unprepared for its demands. If all you're providing is development, your current operation will never perform at its potential, because today's demands are not being fully met.

As you might expect, it's development that's more important for strategy implementation, because it concerns the very issues that a good strategy considers: what should we look like tomorrow and what skills will be required to get us there?

As shown in figure 1.5, strategy requires the development of intermediate skills, which move the organization from where it is to where it wants to be, *and* future skills, which represent the needs of the attained strategic profile. These two sets of skills may be quite similar—particularly for an organization whose strategy calls for only mild change—or quite dissimilar for an organization whose strategy demands "transformation" of its current profile. The makers of Cross Pens, for example, are in a stable industry whose largest shock over the last several years was the happy reemergence of the fountain pen. One would suspect its strategy demands very few changes to the basic skills that it seeks to provide for its people. Conversely, the skills required at AT&T postdivestiture were often radically

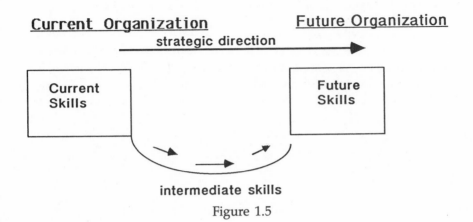

intermediate skills

Figure 1.5

different from those required before. (For example, this was a huge organization essentially without any marketing expertise!)

Training and development, and especially the latter, are indispensable for an organization seeking to implement a coherent strategy. These "human resource" aspects are integral parts of the process, because any strategy is only as good as the people responsible for implementing it, and that implementation and those skills must be congruent with the strategic direction. There is a probably apocryphal story about a school in the Midwest that trains the finest steam locomotive firemen in the world. They are the unassailed leaders in their field. Of course, there are no more steam locomotives.

Is your organization training and developing people for today's jobs (or, worse, *yesterday's*) or for tomorrow's? The locomotive firemen are not so far-fetched. Banks were very slow to change their procedures in the hiring, training, and development of loan originators, for example, even after the job had changed substantially, and the banks' strategies reflected the new sources of competition spawned by deregulation. The old style originator, who sat in a room visited by supplicants to be accepted or rejected, was still the model in many institutions, even though the marketplace was demanding more entrepreneurial, independent, overt sales types who visited prospects in the field and sold the bank over acknowledged competitors. The banks slowest to realize and implement the transition were also the poorest performers.

In their heyday, the Dallas Cowboys never drafted a guard or a halfback or a linebacker. They simply drafted the best available athletes, confident that they would find the right positions for such gifted individuals. Eventually, all the years of winning denied the team access to the top athletes in the draft. But the strategy worked for a long time, and it produced consistent winners. Their implementation—their training and development—was geared to their strategy in perfect synchronization. For decades, the Dodgers have believed in an expensive, comprehensive farm system.

The Dodgers would "grow their own" and not rely on trades or luck. The strategy worked tremendously well because *development* in the minors was in concert with the strategy of the parent club.

Business and industry—and all organizations in general—are in the same league as the Dodgers or the Cowboys. Training and development should be receiving top priority and top investment in good times *and* bad, because there is no other way to prepare people to implement strategy.

2

Why the Best-Laid Plans *Always* Go Awry: Strategy Turned Inside Out

There are as many potential obstacles to successful strategy implementation as there are days in the year and employees in the organization, but there are several primary organizational stumbling blocks which are the equivalent of shooting yourself in the foot. You might as well avoid these first, since they could ruin your whole day. And, as in so many pursuits, you must unlearn bad habits before you can learn the good ones. There's no sense in attempting to implement a strategy with the best of intentions and improper techniques. That would be the same as searching in the restaurant for the wallet you know you lost in the theater because the light is better in the restaurant. The best effort in the world still won't meet the objective. Therefore, in our search for the best light in the right location, here are five land mines that can blow strategy up before it takes shape.

The Handcuffs of Overplanning

The majority of managers and executives we've encountered tend to confuse strategy with planning, with the result that the latter kills the former. Then we get a grammatical paradox like "strategic planning," and awkward attempts to "plan our strategy." I heard one group of marketing people argue over whether the department needed a strategy, a strategic plan, strategic objectives, marketing objectives, a planning strategy, an operating strategy, an operating plan, and/or an implementation plan—all in the same 30-minute meeting! What they needed was a road map through the minefield.

We've established in chapter 1 what some common definitions for strategy might be, and we'll paraphrase them here as "a framework within which the decisions are made that guide the nature and direction of the business." So what about planning? Well, planning is operational in nature. It's on the "how" side of our chart. Planning *is not* the primary vehicle by which strategy is implemented. Strategy requires its own implementation plan. (More about that in later chapters.) However, planning does assist in the implementation of strategy, and it provides for the systematic accomplishment of goals and objectives that are part of the larger strategy. It is the bridge between strategy and daily operating realities.

25

Strategy
  Become the leaders in mail-order software
  Cater primarily to business travelers
Sample Plan Step
  Assess competitive techniques
  Reconfigure aircraft for all business class amenities
Operating Reality
  Requires additional hiring of market researchers
  Longer periods of out-of-service aircraft

Since strategy and planning are often confused and combined, neither emerges with any clear-cut direction or shape. Here are some of the reasons why strategy must be conducted prior to and apart from planning.

1. Planning usually begins at the lower levels of the organization. Projections are based upon people who work where the rubber meets the road. Rather than an eagle's-eye view, there is a two-dimensional view of a nimble animal trying to look ahead while dodging the oncoming traffic. (If it's not nimble, well. . .) These road's-eye view projections are combined by people who are sitting at slightly higher levels but are still bound by the original viewpoint. By the time these accumulated visions reach top management, there is no opportunity to provide for a new direction—to consider different highways altogether. The quantitative thoroughness and accuracy of the projections overwhelm the qualitative considerations of whether the view is valid. Flexibility is lost, and a *fait accompli* has been created by management for itself.

2. In part because of its nature, and in part because of who's involved, planning is almost always excessively positive and optimistic. After all, the prior year or period should be bettered, or what are we being paid for? Strong and weak areas share this rose-tinted view (the strong are not expected to decline, and the weak can only improve). As a former sales manager, one of my primary jobs was to take the individual sales forecasts and try to haul them down to earth. No amount of training, threat, or incentive could achieve reasonable sales forecasts from the troops. If I had simply forwarded the total, each year would have been a several-fold increase over the previous one until, of course, the actual numbers started to come in. Yet my "handcuffs" were such that I couldn't alter the numbers too much, because my superiors would accuse me of "low-balling" for safety's sake! The result was good news–bad news: We always had better years than the prior years, but we never achieved that optimistic plan. (One other significant problem was that many departments' resources were tied to the aggressiveness of the plan—a perfect Catch 22).

3. Planning is much more transitory than anyone really considers it to be. Whether it's a 6-month plan, a 1-year plan, or a 5-year plan (finding an example of the last in the real world is right up there with the Loch Ness Monster and Bigfoot), it tends to change, often abruptly, with cir-

cumstances. Performance evaluations of management are usually made on the basis of "what have you done for me lately," and there seem to be more old planning documents gathering dust in desk drawers and task force meeting rooms than any other type. In the sequence above, planning is much closer to the operations than the strategy, and it is usually subject to extremely short time frames.

4. Planning takes the shape of detailed, rather stringent, projections. Every department and area is supposed to participate. The result is an elaborate construct that prematurely creates the future as an extension of today rather than provide a means to reach a truly strategic vision of the future. This makes for a cumbersome vehicle with which to manage change, which is why planning is so abruptly altered at times: It doesn't accommodate change well. These iterative and linear projections can constitute an ironclad constraint on growth. For example, if sales increased (or returns decreased or turnover improved) by 4 percent 2 years ago, 5 percent last year, and 5.7 percent this year, one might "safely" look at the environment and project a 6.5 percent increase for next year. Of course, this always assumes roughly the same methods, procedures, and interventions. It is not based on the innovative model shown in chapter 1; instead, it is based on the problem-solving model: here's what might go wrong, and here's how we think we can fix it. Strategy, and its implementation, must be innovative.

5. Planning is *activity-based*, not *objective-based;* that is, it involves means and not ends, alternatives and not goals. We said earlier that it resides on the "how" side of our graph. Thus, it usually takes current activities and attempts to extrapolate how they can reach certain goals rather than take the *vision* and determine "what do we have to do to get there?" Implementing strategy requires that you start with the vision and then determine what must be done organizationally to move toward it. Perhaps the best illustration is the difference we would see in the profiles of some organizations if the goals involved the activities the organizations are engaged in rather than their vision. I'll leave the difference to the reader's imagination:

Activity	Vision	Organization
Making watches	"We create fine jewelry."	Rolex
Making automobiles	"Engineered like no other car in the world."	Mercedes-Benz
Delivering packages	"Absolutely guaranteed overnight delivery."	Federal Express
Making film	"We provide memories."	Kodak

Those visions allowed Rolex to survive the Japanese usurpation of the Swiss watch industry (the status watch in Japan is a Rolex), Mercedes to virtually dictate its pricing and become the paradigm of quality (remember, long ago, when an organization might like to call itself "the Cadillac of the business"?), Federal Express to spawn an industry that takes its lead from its own quality standards, and Kodak to dominate its industry (for many years I thought film came only in yellow boxes).

Planning has its place, but that place is not at the head of the line. Strategic implementation will fail if it is confused with the planning process or is subordinate to it. Here's a simple priority-setter: If you have to abandon either the strategic implementation process or the planning process, discard the latter. If the former has been done well, you'll feel much better in the morning.

Executive Abdication

The best executives understand that, once they walk out of their final strategy-setting meeting, having reached agreement and battled through some tough issues, their work is just *beginning*. Setting strategy is easy; it's making it work that's difficult. (My theory is that this is why professors of management are in universities and not running major organizations. It's far easier to spin out strategic advice if you don't have to be around to make it happen.[1]) Yet it's precisely at this critical juncture that executives tend to wash their hands as they leave the dirty work to others.

Why do the very people who have perhaps the greatest vested interest in seeing their strategy successfully implemented abandon the offspring so soon? It's generally not malicious, but it is terribly short-sighted. In my observations, these are some of the reasons:

1. Executives spend most of their time on *operational* issues, even though they shouldn't. They do that because of human nature and because of organizational exigencies from which they have not shielded themselves.

2. It's more gratifying to work on operational issues because they are shorter-term, more tangible, and easier to delegate and to involve others in. There is more of a sense of accomplishment. Many executives, ironically, have difficulty dealing with ambiguity such as that often found in the implementation of strategy. There is simply more sense of accomplishment at the end of the day when one deals with operational issues. Finally, there are usually tried-and-true *processes* for dealing with operational issues that don't necessarily apply to strategic ones.

3. Executives feel the flames licking at their shoes. Even at that level, firefighting is as contagious as the flames themselves. I have observed executives who do literally one thing all day long: combat problems. Although they wear their firefighting badges proudly ("If you want this taken care of, you'd better see Harry"), they develop a mind set and operating habit that quickly constrain them from doing anything else.

---

[1]For an actual example of an academic called upon to practice what he preaches in a large organization, Warren Bennis provides a candid view in his *The Unconscious Conspiracy: Why Leaders Can't Lead*, AMACOM, New York, 1976.

Looking after the implementation of strategy "will just have to wait" until the current rough seas are navigated. Of course, there's always another storm on the horizon. Simply putting in the relatively brief penance of setting the strategy is sacrifice enough for a problem solver who can't otherwise be spared from the front lines.

4. They are caught in the crack. One of my favorite words is "interstitial," which refers to the area between two linking components. Unfortunately, it just doesn't work to say, "Don't let this fall interstitially." It does work in this case, however, because executives walking out of that meeting have just entered the strategic twilight zone.

There are processes to help set strategy. And there are processes to help establish plans. And there are processes to help in the daily operations of the endeavor—things like delegation, decision making, time management, and negotiation. But executives aren't generally in possession of a process to use to *implement* their strategy. Consequently, they either deliberately begin to abdicate the task at this point or they mistakenly believe they have already accomplished it. We hope to provide that key interstitial process during the course of this book.

5. Executives seldom monitor the strengths and weaknesses of the implementation of the *previous* strategy. Because the implementation process is not understood, it's hard to monitor. Also, deviations in achieving strategic goals immediately lead to problem solving, not to a deep understanding of how to improve the implementation process. (Or worse, there's a hunt to find the culprit who screwed things up and assess blame.) If you can't learn from your past mistakes and successes, you'll probably repeat the mistakes and be unable to exploit the successes.

Abdication occurs insidiously because the best-intentioned executives fall prey to it without knowing. There's always the assumption that "someone" has picked up the ball or that the strategy includes provisions for its own implementation. It's just not so.

Cultural Obstacles

Every organization has an "immune system" that tends to reject foreign objects. If a strategy is seen as alien to the current systems and beliefs, then the immune system will kick in. We can see the role of culture and beliefs in figure 2.1.[2] There are two kinds of beliefs to be concerned about. What we are calling "basic beliefs" are the values that represent the core ethos of an organization. "Perform at the highest standards of integrity." "Bring modern research to the areas of greatest human medical needs." "Be the leader in innovative support for the business traveler." Operating beliefs—those within the organizational boxes in figure 2.1, are the values that tend to guide day-to-day decision making:

---

[2]Adapted from *Managing Corporate Culture,* by S. Davis, The Human Resource Planning Co., Ballinger Publishing Co., Cambridge, Mass., 1984, page 6.

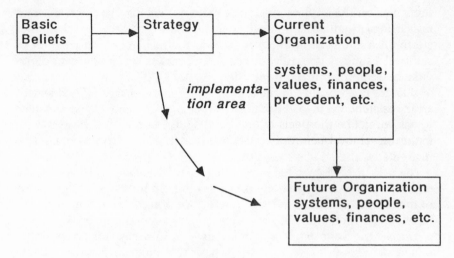

Figure 2.1

"Support my colleagues." "Do everything possible to answer customer inquiries thoroughly and rapidly." "Protect myself at all costs." Notice how the latter two will have vastly different impacts in exactly the same organization.

The organization whose employees follow daily operating beliefs consistent with the strategy that is to be implemented has already cleared an initial hurdle. But the organization whose employees do not share congruent beliefs will have to attend to that reconciliation before strategy can be successfully implemented. If a bank's tellers share a belief that they are there to provide customer service, then a bank strategy to create more comprehensive customer relationships utilizing a variety of products has a toehold. But if those same tellers hold the beliefs that their most important responsibility is completing all paperwork and reconciliations for the home office by day's end, then customers will get short shrift and so will the strategy.

What do you think are the three most important operating beliefs that your employees now hold? Jot them down:

1. _____

2. _____

3. _____

Are these consistent with your current strategy? Are they consistent with a proposed or tentative strategy? If not, what reconciliation steps are required in the feedback, reward, and management systems? (For example, are the tellers promoted to head teller on the basis of superior customer service or on the basis of superior reporting? Which tellers get the best raises? Which are used to train new tellers?)

In implementing strategy you can't start off by saying, "Let's change our culture." Culture change is an end, not a beginning. In chapter 1, we discussed the relationship shown in figure 1.3. Culture change is the *result* of changes in attitudes; it is usually prompted by constructive, rewarded, and consistent changes in behavior. Another way to look at this sequence of change is like the peels of an onion, figure 2.2, with the outer ones requiring removal before the inner ones can be reached intact.

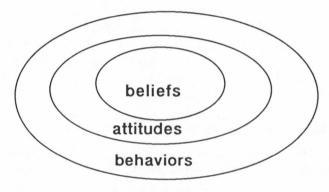

Figure 2.2

The bank teller might not believe at this point that customer service is paramount, and the teller's behavior will reflect that value and attitude. He or she will allow customers to wait in line while paperwork is completed and the total is reconciled. But, if the branch manager provides incentives for the teller scored highest in customer service as monitored by the assistant manager and head teller, behavior should change. If that is reinforced and the superiors serve as exemplars, the teller's attitude might change to "Well, why not? This is no more work than number-crunching, and I like the variety." Ultimately, as the teller experiences customers who are appreciative of the attention or who are genuinely helped by personalized guidance, he or she may come to believe that customer service is the reason for doing the job.

There are only three ways in which behavior can be modified.

1. *Power or coercion.* This is the big-stick technique by which the employee is threatened. "You will turn in expense reports every second Friday or face suspension of charge privileges. Three such suspensions will result in termination." The problem with the power approach is that it lasts only as long as the big stick is present and feared. Moreover, it builds movement but not commitment, let alone enthusiastic support.

2. *Peer pressure.* This is the in-crowd approach in which the employee is cajoled to be a part of the team. "We want a perfect record on expense

reporting, and you don't want to be the only one with outstanding reports, do you? Don't let us down." The problem here is that the in thing to do can be fickle and subject to the priorities of personal agendas.

3. *Rational persuasion*. This is the self-interest approach in which an individual changes because he or she really believes it will be rewarding to do so. "If you get your expense reports in by the deadline, we can have your reimbursement to you by the following working day. But if it's late, it will require a week to get into the next cycle." This approach is the longest-lived in creating behavior change because it relies on internal motivation and is therefore self-perpetuating.

So strategy implementation requires that the culture be conducive to the direction being sought. To make it conducive, the immune system may have to be suppressed and ultimately changed by modifying behaviors, attitudes, and values. Too often this requisite is ignored and the land mine explodes when the executives tread on deeply held beliefs that they chose to ignore.

Profits Keep Getting in the Way: "Line up here, on the bottom line."

All right. The culture could be as receptive as possible, the executives have remained closely tied to and responsible for strategy implementation, and the planning process has been kept in its proper perspective. So what can go wrong now? Success, that's what.

The best time to examine and change strategy is when there is a position of *strength*. Basically, strategy is not a remedial process. Oh sure, we hear of firms saved from disaster because of changes made in their strategy, but we hear of them precisely because they are exceptional situations. In most cases, implementing a new strategy is like leaving the landing lights on at Kennedy Airport for Amelia Earhardt—it's much too little, far too late. Moreover, we virtually never hear of all the firms that have remained consistently excellent *because* they've known when and how to adjust their strategies. Even on a slow news day, that just isn't news.

The fact is, strategy implementation is usually unsuccessful when done from a position of desperation, as in "If we don't change the way we do business, we won't have a business." Some examples of each:

A. Organizations that are consistently strong and adapt their strategies to the times
- GE
- Delta Airlines
- Banc One Corporation
- Marriott Hotels
- American Express

B. Organizations in trouble whose recovery was aided by strategic change
- Chrysler
- Caterpillar
- Bank of America
- Property/casualty insurance industry
- U.S. steel industry

C. Organizations whose position requires very little strategic change
- Merck & Co.
- Bloomingdale's
- Toys 'R Us
- UPS
- 3M

D. Organizations in which strategic change has caused problems
- Braniff Airlines (pre-Chapter 11)
- The New York *Daily News*
- Sears
- Bonwit Teller
- NASA

E. Organizations which failed through resistance to strategic change
- Eastern Airlines (prior to to its reemergence)
- Savings and loan industry
- Penn Central (pre-Chapter 11)
- Wickes (pre-Chapter 11)
- Frieden

Here's just one example to explain these categories. We'll use Sears once again, since it's so visible and is present in virtually every community. Sears' strategic change (into a "one low price" operation) has not occurred with a very smooth implementation (further suggesting that Sears is at the juncture which will lead it to either category 1 or 4, as noted in chapter 1). Its very size and structure, which might be advantages, have emerged as handicaps:

> As it blanketed the country with stores, its management structure turned into a balkanized mess. Cliques in the buying organization at headquarters tended to smother creativity at the top. Worse, power struggles between the buying groups at headquarters and store managers in the field slowed down and distorted implementation of even the simplest new ideas. Store managers often neglected or flatly ignored new merchandise and promotions. "By the time you got to the store, you had only a reflection of the original idea," says one longtime store manager.[3]

Most good organizations and all excellent ones are continually examining their strategy in the midst of their success and implementing change to it during the good times. Organizations that fail, or get into trouble, often look to strategy as a last resort. But implementing a new strategy is not something that's done after all else fails; it's an initiating action. It should be proactive, not reactive. Although it can sometimes work as a last, desperate measure, it clearly works best when it's managed and nurtured under management control with the flexibility and patience attendant on success. Not many teams rally from 10 runs down with 2 out in the ninth, no matter who's coming to bat. The errors of the first eight innings have already killed you.

Why do people in the organization tend to be better implementors of strategy in good times? Here are a few of the reasons:

- The strategy is perceived as a proactive, managed, confident move.
- Resources are available to invest in success of the strategy.
- There is more of a freedom-to-fail and experimenting attitude.
- There is an atmosphere of innovation, not defensiveness.

---

[3]"The Big Store's Big Trauma," by Brian Bremner and Michael Oneal, *Business Week*, July 10, 1989, page 51.

- There is the luxury of plotting alternative strategies and contingent actions.
- Rewards can be connected to strategic goals.
- There is a long-term horizon by which to judge success.
- Patience to effectively evaluate results is available.
- People are focused on the business (not personal escape).

And here is the rub: Many successful organizations, exactly those in the best position to examine and implement strategic change for all the reasons cited above, are seduced away from it by the bottom line. Short-term goals overwhelm longer-term considerations because the organization "wants to make hay while the sun shines," or "will never see this opportunity again," or "wants to reap what it can before the economy goes sour." This emphasis on the bottom line, the quick buck, the short term, makes strategy implementation subject to all of the weaknesses of inattentiveness, low priority, and the attitude "Who needs it—we're doing great!"

Two examples from the same industry should prove the point. In the aftermath of the fuel crisis of the 70s, GM's fortunes took a serious turn for the worse and Honda's for the better. Here are two salient facts:

1. When Honda was in the position of selling every car it could export to the United States (these were prequota days) the company applied tremendous self-restraint to its export volume. During a strategy session, in response to the question "Why aren't you increasing production and selling everything you can in the United States while the opportunity exists?" the Honda CEO replied, "We do not think we can maintain our quality standards much beyond current levels. So our strategy calls for a maximum of a 5 percent increase in exports to the United States over the next two years." That restraint wasn't imposed by production or by buyer demand, it was a strategic component critical to long-term success—future reputation. The opportunity, of course, didn't disappear, it actually increased, and the decision turned out to be a superb one. Of course, Honda executives (and Japanese executives in general) are paid to think in the long term.

2. As GM lost market share and its reputation took a justifiable beating, both in the strategic realm for failing to anticipate events and in the operational realm for producing inferior cars, there appeared to be genuine confusion over how such a powerful organization could have had the rug pulled from under it. During those years, GM executives were not compensated for their ability to think in the long term. In fact, they were compensated almost exclusively on the basis of the current bottom line. For example, top executive retirement benefits incorporated a formula utilizing the prior 5 years of profitability. Now, if you're a senior GM manager with a few years before retirement, are you going to invest in long-term projects, such as more fuel-efficient cars and superior safety features, or are you going to invest in short-term cosmetics, such as styling and promotion? No contest. We've previously discussed self-interest as being the

most powerful and long-lived behavior modifier. It certainly worked in GM. (GM seems to have a penchant for discordant acts. A couple of years ago it announced a cutback in employee benefits and a desire for union concessions at the same moment that it was handing out huge executive bonuses. You don't need to avoid land mines if your plan is to carry a time bomb in your pocket.)

Consider the case of PPG. A traditionally solid, conservative company with an excellent track record of success saw its new CEO, Vincent A. Sarni, initiate radical changes upon his appointment in 1984. The company's prospects involved continued slow growth, with annoying competitive pressures in standard marketplaces, and a return on investment that had fallen for 5 straight years. Sarni created a "Blueprint for the Decade," a pamphlet containing the mission, objectives, and performance goals he saw as vital to a renewed PPG. *To hit numbers, such as 18 percent return on equity and 4 percent real growth, the company had to do better than its own long-range projections said was possible with the existing products and services.*[4] Sarni showed what a CEO can do with a new strategy played from a position of strength, how the organization and its people can be mobilized, and how such dramatic change isn't possible as an outgrowth of the planning process and its limiting projections.

The moral is, don't allow yourself to become too fat and happy. Good times are simply the stepping stone to more good times *if* they are used to examine and implement strategy from a position of strength. How are your executives rewarded? How are your managers rewarded? The more the emphasis is put on short-term performance, the more strategy will fall by the wayside. You need milers for this event, not sprinters.

Competitive Gridlock: "We can do anything you can do better."

In the late 70s I visited a Honeywell site in Phoenix. Once past the receptionist's desk it was easy to see that the normally staid place was in a tizzy. Conversations were going on in the halls; names were being called out; and relatively few people were hunched over desks working. When I arrived at my meeting room, I asked my local contact what was going on.

"Don't you know what day it is?" he asked incredulously. Now, as far as I knew, there was no offer to buy the company, nor did Honeywell have any product announcements due out, nor was there anything especially dramatic occurring in the economy.

"I'm afraid not. What's up?"

"*Today* is the *day*," he articulated slowly, as if talking to a preschooler, "that IBM announces its plans for the coming year."

My first reaction was, "So what?" which I wisely withheld. After all, Honeywell would be well underway with its own plans, implementing its own strategy, setting its own course....

Wouldn't it?

---

[4]For details see "PPG: Shiny, Not Dull," by Bill Saporit, *Fortune*, July 17, 1989, page 107.

I was quickly disabused of that lofty notion. Local management informed me that IBM's announcement, being anxiously monitored and evaluated by every Honeywell manager on earth, would either "justify" or "dismantle" Honeywell's strategy for the next several years. I was startled by this enormous company, with vast resources and wonderful talent, being completely controlled by the actions of its competitor. Not only was IBM dictating Honeywell's strategy, it was forcing the weaker competitor to compete on its terms and adjust to what it did rather than carve out an appropriate niche.

I'm not privy to what Honeywell does today, but I do know that there are frequent explosions out in the mine field caused by still another organization attempting to implement strategy based on what its competition is doing. Certainly, competitive actions should be a factor in any strategic process, and alternatives of product, service, timing, pricing, market share, and so forth ought to be debated and discussed. But a strategy should stand on its own and be appropriate for your organization in any case. "Current industry structure reflects the strengths of the industry leader; and playing by the leader's rules is usually competitive suicide," say Hamel and Prahalad, writing about the fallacies of strategic intent.[5] If your strategy is dependent on the strategy of others, a "strategic gridlock" can develop, which means you can't get maneuvering room until somebody else moves, and they can't move until somebody moves, and, ultimately, there is no movement, only a bunch of overheated organizations stalled in their journeys and losing precious time.

Strategy implementation is sensitive to this reactive mentality because those responsible for making it work are fully aware that things can change tomorrow if the competition sneezes or clears a throat. Consequently, implementors become quite tentative. Decisions are hedged, and "relief valves" are established. The strategy might call for the creation of a new product task force with the charter to create a do-it-yourself line. But the funding isn't fully committed because it might have to be shuffled elsewhere, and some of the top talent isn't released because there are other areas that might need the expertise, and the executives don't provide enthusiastic support because they're busy in the crow's nest trying to plot the competition's course. All of this means, naturally, that the organizational immune system will reject the new product task force (or its output) because nothing has been done to suppress the immune system and the implementation is based not on a position of strength, but on one of fear. ("What are they going to do to us?")

Implementation can only be as strong as the commitment to the strategy itself. If the precedent indicates that the strategy will change quite abruptly in reaction to financial performance, competitive actions, internal personnel changes, and/or customer reaction, then that implementation will

---

[5]"Strategic Intent," by Gary Hamel and C. K. Prahalad, *Harvard Business Review,* May–June 1989, page 73.

proceed only as far as people think they need to go to protect themselves. "The task force? Yes, we're working on it. We've identified some potential members, but we need several additional meetings to specify the conditions under which we'll operate and when members can be released from current assignments. But things are progressing well—I'll have a monthly report on your desk." Uh, oh.

Every organization needs a clear sense that it has established its own direction, that someone is at the helm and someone is navigating the seas. If the executives do not provide that confidence—as expressed in the actions or lack of action detailed above—they have no one to blame but themselves if strategy implementation is subject to whichever way the wind is blowing.

These have been some of the major reasons for the failure of even fine strategies to be successfully implemented. It's important to bear them in mind as you continue through this book. They are probably the reasons behind "It just doesn't work here" and "Why doesn't it get *done?*" Let's turn to what will work.

3

Everyone a Strategic Thinker: The Shortest Distance Is Never a Straight Line

In order to implement strategy successfully, employees must know what strategy is as distinct from other pursuits, they must be familiar with what *your* strategy is so they can adhere to and support it, and they must know how they are expected to support it. In figure 3.1 let's look at each of these needs.

Knowing What Strategy Is

It is an educational function to know what strategy is. Training in what strategic thinking is should be a requisite for *every* manager during his or her career development. Just as training programs are provided in problem solving, planning (!), time management, leadership, and the like,

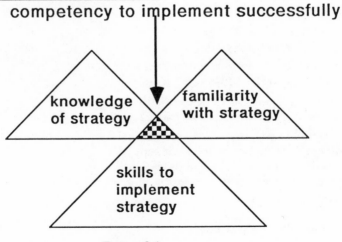

Figure 3.1

specific training in strategy must be provided. The components of such training, which may be nothing more than a relatively brief classroom experience with selected reading, should include:

- A common definition of strategy
- The role of strategy relative to planning and daily operations
- The inputs to and components of strategy
- The concepts of vision, missions, and goals
- How strategy is formulated, reviewed, updated, and evaluated

Our ongoing surveys reveal that fewer than 10 percent of all organizations provide for any formal training in the area of strategic thinking below executive level. This means not only that, in most cases, managers are woefully unaware of the exact nature of the beast but also that, as they progress, the ignorance is multiplied! They are increasingly unable to support strategy from loftier positions; they cannot adequately train subordinates in the discipline; and, should they make it to the executive suite and be expected to participate in strategy formulation, they have to learn on the job! That's hardly the time to make a beginner's errors.

Our purpose here is not to provide the details of strategy formulation, but to emphasize that *all* managers need to know what strategy is if they are to be expected to implement and support it. How well is it done in your organization? Or do you believe it occurs through osmosis and no formal training is required? Here's a quick test:

Strategic Knowledge Assessment

Your managers should articulate a common definition of strategy	☐ some ☐ most ☐ all
Your managers don't confuse strategy with the planning process	☐ some ☐ most ☐ all
Your managers clearly separate "what" and "how" when analyzing issues	☐ some ☐ most ☐ all
Your executive-level meetings focus on strategy as well as operations	☐ some ☐ most ☐ all
Your managers consider competitive threats in terms of both strategy and tactics	☐ some ☐ most ☐ all

Simple test, isn't it? Yet very few get five "alls." Your goal should be to orient your managers and their support systems so that you can confidently check off every "all." Unless everyone is operating in concert, with equal knowledge of what strategy is, successful strategy implementation is haphazard at best.

Familiarity with Strategy

To be familiar with strategy is to be aware of and understand your organization's particular strategy. Becoming familiar with strategy is a communication and comprehension process. And this is one of those instances in

which it is quality *and* quantity that matter. The president of a major apparel company put it quite succinctly:
"Strategy poorly defined, leaving room for different [personal] interpretations, is the greatest cause of poor implementation."[1]

I was called into a nonprofit organization of high visibility. The senior management had a concern that the organization was performing well enough, but it was getting by on past successes—there was little enthusiasm for or commitment to the new direction which the executives thought was vital for continued dominance in their field. The senior vice president, who was spokesperson for the seven-man executive council, gave an exact description of a category 2 company. The organization was operating well, but the vision for the future wasn't shared or supported by its management. I asked if a strategy had been prepared.

"Yes, of course. It's the best we've ever done." And I was presented with a pristine binder, indexed and tabbed, covering past strategies, external and internal considerations, environmental realities—the whole nine yards. The new strategy was spelled out in all its glory.

"Has everyone read this?" I innocently inquired.

"Of course."

"And what has been the reaction?"

"Unanimous support."

"'Unanimous support'? From *everyone*?"

"Well...yes. All seven of us fully agree!"

The strategy had never gone beyond those magnificent seven. They felt there were legitimate reasons not to circulate such a "sensitive" document: employee irresponsibility, confidentiality, misinterpretations, and so on. Nor did they feel that formal discussions (remember those "face-to-face" meetings?) were necessary. Their solution was to train people (in what?) and to motivate people (for what?) and to reinforce people (with what?). Ludicrous, perhaps, but not unlike similar circumstances in organizations large and small, all over the map.

Strategy must be communicated accurately, regularly, honestly, and *loudly*. Every formal interaction between managers and their staffs should include a strategy update. Management emphasis areas should be tied into the strategic business goals of the organization. When managers prepare plans, the plans should be assessed for strategic fit. In figure 3.2 is a grid developed by one of our clients to assist in the assessment of new ideas relative to strategic fit and cultural acceptance.[2]

Any opportunity, issue, or general plan is evaluated in terms of how well it fits the current (or future) strategy and how well it fits the current culture—"difficulty of implementation." This latter criterion addresses

---

[1]Correspondence with the author.
[2]©Decision Processes International, Westport, Conn., 1988. All rights reserved. Used with permission. See *The Innovation Formula: How Organizations Turn Change into Opportunity*, by Michael Robert and Alan Weiss, Harper & Row, New York, 1988, page 74.

	high	possible	fair	poor
Difficulty of Implementation	medium	probable	possible	poor
	low	excellent	probable	poor
		high	medium	low

Strategic Fit

Figure 3.2

cultural issues raised in chapter 2. Obviously, anything finishing in the lower left box of figure 3.2 is an excellent plan, because it will fit both the culture and the strategy excellently. Beyond that there are shades of acceptability down to "poor" fits. Management has the option of trying to improve strategic fit (very difficult and often a rationalization) and/or improving ease of implementation (somewhat easier to accomplish). In any event, the grid provides an objective and coherent framework within which to compare plans against strategy. In so doing, one must be familiar with the strategy to make accurate evaluations within the grid. In presenting results of the assessment for review, managers will quickly learn whether or not their interpretation of strategy has been correct.

Here is a test to evaluate your managers' familiarity with your organization's particular strategy.

Strategic Familiarity Assessment

Your managers could articulate your organization's strategy in a uniform, consistent manner   ☐ some ☐ most ☐ all

Your managers share the same vision and concept of the business you are in   ☐ some ☐ most ☐ all

Your managers make key operating decisions that are consistent with the strategy	☐ some ☐ most ☐ all
Your managers share a single concept of your key strategic area, i.e., products, method of sale, technology, and growth	☐ some ☐ most ☐ all
Your managers' emphasis areas are tied into the strategic direction and are consciously evaluated in that light	☐ some ☐ most ☐ all

Another simple test. Of course, performance on this one is keyed into that on the first—it's tough to be familiar with your strategy if you're not clear on precisely what strategy is. It's unusual to have a high score on this one and a low score on the prior one but quite common to score low on both. The beauty of this test is that you can take it periodically and validate it immediately simply by asking a few questions in the hallways and at meetings and observing how people are reinforced and rewarded. Your findings will tell you how much you need to concentrate on in the third part of our triad.

Skills to Implement Strategy

The first two questions above have dealt with the "what" aspect. Do your managers know what strategy is, in general, and what yours is, in particular? Once those have been answered satisfactorily, you can address the how-to.

The skills required to implement strategy, and their application, will be the topic of the remainder of this book. As an overview, we are talking about a combination of skills, knowledge, and experiences that create a *competency* to implement a given strategy effectively. A simple knowledge of the strategy is insufficient; experiencing the implementation of a strategy is inadequate if the process hasn't been understood and, therefore, can't be repeated; and the skills are wasted if they are not based on accurate knowledge and rooted in the experience of having applied them. It is the combination of those elements that creates *wisdom*, and that makes one competent. We can fairly state that we have an awful lot of knowledge about strategy—models and matrices, seminars and research, consultants and professors—but precious little wisdom about it, as reflected in the fact that so few firms, despite these resources, effectively implement their strategies.

What's your organization's skill level? Our third test:

Strategy Implementation Skills Assessment

Your managers are able to set departmental goals in support of the strategy	☐ some ☐ most ☐ all
Your managers lead meetings in which strategic issues are discussed in relation to operations	☐ some ☐ most ☐ all

Your managers, if asked, could provide a priority list of issues directly related to strategy implementation for which they are responsible   □ some □ most □ all

Your managers set their subordinates' goals and objectives according to the strategic goals that relate to their operations   □ some □ most □ all

Your managers evaluate, reward, and promote their people with strategic goals in mind   □ some □ most □ all

How well are your people doing in those areas? If they are uneven, or if "some" is the best you can do, whose responsibility is it? Obviously, these are self-tests before they are assessments of anyone else! Let's proceed by examining the *individual* skills that are required as a basis for developing the competence needed to implement strategy from the individual's standpoint.

Decision Making

On every list I've ever seen of "future leaders" or "key emphasis areas" or "skills required," decision making is present. However, let's make sure we're all talking about the same thing. For our purposes, decision making is: "The ability of the individual to evaluate options against established criteria in order to select a course of action that maximizes benefit and minimizes risk." So decision makers don't just choose, they choose *selectively*. And they don't merely consider benefits; they consider risk. (We've all seen decision makers at either end of the spectrum: The benefits-seeker jumps on a bandwagon without ever checking its direction; the risk-avoider won't opt for any alternative unless there's an ironclad, risk-free guarantee. Both extremes are worthless.) When I asked one executive why he spent so much time and money trying to provide his people with decision-making skills, he replied, "If my managers aren't paid to make decisions, then why are they paid?"

Decision making might be *the* most important individual component involved in building strategy implementation skills. That's because one of the most crucial tasks that the decision maker performs is to choose between objectives and alternatives, ends and means, goals and routes. Here's a conversation between a vice president (VP), marketing director (MD), sales director (SD), and training director (TD). Read it and then answer the questions that follow.

VP: It's clear that our chain of copy stores is imperiled by the new "private post offices" that are going to be launched next month. They're offering copy services as an adjunct to all kinds of packaging and mail services. What do we do about this?

MD: I think our strategy has to be based on price. We're not interested in the person with three copies. It's the local business that needs several hundred at a time that we want to retain. Those customers will be price-sensitive.

SD: We're going to have to raise our profile as well. The market should expand as a result of all the publicity over the private post office concept, so we might as well spread our name around during all the hoopla.

VP: Those sound like legitimate approaches we ought to explore. Anything we can do on the local level?

TD: I've always believed that the local franchisee needs training in marketing skills. These people are basically entrepreneurs and refugees from large companies. Some are early retirees from completely different industries. We need to provide them with some skills to retain customers, sponsor local events, put out direct mail. Right now, very few understand that running the store itself is just one component of the business.

MD: That sounds promising. We could deliver something regionally to minimize travel expenses. . . .

SD: And maybe while we were doing it we could introduce some new pricing alternatives face to face to get their feedback.

VP: All right, we've got our work cut out for us. These are all good ideas. I'd like each of you to put your thoughts on paper, and we'll meet again after I've had a chance to review them.

Questions:
- What were the objectives discussed in the meeting?
- What were the alternatives discussed in the meeting?
- What was the group's approach to benefits?
- What was the group's approach to risk?

First, I think we can agree that this brief dialogue accurately represents meetings going on in every organization, every day. It wouldn't be unusual if you were engaged in one yourself during this week. Yet despite its brevity, and despite your ability to reread it, and despite the fact that you've been in many of them, was it easy to generate answers to the questions? Probably not, because the meeting never focused on them to any great extent, and certainly not in a systematic manner.

There were never any *objectives* established by the vice president. There was no statement of the *goal* of the group, that is, "To select a competitive strategy for use against private post offices," or "To choose a way to involve franchisees in responding to the new competition." Such decision statements define the range or scope of the decision. For example, a simple statement such as "to buy a new car" implies that several decisions have already been made: a car is needed for transportation; it should be purchased (not leased or borrowed); and it should be new (not used). Similarly, business decisions require a starting point to establish the scope of the decision: the broader the scope, the wider the range of alternatives to be considered; the narrower the scope, the narrower the range of alternatives. Here is an example of decision statements, and the increasingly narrow range of alternatives they demand:

To improve profitability.

(Raise prices; cut expenses; add services; defer spending; open new markets.)

To cut expenses.

(Cut staff; reduce shifts; shorten hours; reduce travel; terminate rentals.)

To cut staff.

(By attrition across the board; close poor operations in headquarters; part-timers.)

To cut staff by attrition.

(Immediate job freeze; early retirement offer.)

We have progressed from a wide charter—improved profitability—and equally wide alternatives to narrow goals—attrition—and specific alternatives. If you were told that profitability was going to be enhanced through an immediate job freeze, you would hope that the preceding steps had been examined.

Similarly, in our brief drama, there must be a goal that the group agrees to so that their approach is common. Only then can objectives be set.

The objectives for our group might have included:

- Launch program within 3 months.
- Cost to be no more than $150,000.
- Franchisees must have involvement in their communities.
- Not subject to countermeasures from private post office group.
- Self-perpetuating.
- Upholds our image of customer service.
- Applicable nationwide.

A more "effective" and potentially higher-quality discussion might have gone like this:

VP: I've called this session to discuss the subject of our strategy for the next year with the franchisee business. As you're all aware, a new consideration for us this time is the announced opening of the private post office business. For our purposes today, I suggest we focus on the following decision: "To select the best franchisee interventions for the next 12 months." Let's begin by examining our objectives. Suggestion?

SD: Because of the nature of the marketplace, I'd say it's important to actually implement our ideas within 90 days. We can't take the luxury of a year just to get things in place because of the increased volatility of the market with the new competition.

MD: It's also vital to stay within the budget that's been approved. The president has made it clear that there will be no additional funds forthcoming, and *no* excuse will be tolerated to justify any.

TD: It seems to me that we need something absolutely uniform—applicable to all franchisees, regardless of location, size, and experience. And since our staff clearly isn't going to grow, as much as possible has to be effective without our personal presence.

MD: And let's face it, we have to be extremely cognizant of the new competition. But let's not let them dictate to us. We have design interventions that can't be countered by competitive actions from any source. I mean, they should be based on the unique strengths of our business and organization.

VP: OK, let me summarize to this point. Here are the objectives I've written down thus far:

- Implement within 90 days
- Within current budget constraints
- Not dependent on our staff's physical presence for effectiveness
- Not subject to deterioration due to competitive countermeasures
- Applicable despite geography, experience, and store volume.

Let's begin to put these in priority while we're together, then I'd like each of you to generate some alternative you think would satisfy our objectives to accomplish the decision goal. We'll meet again in two days to discuss the alternatives you've come up with.

In this discussion, the *focus* is clear, proactive, and organized. For my purposes, I've broadened the group's ability to generate alternatives by providing a much wider decision—franchisee intervention for the next year—rather than the reactive and narrow—what to do about private post offices. The second meeting also organized their *resources, expectations, and constraints* by organizing their objectives and not trying to produce arbitrary alternatives until the objectives were understood and agreed upon. (For example, time is both a resource and a constraint, uniformity in approach is an expectation, money is a constraint, and their unique business strength is a resource.)

Which meeting will tend to produce a better decision? Which will tend to produce a better strategic approach? Although there are no guarantees, the second certainly has better prospects at this point. Which of the two characterize your meetings? How would you fare with this checklist?

Decision Making in Meetings

Do your meetings begin with a clear statement of the goal to be met?   ☐ yes ☐ no

Do you refuse to consider alternatives until objectives have been established?   ☐ yes ☐ no

Do all interested parties to the decision have an opportunity to contribute objectives?   ☐ yes ☐ no

Is there an effort to set priority among the objectives?   ☐ yes ☐ no

Do you consider only alternatives that you believe will satisfy the objectives?   ☐ yes ☐ no

Do successive meetings build on prior ones rather than reiterate "old" issues?   ☐ yes ☐ no

Do you assess the scope of your decision to determine the
range of alternatives to consider?   ☐ yes ☐ no

If asked, could you readily tie your decision goal into your
overall strategy?   ☐ yes ☐ no

Are your decisions more proactive and positive than reactive and "desperate"?   ☐ yes ☐ no

Decision making is a crucial individual skill in the strategy implementation process. Let's now examine how it can best be made effective among
groups.

Communicating

"Poor communications" and "a failure to communicate" are rubrics used
to disguise a variety of interpersonal ailments. The accuracy of communications, however, *is* a crucial component of strategy implementation. The
trouble is, with the best of intentions, what you "say" is not always what
I "get." The children's game of "telephone" is at work every day within
all of our organizations:

1. "Joe, make sure that we get the Conway proposal to the boss by Friday. He wants to study it over the weekend."
2. "Mary, we need to get moving on the Conway project. The general
   manager wants it by Friday at the latest, and it sounds like he's got
   it on the top of his list."
3. "Joan, what's your progress on Conway? The GM is hot to trot about
   it, and he wants it ASAP."
4. "Jim, drop everything. The Conway account is the hottest thing in
   the company and it sounds like the big shots aren't real happy about
   it. And they want the proposal yesterday."
5. "Hey, Sue, are we in trouble with the Conway thing. Sounds like
   we've lost the account!"

Sound remotely familiar? In actuality, the typical communications process at work is as shown in figure 3.3.

There are two types of interference in this process: internal and external. We'll take a brief look at each.

Internal.   Internal interference can occur during the communicating process in the shaded areas of figure 3.4. The items in each of our "personal"
boxes (values, experiences, etc.) create what we popularly call our own
"frame of reference." These personal filters, left unchallenged, allow certain messages through, but not others. If our value system dictates that
"anyone over 50 can't possibly relate to me," then anything such a person
has to say, regardless of its intrinsic worth, probably will be muffled by
that filter. If employees believe that "strategy is nonsense, and the

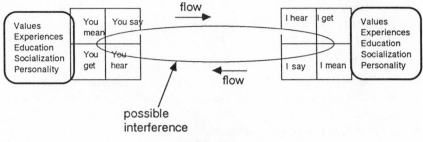

Figure 3.3

Internal Interference

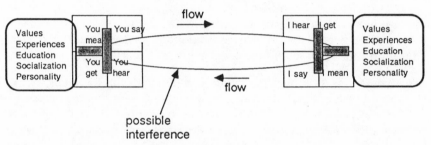

Figure 3.4

give it lip service—what they *really* want is today's sales figures to be bet-ter than yesterday's," then the chances are that the most sincere and sup-ported strategies will not be comprehended.

And "comprehension" is the operative word. They might hear you, but they won't understand, which is why the communications skills are so critical to successful strategy implementation. The transitions, as shown in figure 3.4, between what I hear and what I get, what I get and what I mean, and what I mean and what I say contain any number of filters and evaluation devices which color the communication (as do those in the other person's sequence). For successful strategic communication, the filters must contain the correct criteria. The personal "boxes" of values, experiences, education, organizational socialization, company education, and personality must have a positive influence. If the organization's for-mal and informal educational system, for example, repeatedly reinforces the lack of follow-up on strategic goals, an individual "filter" is affected accordingly. If the socialization process supports "do as I say, not as I do" or "pretend you go along, then do what you have to," appropriate filters will be established.

These filters of and influences on one's internal interpretation of com-munications can be changed, but as we stated earlier, it is virtually impossible to begin with values. The values generally change last, once the individual has experienced the self-interest in changing them. These are some of the ways in which internal influences can be affected to accentuate positive interpretations of strategic goals and directions. (They should be further modified to fit your organization's particular goals.)

1. *Education.* As we stressed earlier, *every* training intervention must be oriented toward strategic goals. The organization's management should be formally trained in what strategic thinking is and what the strategy for the organization is. Managers should have advisers and mentors who can help them develop goals for their operations and departments that support and augment the strategy. Managers require ongoing feedback, preferably not relegated to salary review time, to help them "keep on track" as they manage within the strategic framework.

Any formal education, such as seminars, tapes, business school offerings, and related opportunities, should include strategic issues. Career management and succession planning systems (the first is individually focused, the second should be organizationally focused) must take such education into consideration in an organized, proactive manner.

2. *Experiences.* As a manager progresses through the hierarchy, he or she should receive the opportunity to serve on various strategic subcommittees and task forces and, ultimately, strategy input groups. The manager should see the process at work firsthand and understand how it relates to day-to-day changes. As jobs change, every effort should be made to provide for contact with the mentors and advisers referred to under "Education" so that the individual acquires several role models to help create the right approach to strategic understanding and implementation.

3. *Organizational socialization.* The organization has to practice what it preaches. Top management has to serve as the exemplar for direct reports, who in turn must set the example for their subordinates. Individual departments and sections cannot be excused from strategic inputs or strategic evaluation because the top manager has clout or because they are performing so well that they "can afford not to pay attention to it" or because "their work isn't approriate."

People heed what they see, not what they hear or are told (the latter two elements are supportive but not directive). Consequently, the organization has to visibly demonstrate that it supports and rewards strategic thinking and successful implementation and discourages and punishes ignorance of it, circumvention of it, and unsuccessful attempts at it. If the organization says that strategy is important but consistently rewards those who achieve short-term goals and openly ignore strategic issues, people will respond to what is actually happening. The only way to stop the grapevine from spreading that "no one really cares about strategic goals" is to clearly demonstrate that the organization cares about them and acts on them.

4. *Personality.* Although personality can't be changed, and this is not a book on hiring, it is important to point out that the filters are affected strongly by personality and that hiring managers whose personalities are not conducive to strategic thinking and implementation is a weak link that no amount of later actions can strengthen. Especially in organizations which tend to hire people in the same mold, such shortcomings can create a "critical mass" of managers who aren't comfortable in dealing with strategic issues.

What kind of individual is most comfortable with strategic issues? Here are some specific personality traits that are generally compatible with strategic skills:[3]

- Comfort with ambiguity
- Risk taking
- Moderate to high patience levels
- High persuasiveness
- Moderate to high self-confidence
- Flexibility and lack of stubbornness
- Comfort with change
- Openness to innovation
- Willingness to serve as formal or informal leader
- Moderate attention to detail
- High energy level
- Team orientation

Are these traits absolute requisites for successful performance in implementing strategy? Of course not. However, the more of them that individuals possess, the more *likely* it is that those people will have an affinity for the tasks and responsibilities inherent in strategy implementation. Thus, the more of such people you have in key management positions, the better you've "stacked the deck" in your favor. On the other hand, if there aren't many of these people around—that is, your hiring practices have rejected them—the more likely it is you are about to shoot yourself in the foot.

As you make appointments to key positions, and as you are called upon to formulate task forces and committees, it's a good idea to consider if you're including enough of the right "raw material" to begin with. It's difficult to be an exemplar if your predispositions mitigate against the content, and no amount of company training, encouragement, or incentive is likely to overcome that basic human reality. Make sure the personality fits the job, and in this case the "job" is successful strategy implementation.

---

[3]See *Managing for Peak Performance: A Guide to the Power (and Pitfalls) of Personal Style*, by Alan Weiss, Harper & Row, New York, 1989, pages 58–61, for a discussion of individual and job compatibility.

There have been some techniques for influencing the factors which, in turn, establish the types of filters that can cause internal communications success or failure in the strategy comprehension process. Most are manageable and can be affected by organizational and individual interventions. Too often, they are merely left to chance. Although it's true you can't "get into someone's head," you can certainly influence what goes on in there. Are the filters filtering out your strategic messages or encouraging them by filtering out extraneous and contradictory messages?

External.   External interference in the communications flow can be caused by a wide variety of factors, but it is not our intent to focus on the obvious ones here: noise, insufficient time, interruptions, and the like. In the strategy implementation process, external disruption of communications should be viewed in more of an organizational context.

The shaded areas in figure 3.5 show where the disruption takes place: at the times when you and I are actively saying something or trying to hear something. The internal aspects above are cognitive; these external factors are mechanical. And since they are mechanical, they are even easier to affect, control, and improve.

External Interference

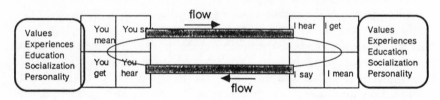

Figure 3.5

We spoke earlier in the book about a client's "face-to-face" meetings, and how the meetings were to be prime communications vehicles but were undermined by a focus on quantity rather than quality. External communications, whether oral or written, would have the following characteristics:

1. *Clarity and brevity.* Tell people what you're going to tell them; tell them; and then tell them what you've just told them. Be brief and concise. Use words as though they were corporate assets. A one-page memo has a good chance of being read. How many people do you think actually read the three-ring binders holding corporate strategy? A simple phrase has a superb chance of being remembered and *used as a guide* for subsequent

behavior. Remember our example of "Beat Benz"? The key to communicating with a minimum of external interference isn't length; it's repetition and consistency. The same message must be delivered in a variety of ways repeatedly (and, of course, supported by actions, as previously discussed). This brings us to our next point.

2. *Variety of the message.* People learn and absorb in dramatically differing manners. Some of us are visual; some are more sequential. Some of us prefer the written to the spoken word, and some are just the opposite. You simply can't trust a single method to reach everyone equally; and with a subject as critical as strategy implementation, it's an excellent idea to stress diversity. Communications about strategy, including its current status, progress toward goals, and departmental responsibilities within it should be frequent and diverse. Here are examples that organizations utilize to get the message across in as distortion-free and varied a manner as possible:

- A 10-minute video update by the CEO once a month
- An ongoing column in the house organ written by the CEO
- A "strategy update memo" on one page circulated monthly
- Strategy discussions as an agenda item at regular department meetings
- Quarterly, interdepartmental focus groups convened and led by senior management
- "Personal updates" periodically mailed to employees' homes

The variety should be wide enough to ensure that everyone has an equal opportunity to hear the strategic message and to be able to act upon it in his or her area of responsibility. There is probably no such condition as "too much variety" in this endeavor.

Feedback and testing. Don't trust that the message you want conveyed has been conveyed simply because you've been brief, clear, frequent, and varied in your communications. Test to see what, in fact, has been heard. Then provide constructive feedback to orient the other person precisely in the direction you have taken.

Leader:	Ladies and gentlemen, we've just heard the president talk about our goal to be perceived as offering the finest customer service in the appliance repair business. What do you think that means to us right now and in the immediate future?
Subordinate number 1:	Well, it means we have to respond more quickly. We know that our competitors' response time is averaging two days, and ours is sometimes up to four. It's a source of chronic complaint.

Subordinate number 2: And I think it means more cross-training for repair people. Part of the slowdown is caused by the delay in matching the repair person to the problem description—which is sometimes inaccurate anyway. If all repair people could repair vitually all problems, then we could simply assign the first available person.

Subordinate number 3: What about that idea to provide "loaned appliances" while a major repair was underway? That would probably enhance our service repute. . . .

Leader: OK, these are the kinds of issues that need to be raised from the repair function. Now, let's focus a bit more if we can. The perception of quality is more than just speed, isn't it? What about these issues: fix it once, not repeatedly, repair person demeanor and courtesy, toll-free numbers to call. . . .

In this example, the leader was able to test what the subordinates heard, determine that it was on track with the overall strategy, but he found that too many single ideas about speed of repair might tend to overwhelm the larger issues. So the leader was able to focus the subordinates on the key issues. (Similarly, the leader's superior should be pursuing the same ends with his or her direct reports.)

Unless strategic communications are continually tested, both for accuracy of reception and appropriateness of application, the odds of some external interference distorting comprehension remain high. The kinds of testing questions to use relative to strategy application and implementation are:

- What does it mean for us, in this particular operation?
- What would you do differently tomorrow, now that you've understood this?
- What will be the impact on our customers?
- Who can best contribute to these strategic goals?
- How will you reallocate resources?
- What does this do to your priorities?
- How will you reflect this in performance emphasis areas?
- What are the key problems that must be overcome to implement this?
- What are some innovative techniques we can use to implement this?
- How will you educate your people about these issues

Note that none of these questions call for yes or no responses. They are all open-ended and reactive. Upon hearing one of your subordinates reply, you can judge whether he or she is in line with your thinking about the issues and provide the intelligent management direction needed to successfully translate the strategy into reality in that area. There is nothing arcane or mystical about communicating strategy—only the tough work of preparation, discipline, and follow-up in the communication process.

Leadership

The final individual skill we'll examine is that of leadership. There are, of course, those who claim that this isn't really skill at all, but rather a talent that one does nor does not possess. However, for strategy implementation purpose, we will define leadership as: "The willingness and motivation to serve as an exemplar, in a formal or informal capacity, in the implementation of strategy."[4]

Being a leader in strategy implementation means:

- Being able to translate the strategy into local operating reality.
- Championing the strategy *and* the people who must implement it.
- Constructive critique—lighting candles, not cursing the darkness.
- Focusing on the future, not today's fires.
- Evaluating present actions in terms of tomorrow's impacts.
- Establishing the coalitions and cooperation that implementation requires.
- Sacrificing short-term gratifications in favor of long-term success.
- In the long term, demonstrated loyalty to the organization and its goals.[5]

There are five ways in which leaders can implement and demonstrate these characteristics. Here they are, in increasing order of preference:

1. *Autocratically.* In this case the leader acts independently and alone. He or she dictates to others what the strategy implementation entails. Virtually all key decisions are made by the leader and are dictated to others for implementation.

Advantages: Time-efficient; consistent with one vision; clear source.

Disadvantages: Does not foster ownership of others; cannot test communications; will generally fail in instances in which the leader does not have adequate information to act so unilaterally and obtain a quality result. Here's what the president of U.S. operations of one of the world's most prestigious clothing and accessory organizations said about an autocratic style: "Involvement of the implementing parties at the time strategy is formulated is the best guarantee of successful implementation. Dictating [implementation] can pose problems to successful implementation."[6]

2. *Inquisitorially.* The leader still acts alone but solicits some information from others to fill in areas in which he or she lacks data. The questionning of others, however, is done without acknowledging why the responses are needed. This type of leadership often claims the involvement of others, when others have actually been interrogated.

---

[4]For the best discussion I know of concerning leadership as an acquired, learnable skill, see *Leaders: The Strategies for Taking Charge,* by Warren Bennis and Bert Nanus, Harper & Row, New York, 1985. For a provocative viewpoint of leaders as born, not made, see *The Managerial Mystique: Restoring Leadership to Business,* by Abraham Zaleznik, Harper & Row, New York, 1989.
[5]For a discussion of specific leadership qualities, see *Tough-Minded Leadership,* by Joe D. Batten, AMACOM, New York, 1989, particularly pages 26–41.
[6]Correspondence with the author.

Advantages: Time-efficient; focused; tends to acquire needed data; single source.

Disadvantages: Data acquired might not be useful, since providers don't know context and may unwittingly withhold information; doesn't support involvement or commitment; no feedback or testing is possible.

3. *Collegially.* This style of leadership is based on personal persuasion. It involves one-on-one interactions during which the leader reveals the issues and solicits information and opinion from the subordinate. The leader is expected to discuss strategy and its implications for the operation and review alternative implementation options. The leader retains the decision-making prerogative.

Advantages: Subordinates become part of the process; ownership is initiated through their inputs; time can still be controlled by the leader; ideas, as well as information are gathered.

Disadvantages: Each person hears things individually and distortion can result from person to person; ideas don't receive the leverage of several people building on them; too much depends on the leader's influence with each person; decisions are retained by the leader.

4. *Participatively.* The leader communicates in group settings (as well as individually) and actively reveals the issues and seeks recommendations and opinions. The leader controls the meeting and sets the agenda but allows the group to interact freely. The leader either makes or "passes on" decisions reached by the group.

Advantages: Significant ownership; ability to freely diagnose and question issues; "leveraging" of people building on each other's ideas; opportunity to test and provide feedback and for the group members to test each other.

Disadvantages: Leader is still seen as final arbiter and might push personal views over group findings; more time-consuming process; potential for conflict within the group.

5. *Synergistically.* The leader uses group and individual communications and interactions to implement strategy. The leader may or may not attend the group meetings and may be only a participant when he or she does attend. The group discusses the strategy, creates implementation plans, and self-critiques and monitors its performance. The leader serves as a resource and "parameter guard" suggesting boundaries that can or cannot be crossed.

Advantages: The group has total ownership; it is self-testing and provides for its own feedback; the implementation is not leader-dependent; conflict about strategy must surface within the group; progress is subject to peer expectations.

Disadvantages: Most time-consuming process; can be undermined by leader insecurities and/or lack of trust.

These are the basic postures and positions a leader can adopt to help the strategy implementation process.[7] All can be effective, but the fifth presents the best chances for success, especially with a changing strategy, because it allows for the elements we've established as important to this point.

These three skills—decision making, communications, and leadership— are crucial individual competencies required for successful strategy implementation. The more they are possessed and the more people who possess them, the better equipped your individuals are to implement strategic change. E. Douglas Huggard is the president and CEO of Atlantic Electric, a utility that faced enormous strategic change when its base area, Atlantic City, New Jersey, metamorphosed from a fading single-season resort town to the most popular U.S. gambling center, with attendant dramatic growth of his organization's services. At this writing, the company has completed its most successful year in its history. The organization prides itself on its ability to capitalize on a relatively small size in order to be acutely aware of what's happening within the company at any given time. Here's what Huggard says about the effective leader in strategy implementation: "You need a clear and consistent signal from the CEO; an effective program of consensus-building; assignment of accountability, authority and resources to the *right implementor* (not all executives are really good implementors); and follow-up by the CEO."[8]

In the chapters ahead, we'll look at organizational requirements.

---

[7]For a detailed treatment of such situational leadership styles, see *Leadership and Decision Making,* by Victor H. Vroom and Philip W. Yetton, University of Pittsburgh Press, Pittsburgh, 1973, particularly pages 10–31. Also *The Situational Leader,* by Dr. Paul Hersey, Warner Books, New York, 1984.

[8]Correspondence with the author.

4

Churchill and Machiavelli: "We Make Our Houses and Then They Make Us"

The remark about our houses was made by Winston Churchill. He was referring to Parliament, but he might as well have been speaking about modern organizations of all types. Years ago, the terribly weak hitting Los Angeles Dodgers configured their stadium to the realities of the team: Home-run fences were impossibly far away, and the infield was kept groomed in such a way as to benefit the team's bunt and chop-swing batting habits. Combined with some excellent pitching, their house was tailored sufficiently close to their strengths to allow them to generally remain among the stronger teams in the league, even though individual talents didn't always match those of competitors. Of course, when the configuration of the team eventually changed, the ball park didn't, and it became as big a handicap for them as it was for their rivals.

Fortunately, the Dodgers were able to build a new stadium. Unfortunately, most organizations can't build new structures so easily, nor should they attempt to. Organizational "houses" should be organic affairs changing with the times through policies, procedures, and change agents that are adaptable and flexible. An organization isn't subject to its minor league farm system or what talent is available through player trades. Organizations should be hiring today with the objective of obtaining the talents required to realize their visions for the future. Structures and their internal workings shouldn't be changed to accommodate people who have been hired, promoted, and trained without such a vision in mind.

Niccolo Machiavelli wrote during the sixteenth century, in *The Prince,* that "I have often reflected that the causes of the successes or failures of men depend upon their manner of suiting their conduct to the times." In an age when it is now trendy to examine the wisdom of the ancients, from the strategy of military tactics to the people skills of Attilla the Hun, a few minutes with Machiavelli are probably well spent. But just as *The Prince* was not the obvious advice on how a monarch should govern, but rather subtle direction for how to overthrow him, the quote is not as simple as it first appears. Suiting our conduct to the times does not merely mean looking around and deciding how best to cope with our surroundings. It really means to *create* our future, consciously and deliberately, and to plan for our success once that future is realized. We can't allow our houses to make us—we have to create the structure that will best serve us as we perceive and create our future living conditions.

In this chapter we'll deal with the variety of organizational components— the bricks and mortar—which should reflect strategy and not determine it. These are the key building blocks involved in successfully implementing strategy. The trick is to configure them as the architect and not to become a frenzied strategic messenger who encounters the blocks as obstacles that have fallen randomly in your path. An example of successful architecture can be seen at Kodak. About a decade ago, the organization was hiring ten chemical engineers for every electronics engineer. Today, the proportions are reversed. It's clear to even the casual observer that Kodak's strategy includes the belief that its future is in the improvement in user-friendly cameras and their options, not in further refinements in film emulsions and production. Consequently its hiring—some of its building blocks—are being assembled with that configuration clearly in mind.

Many strategic structures suffer because the organization's vision is tied to the bottom line. At various times, and with various projections (the legacy of "planning" in place of strategy), differing components can seem appropriate. Ultimately, no structure is ever fully developed, because financial projections vary and the organization is left with disparate building blocks that management can only attempt to force-fit into a coherent structure. But try as they might, managers simply can't make those components compatible. Here's a better approach:

> These creative strategy-makers succeeded by focusing on secondary, and even tertiary, benefits from their strategic initiatives, *apart* from boosting profits directly or immediately...At times this form of intuitive thinking has far more impact on the company's growth than the conventional economic analysis.... *Important:* Successful business strategists know that their thinking is only as good as the people and corporate structure available to act on it. Entering a whole new market, for example, requires new resources, changes in decision-making priorities, shifts in emphasis on quality or service, as well as increased employee participation.[1]

Ironically, structures commensurate with strategic vision are not complex nor are they intricate. They are *appropriate*. That usually means a minimum of hierarchically based "bricks" and a maximum of cross-functional "mortar." In an address to Manchester Business School, British Airways CEO Sir Colin Marshall commented on the need for streamlined management to meet strategic goals: "It is perfectly possible now to postulate companies with only three levels of management: that which runs the tasks, that which both plans the operational policies and acquires the resources and that which deals with the strategy and the people-policies involved."[2]

---

[1]"When Strategic Planning Isn't Strategic Planning," by Dr. Leonard R. Sayles, *Boardroom Reports*, July 15, 1989, page 8.

[2]As quoted by Godfrey Golzen, "Management Strategy and Culture Change: A Chief Executive View," *The Sunday Times*, as a reprint in *Vital Topics* from the Manchester Business School, Manchester, England, 1989.

Dr. Thomas Brown, a strategic consultant, supports an even more basic configuration:

> Two tiers of management are essential for corporate vitality. An executive committee manages the long-range direction a company needs. A management committee then expedites that vision in deployment of employees and resources. This second echelon of management is what makes the executive committee's dreams happen. It decides the who, what, where, when and how that brings about real change.[3]

Let's examine the organizational building blocks that will allow us to erect organizational structures that suit themselves to our vision of our future.

Selection

Nothing influences the future of an organization as dramatically and pervasively as the kinds of talent it recruits, promotes, and rewards. No amount of sophisticated strategy setting will overcome inadequate or inappropriate people. Conversely, it takes a ton of poor direction before superb people are worn down. Yet few people can be interviewed and observed with a conclusion such as "mediocre" or "excellent" immediately reached by the evaluator. Mediocre for *what*? Excellent for *whom*? Unless objectives are established for the selection of people,* how can you know if you are selecting the "correct" talents? And unless the organization's strategy is used to determine those objectives, how can you know that your selection *criteria* are correct, irrespective of whether you're finding people who satisfy them?! That is why we advocate common definitions and applications for concepts such as "strategy" or "planning" or "tactics." The notion of a "hiring strategy" in most organizations is an endeavor unto itself; it is not tied into the organizational vision. Simply stated, the relationship should look like this:

Strategic Component	*Implementation Plan*	*Implementation Tactic*
Become a multi-service financial institution	Develop sales and marketing expertise to complete aggressively	Hire search firm to recruit marketeers from retail industry
Be the leaders in support of software application	Maintain a comprehensive customer service support unit	Assign top-flight technicians to unit and provide with training in telephone skills and intepersonal skills

---

[3]As cited in "Managing by Committee—The Trick Is Synchronizing Roles," by Tom Brown, *Industry Week*, Feb. 6, 1989, page 36.
*I am going to use "selection" to include initial hiring, promotions, transfers, and any job assignments for which there is a qualitative consideration.

The first example is taken from the banking industry, which actively began hiring nonbankers with significant retail sales and marketing experience in order to position them for the financial product, sales-driven future it foresaw. When that began a few years ago, such hiring was precedent-shattering in most institutions, which had never hired nonbankers and seldom even stole talent from other banks. Banks which continued their selection policies of exclusively hiring trainees and nurturing them over decades were soon far behind in the new world of banking. The better institutions understood that it was far easier to teach bank products to people with marketing skills than it was teaching marketing skills to traditional bankers (which many liken to teaching goats to fly).

The second example is one I've extrapolated from Microsoft. That software provider's support service is simply superb. Questions are answered by individuals who are knowledgeable about the caller's system and use their own computers to replicate the caller's problem. The combination of technical expertise and unfailing customer courtesy are rare in *any* business. The connection to strategy, and the contribution to the bottom line that Sayles alluded to above, is manifest in this consumer's choice, because of that service, to purchase only Microsoft software whenever the option is available. (Conversely, as thrilled as I am by the performance of my Apple computer, that company's decision to force consumers to rely on local retailers for technical help rather than provide a centralized service will affect my choice of peripherals in the future. Is Apple organizing to be a personalized provider in its own niche or to be an alternative to IBM? At the moment, it seems muddled.)

Here is an analysis that few organizations score very well in. Having been warned in advance, check off the boxes that apply to your organization as a whole:

Selection Procedures Linked to Organization Strategy*

Criteria for hiring are established by line management. ☐

Criteria for hiring are reviewed at least yearly and whenever strategy is modified or changed. ☐

Criteria for hiring are reviewed by senior management for compatibility with strategic goals. ☐

Candidates for management positions are apprised of strategic goals and evaluated against them. ☐

Candidate evaluation includes an assessment of long-term contribution. ☐

High-potential managers are determined by contributions to *future* needs. ☐

Whenever possible, promotions are granted to the people who are deemed promotable *beyond* that next level. ☐

Succession-planning procedures do not simply seek to fill existing boxes, but anticipate future needs and positions, which may not exist today. ☐

You will readily seek outside talent to groom for future positions if current staff does not provide high-potential candidates. ☐

Whenever possible, seniority alone is not a criterion for promotion. ☐

Assignments are made with a goal of developing talents needed for the future. ☐

Performance is evaluated on the basis of potential as well as accomplishment. ☐

Development plans for employees are created with an orientation toward building the skills required for the future, not with the primary emphasis on correcting past mistakes. ☐

The organization regularly reviews the responsibilities of key positions to ascertain whether there are better ways to configure them in light of present (or proposed) direction. ☐

There is ongoing feedback, informing managers of their progress and performance within the context of overall strategic goals. ☐

The first five statements deal with hiring, the second five with promotion, and the final five with assignments. In all the time we've administered this instrument, we've never had a perfect score. This is our recommendation for interpretation:

Excellent: Twelve to fifteen checked, with a minimum of four in each category. The organization's selection processes are closely aligned with its strategic process, and talent is being hired and rewarded to support the strategic direction.

Good: Nine to eleven checked, with a minimum of three in each category. The selection processes are generally aligned with strategy, though there will be exceptions that can cause impediments to successful strategy implementation. The talent won't always be in the right place at the right time.

Fair: Six to eight checked, with a minimum of two in each category. The selection process is hit or miss in terms of strategic intent, and the organization is undoubtedly developing some talent that is inappropriate relative to its direction.

Poor: Five or fewer checked. The organization makes little or no connection between strategy and the development of people, and it will not be successful in its strategic direction for that reason alone (and probably for a number of others as well). Also, be aware that fewer than three responses in any of the three categories is a poor showing despite overall score. That particular area should be addressed and improved. It does little good to hire in line with strategic needs if development then proceeds to ignore those needs.

Of course, all of that must surely seem natural and sensible, so why do so many score so poorly so frequently on this instrument? Because the obstacles to linking strategy with selection are pernicious. Here are the most common:

- Promotions are used as "rewards" for past services and past performance, and the organization's culture and actions support this past-oriented system.
- It's easier (and "safer") to select on the basis of what one knows is needed today rather than speculate about what's needed tomorrow.
- People have a tendency to hire in their own images and according to their personal biases.
- No one ever monitors the success of selection processes down the line. If a hire makes it through the initial orientation and/or probationary period, the hiring decision is deemed to be successful even if the individual leaves in 12 months or proves to be incompetent later.
- Assignments are made on the basis of available bodies, or who is expendable, or to reward or punish.
- People view past tracks of mobility ("She came up through the marketing ranks," "He got to where he is through his financial skills") as indicators of future paths to pursue and reward.
- Selection is made in *reaction to* crisis or competitive threat and not in *anticipation of* future vision and direction. It is, effectively, dictated by external influences rather than controlled by internal ones. (One organization in a highly competitive industry determined it should have better people at all positions than its top competitors had. Finally, after lengthy recruiting at top schools and substantial investment for top talent, the president said, "Wait a minute. We're in the consumer electronics business. Do we *really* need the best legal talent available, or simply competent attorneys? Isn't there the need to be selective about *where* the top talent is actually needed in terms of our business vision?" The weapon of choice for selection is a rifle, not a shotgun.)
- Emphasis areas, upon which promotions are based, are not tied into strategic goals, so even excellent performance might not be a reliable indicator.

The organization's selection systems are the primary building blocks for the structure that will implement corporate strategy and realize strategic goals. With the right blocks, as dictated by the architect's vision, the correct foundation is laid. Once the people are being selected properly, what does the organization have to do to get them to work together toward a common vision?

Team Building and Participation

There is no route I know of that leads from individual contribution, no matter how excellent or innovative, directly to organizational goals. The catalyst that turns individual effort into organizational results by the synergy of teamwork. Here are the mortar and "connectors" that keep the building blocks in place. We've worked with many organizations in which the individual talents were tremendous. Yet, the CEO was mystified at the failure to implement even simple strategic changes and tended to blame "a few troublemakers" or "entrenched middle management." Invariably, we found no such phenomena, let alone conspiracy. Top management had done virtually nothing to meld the talent into a team. And that synthesis can happen in any organization, even with talent that borders on "maverick." If you don't believe it, read the Pulitzer Prize-winning story of Digital equipment producing a new computer in *The Soul of a New Machine,*[4] consider IBM creating a subculture in its very regimented midst in order to create the personal computer, or observe an individualistic, competitive sales force work smoothly together to reach common goals under the guidance of leaders who understand the dynamics of teamwork.

There are some common tenets that should be observed, in both a pragmatic and ethical sense, whenever approaching the issue of improving teamwork. Here are five that we have found to be generic in organizations that foster teamwork in implementing strategic change:

1. Team building is focused on individual benefit as well as organizational benefit. The "rational self-interest," as a change agent we discussed earlier, is a key component. The most effective teamwork is generated by those who derive gratification from engaging in the activity, not those who do it because they "have to or else."

2. The current rate of change is such that traditional approaches to problem solving no longer work as well as they once did. Individuals working alone are generally not the best people to solve problems, and they are virtually never the best sources of innovation. The leveraging of feedback and the group dynamic are an intrinsic part of success in these processes.

3. There is natural conflict in working together that is healthy and should not be hidden. Psychologically, it derives from an inner tension in all of us created by the diverse forces of individuality and the need to belong and between authority and dependency. When people speak of "bad chemistry," it is usually within the individual, not between two parties.

4. The organization is not a zero-sum dynamic. It must be an environment in which everyone can win, rather than one that requires me to lose for you to win. It is not a closed system, like a water bed or a balloon, that must change shape because of forces exerted elsewhere on its surface. It is rather like clay, to be molded. The shape it takes and the dynamic it assumes will be the results of the values, culture, and reward systems established and exemplified by senior management.

5. Teamwork, like individual skills, is not an end in itself; it is a stepping stone to a greater goal: organizational results, business goals met, strategies realized. Teamwork should be emphasized, organized, and reinforced toward that greater end.

---

[4]By Tracy Kidder, Little Brown, Boston, 1981.

Effective teamwork begins in systems that support it. The most basic unit of those systems is the physical environment. Ten or so years ago, a "modular office" approach became popular. Acres of open, unimpeded desks and surrounding space were divided by movable walls into small cubicles for everyone right down to the lowliest clerk. The justification included a "space," and attendant privacy, for everyone. Subtly, one assumes, the goal was also to force people to concentrate on the work, discourage small talk, and make it more difficult to randomly socialize. "Privacy" was not really ensured, since the walls were about 6 feet high and there were no doors, but casual conversation couldn't be conducted unless a person left one cubicle and entered another. (Isn't it ironic that, in some of these very organizations, management had been encouraged to have an "open door policy," "manage by wandering around," and replace sealed-off offices with glass-enclosed ones for greater visibility?) These mazelike configurations hinder teamwork tremendously, because they are physical impediments to people working together: It's difficult to even fit more than three people in one of the cubbies, and seldom are more than two chairs provided! *Teamwork is not something that is scheduled to take place at prescribed times or during certain activities. It is not represented by the company softball team or holiday party. Teamwork should happen continually. It is a way of doing business.*

Here is an example of a physical impediment to teamwork provided by a firm with which we often collaborate.[5] The diagram in figure 4.1 illustrates the physical layout in a client organization in which insurance policies were issued.

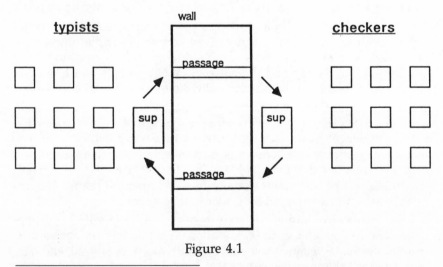

Figure 4.1

---

[5]Roy W. Walters & Associates, Whitney Road, Mahwah, N.J. This organization is a leader in the self-directed team approach. The example cited is from their early work in the insurance industry.

The typists received work from the underwriters and created the insurance contracts. The supervisor collected completed certificates and walked through the passage to the checking area, where the checking supervisor assigned them to checkers. Approved work left the area to go to the policy-holders. Errors were collected by the checking supervisor and walked back to the typing supervisor for correction, at which point the process repeated itself. As you may imagine, it took quite a while for this system to disgorge completed contracts, and typists seldom saw their own mistakes because some other typist usually corrected them. This was a "functional system" or "functional structure" created—as are so many—purely in terms of what the work demands and not in deference to adult learning, teamwork, or effectiveness. It is Taylorism[6] run amok in the information age.

The client requested changes in procedure that would reduce errors, increase the speed with which contracts were issued, and reduce turnover. (There was significant dissatisfaction with the boring work.) My colleagues suggested an environmental, physical change that removed a functional structure and replaced it with the team structure diagrammed in figure 4.2.

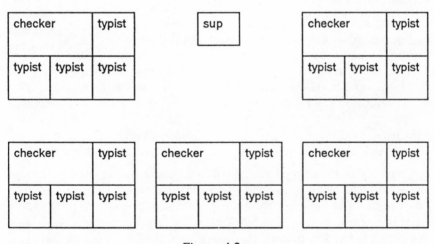

Figure 4.2

In this new structure, checkers were assigned to teams which included four typists. The number of checkers was reduced by three-fourths; each typist received back errors he or she had made to learn from their mistakes; one supervisor was eliminated; and the overall environment was opened

---

[6]Frederick Winslow Taylor was the father of "scientific management," whose work in the 1920s generated a mechanistic, time-and-motion orientation to the nature of work. He timed the motions of ditchdiggers, for example, and suggested more efficient motions and standards for each. His classic work, *Principles of Scientific Management*, was published in 1911 in New York by Harper & Row.

up (the wall was removed) and communication among typists and checker was encouraged. The new arrangement improved speed of processing by 50 percent, decreased turnover by 20 percent, and saved the salaries of a supervisor and all those checkers. The client thought it was magic. My colleague chose to call it a team-structured approach.

I will concede that typists and checkers are not those who are implementing your strategy in any direct way. But consider the physical environment for your people who do influence strategy implementation. Is it open and conducive to people working together? Could they work together if their lives depended on it, or are there too many impediments in the way? The same dynamics that affected these typists affect your service people, salespeople, administrators, agents, technicians, underwriters, engineers, and so on.

Taylorism pervaded management thinking for much of the first half of this century. There are vestiges still with us, even though the standards underlying and governing performance have changed drastically from the early to the late twentieth century:

Old Standards/Values	Current Standards/Values
Technology is king.	Social and technical system synthesis.
People as expenses.	People as assets.
Equipment as assets.	Equipment as expenses.
Narrow tasks, basic skills.	Multiple tasks, broad skills.
External controls and procedures.	Self-control and work teams.
Multilevel, "Roman legion" style.	Flat, participative organizations.
Organization's goals are sole focus.	Inclusion of social and individual goals.
Alienation: "It's just a job."	Commitment: "It's *my* work."
Low risk and problem solving.	Calculated risk and innovation.

Philip Caldwell, former chairman of Ford, states: "Regarding line workers as a *cost* rather than as an *asset* is a traditional mistake of U.S. industry. American firms too often think of industrial workers as single-purpose machine tools. Instead, get workers at all levels to contribute design, manufacturing, and marketing ideas. The more people in the company, the greater the opportunities in having *all* their brains working for you."[7]

As the experts say these days, when the "paradigms" themselves change, we must adjust to keep up with them. Is your organization geared to supporting the left or the right column? Are such standards and values even considered? Strategy cannot be implemented in an organization that is guided by the left-hand column's set of values. It can certainly be *formulated* in that organization, which creates some of the confusion stemming from "If we can establish what our strategy is, why can't we achieve it?" The implementors, you see, reside over there on the right.

---

[7]Cited in *Bottom Line*, "Privileged Information," Aug. 1, 1989, page 2

Middle management has traditionally been the repository of information. Its very power base rested on obtaining data from disparate sources—experience, directives for senior management, reports, competitive analysis, customer feedback, and so on—and interpreting those data so as to create information for the troops. The middle manager was thus in a pivotal role, the linchpin holding together the sources of data and the users of information. If everyone were lucky, some true knowledge might result.

Today the game has changed completely; the paradigms have shifted; the rules have been rewritten. Today, *everyone* has the data! We are a communicating, data-drenched, information-seeking society best exemplified by the state of modern business. Virtually anyone who needs one has a computer nearby—right down to the lowliest of clerks—and those machines provide data in a way that no middle manager ever could. However, the data still are not automatically turned into information, much less knowledge, much less *wisdom*.

And that's where the successful middle managers find themselves today. They are serving as team leaders, helping subordinates (and others) turn data into useful information, applying them and evaluating results to create knowledge, and acting with foresight and intelligence in the future based on that learning: acquired wisdom. Yet yesterday's middle managers weren't hired for their team leadership abilities, they were hired for their *content* abilities and promoted by dint of that content expertise. And there they are today—having been hired, promoted, and rewarded on that set of skills—finding the rules have changed and their future hinges on a new set! That isn't a paradigm shift, that's an earthquake.

Middle-management ranks have thinned by about 15 percent in this country over the past decade (and about 30 percent in western Europe). Teamwork is dependent on team leaders, and that role, whether by design or default, has fallen to the middle managers—and to fewer of them. Organizationally, you should be investigating the roles your middle managers are playing, how they are being reinforced and supported, and whether they are receiving the skills necessary to function as team leaders to build the teamwork required to implement strategic change. Content skills are generally acquired and honed as one's career progresses. But people skills are seldom naturally acquired, and bad habits tend to solidify. This is the "art" of management's art and science, and it's incumbent on the organization to provide the training required.

In the "old days" (Or is this example from your "current days"?) issues would follow the sequence shown in figure 4.3.

This is the "doctor will prescribe your medicine" approach, and it carries the general warning on the label, "Do not screw up again." In the newer days, expert problem solving rose to the fore, with the general sequence shown in figure 4.4.

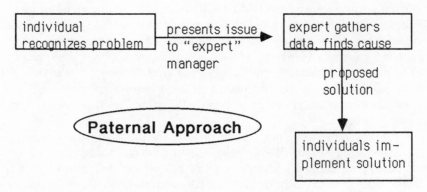

Figure 4.3

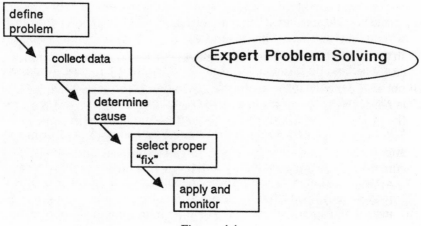

Figure 4.4

This model represents individualistic, person problem solving—highly "scientific," and taught today by any number of training firms to thousands of organizations around the world. Its philosophy includes "Do it yourself if you can—it's faster and more cost-effective," "Solving problems is what you're paid for," and "A manager's job is to take action." Unfortunately, despite their popularity, these approaches are yesterday's news. Managers are not paid to act; they are paid to *think!* And individual problem solving, as we've discussed earlier, must give way to team-oriented innovation, especially for purposes of strategy implementation.

This brings us to the team-oriented sequence of tomorrow, figure 4.5, which the best organizations are doing today:

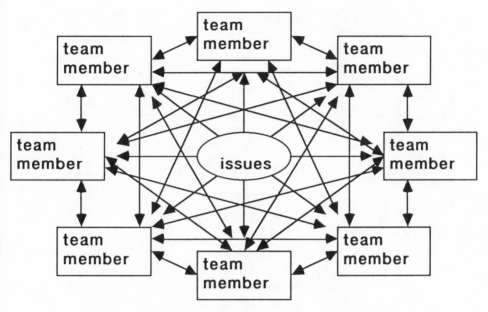

Figure 4.5

In this configuration, issues are tackled by team members alone or in concert with others as the situation dictates. Individual problem solving is not abandoned; it is simply one of many options. And note that the leader is not formally represented. He or she is most likely an intrinsic part of the group. This is the optimal configuration for effectively implementing actions, for achieving ownership, for prudent risk taking and innovation, and for self-directed work. In short, it is the best possible set of circumstances for effective strategy implementation.

Another way to look at the progression we've outlined is:

1900 to 1950s   Experts solve problems.
1950s to 1960s Everybody solves problems individually.
1960s to 1980s Experts improve systems and innovate.
1980s to 1990s Everyone improves systems and innovates.

The ability of your organization to foster such teamwork can be guided by these simple guidelines:

- Focus on the future, not on past problems and frictions.
- Involve everyone, at every level, who has a role in the outcome.
- Structure tasks that people can manage and direct themselves.
- Provide independence, authority, and genuine responsibility.
- Allow for the freedom to fail.

The resulting systems will tend to look like figure 4.6, in comparison with past structures.

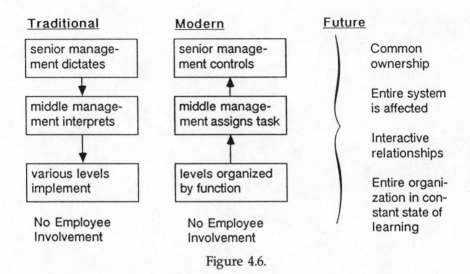

Figure 4.6.

As figure 4.6 illustrates, traditional organization dictated work relationships from the top down. Employees simply did what they were told. If plans weren't implemented correctly, it was someone's "fault," and the person had to be "corrected." In more modern times (although the traditional organizations are still with us), with the emphasis on planning, frontline supervision and lower-level management assign work based on projections. These tasks are formalized by middle management, which might make modifications for the purposes of efficiency or work flow. Senior management, handcuffed by the weight of all of these projections and in-place structures, attempts to control the *fait accompli* with which it's been presented and perhaps, through brute force and iron will, move the monolith toward some strategic goal. In neither of these organizations is there any employee involvement. Employees are extensions of the equipment, machines, and processes.

In the new, open-systems organizations, the environment is interactive and organic. Management levels are flat, and everyone is encouraged to deal directly with whomever is necessary on given issues. As the organization evolves, it uses its learning about itself and the way in which it functions to further improve itself. (The philosophers might call this an epistemological approach.) The strategic process has inputs from everyone; it is explained to everyone; and everyone shares in its familiarity—as discussed in the preceding chapters. So implementation is a natural consequence in which all employees are involved.

The very nature of many organizational structures inhibits—or prohibits—this process. It has nothing to do with people or competence primarily; it has to do with the way in which teamwork is frustrated. The traditional structure does not encourage lateral communications or cross-functional ones. Contrast that to the team-oriented sequence of figure 4.5.

The differences represent the essence of effective teamwork. We should be moving away from:

- Solve the problem
- Give it to the expert
- Get a task force together
- Protect yourself
- Do it now—take action

and toward:

- Create the future
- Help everyone to learn
- Involve everybody
- Take measured risks
- Think and contribute.

To what extent do you and your organization foster the teamwork and participation necessary to synthesize people into a strategy implementation team? How well does your organization *live* these ideals and not just talk about them in annual reports and press releases? How well do you do the following?

Assessment of Teamwork Support

We manage according to our values and our vision of the future.	☐ yes	☐ no
We focus on our customers needs, not our internal activities.	☐ yes	☐ no
We institutionalize processes to continually scrutinize and improve our operation.	☐ yes	☐ no
We treat everyone in the organization as a business partner, not an employee.	☐ yes	☐ no
We place our highest priority on developing people and their relationships.	☐ yes	☐ no
We actively seek out and eliminate barriers to teamwork and success.	☐ yes	☐ no
We deemphasize hierarchy and encourage open communications.	☐ yes	☐ no
We visibly support the freedom to fail.	☐ yes	☐ no
We support teams in setting their own objectives, standards, and procedures.	☐ yes	☐ no
We ensure that everyone is involved in the strategic process in some capacity.	☐ yes	☐ no

It would be rare to find an organization that can respond yes to all ten questions that is not successfully implementing its strategy and meeting strategic goals.

Institutionalization

We've now erected two-thirds of our house. We've provided for the right people and created an environment in which they can work together productively, communicate openly, and be a part of the strategic process. The bricks and mortar are working well. But it's time to put a roof on the structure to protect it against the elements. This protection comprises the policies, procedures, and reinforcements required to maintain the structure. Organizationally, it can be called "institutionalization."

Once a process or pursuit is institutionalized, it is self-perpetuated. This is the organizational equivalent of an individual being motivated, since true motivation can come only from within the person. I can't "motivate" you; I can only try to establish an environment in which you motivate yourself. Hence, motivation is of high quality and is long-lived because it is internally produced, not externally forced, and is self-perpetuating.

The same holds true for institutionalizing ideas, beliefs, and practices. Once the organization has implemented and reinforced them, if they are adopted as a natural consequence of the work, they will be long-lived and self-perpetuating. That isn't to say that they can't be examined and changed, just as our personal motivation is subject to scrutiny and change. But they needn't be reestablished every working day, nor are they vulnerable to a particular personality or event ("I'll gladly do it for Joanne, she has a special way of involving you." "I certainly wouldn't have done this before the merit increase!").

What specifics are included in institutionalization? They include the following:

Daily Operating Beliefs. Some organizations have superb customer telephone service. The employees are courteous and patient, and they will gladly look up catalog numbers or shipping charges. Other organizations employ people who view each call as a burden and are prone to critique the customer for failing to have a credit card number ready or not knowing what color he or she prefers. There are other organizations in which people openly experiment and seek help with a unique problem or unprecedented request, and there are those in which people scramble to move the issue to someone else's desk and to cover themselves at all costs.

These actions are based on beliefs which govern daily activities. They are the tactical equivalent of strategic core beliefs. Often they can't be articulated, and third-party observation or surveys are required to identify what they are. When operating beliefs are fractured—that is, different beliefs are manifest by different departments or, worse, by different individuals within single departments—that is a sign that the organization has failed to institutionalize a set of operating beliefs consistent with its strategic beliefs.

Merck & Co's strategic beliefs include "acting with the highest degree of honesty and integrity" and "bringing the best medical research and science to the greatest areas of human need." A daily operating belief, held throughout the 32,000-person organization, is to "do the right thing."[8] Thus, Merck sales representatives, researchers, manufacturing employees, and others are constantly acting in concert with the strategic direction and implementing it every day as a part of the work ethic. That is manifest in the environment in a variety of ways. It's no accident, for example, that surveys indicate that Merck field representatives are considered the best in the business in comprehensive, honest comparative information provided to doctors.

Recently, I wrote to Texas Instruments to tell them that one of their desk calculators had finally failed after 19 years of yeomanlike service and that I wished everyone made products of such quality. They wrote back to tell me that they wanted to send me a complimentary new calculator, and would I please return the old one so that they could see what had happened after 19 years. I sent it, but I told them I had already purchased a new model and I hadn't written with the intent of getting anything for free. They responded with a check to reimburse me for my purchase!

Now for the real satisfaction. The person on the other end of my letters was an administrative assistant in the executive offices! She was the only one who dealt with me and clearly had the pride, authority, and incentive to act as she did. I am a Texas Instruments fan for life. (When I told this story to management of Hewlett-Packard, one of our clients, their response was "We hope we would have acted like that. It was the perfect response.")

On the down side, I visited a local department store recently with the full intent of purchasing a miniature color television I had seen advertised. Not browsing, buying. After 15 minutes of hearing people say "It's not my department" and watching salespeople ignore me in a nearly empty store, I went elsewhere, and I will never return to that store or the chain to which it belongs. That was more than individual failure on the part of a salesperson, or even collective failure of the store personnel. The institutionalized belief system is "Why break my back when nobody else is?" or "I'm not doing anything special for this place!" And it shows.

Have you methodically sampled and attempted to mold the daily operating beliefs of your organization so that they are in concert with your strategy? Are your employees *at every level* helping to implement strategy each day through their respective actions and decisions, or are they undermining it even as you read this sentence? *Daily operating beliefs are subconscious guides, but they result in conscious choices of behavior.*

---

[8]These beliefs at strategic and operating levels were identified in studies conducted by Summit Consulting Group, Inc. for Merck & Co., during 1986–1990.

Feedback. Every organization needs a continuous feedback loop. The arrows in figure 4.5 represent two-way communication from which no one should be exempt. The communication should be both external–internal (with customers, vendors, agents, trade groups, community) as well as internal–external, as in figure 4.5. Note that such feedback is virtually impossible in the traditional pyramidal structure and, if attempted, usually results in "What! You talked to my boss!! Listen, anything he needs to hear comes through me, got it?!" Management consultant Bill Reddin has the best line I've ever heard on the ubiquity of feedback: "After all, even St. Paul had clear key effectiveness areas, though Judgment Day does represent a long-performance feedback loop."[9]

There are really no such things as "negative" and "positive" feedback, there are simply consequences of actions that the perpetrators of the action (or those affected by the actions) ought to know about for future consideration. All feedback should be viewed as improvement-oriented. Military academies study great losses to learn what went wrong so as to avoid the same mistakes in the future. The great athletes study their moves to determine what's working well and how to perpetuate it. Management's philosophy should be similar: What have we done; what has resulted; and what can we learn from it? These are the key components in the "continual learning" cited in figure 4.6. The best sources of learning are what we have done and what it has meant.

How is feedback institutionalized? Through any or all of the following procedures. How many does your organization provide for and pursue?

- Surveys and face-to-face meetings with customers, suppliers, and other "outsiders" to specifically test service, responsiveness, quality, decision making, and so on.
- Management "shops its own business." You anonymously buy products and test services as a customer to test the normal, daily workings of the system.
- There are at least quarterly reviews of individual performance, divorced from salary review and/or bonus evaluations, in which employee and direct manager compare notes on progress against respective performance goals (which, in turn, reflect the strategic thrust).
- Managers provide unsolicited praise and nonfinancial reward for jobs well done.
- When something goes wrong, teams work on finding the cause of the problem, not the blame for the effects.

Senior management is constantly in touch with the work force through focus groups, meeting participation, common eating areas, social activities, regular (unannounced) tours of the facilities, and so on.

---

[9]As stated in *Effective Management by Objectives: The 3-D Method of MBO,* by W. J. Reddin, McGraw-Hill, New York, 1971.

"Open door" policies mean nothing if everyone is afraid to walk through the door, and "management by wandering around" is futile if managers don't know what to look for and how to act during their wandering. Here are two of my favorite examples of organizations with obvious weaknesses in their institutionalized feedback systems:

1. I was being escorted through the various divisions of an insurance company by the director of human resources in order to understand the current operation. I noticed nervous glances following our trek. My guide finally explained: "Oh, they probably think you're one of the senior officers trying to figure out how to cut staff." "Don't they know what the senior officers look like?!" "Why, no...why would they?"

2. A senior vice president of a utility took me to lunch to explain his problem. "I don't get accurate information about morale and performance," he lamented. "My managers tell me only what they think I want to hear and only what makes them look good."

"Well, look around," I said, "we're sitting in an executive dining room with other officers, while down the hall are a thousand people with the information you seek having lunch."

"What's your point?" he asked.

Feedback doesn't occur naturally. The organization must take pains to make sure it is a way of life that starts at the top and permeates every aspect of the operation. Once feedback is institutionalized—self-perpetuating—you will have accurate, timely information to judge how well strategy is being implemented, how much progress is being made toward strategic goals, and what needs to be done in terms of midcourse corrections. If you don't listen, you won't hear anything, and you can't listen if no one chooses to speak.

Critical Thinking Skills

We talked earlier about the need for ongoing training in basic strategic skills as a precursor to successful strategy implementation—how to achieve it. Once those skills are developed individually and applied with others as the basis for teamwork, the organization must formalize and institutionalize the use of what we'll call "critical thinking skills." These are the skills that are content-independent. They provide for objective, rational approaches to business issues from a neutral base free of bias, politics, and local self-interest. An assortment of these skills can be cited, but we've isolated five that are not only generic across industries, hierarchies, and even cultures but are absolutely the key to successful strategy implementation:

1. *Problem-solving skills.* These techniques go back to the early Greeks, but all good ones revolve around the same themes: Identify the problem; describe the problem's characteristics; hypothesize causes; test the causes; remove the most likely cause (fix the problem); verify that the problem

has gone away.[10] As stated above, successful organizations don't want problem-solving "experts" who tackle these issues; they need everyone to be problem solvers working together toward rational solutions. Institutionalizing problem-solving skills means:

- Rewarding those who find cause, not blame.
- Avoiding witch hunts and focusing on observable and verifiable facts.
- Fostering patience over arbitrary action and punishing "ready, fire, aim" mentality.
- Building systems in which everyone is expected to identify and fix problems.

Honda, the Japanese automaker, long ago installed a system in which assembly line workers were encouraged to stop the assembly line whenever a flaw or defect was spotted, and they were rewarded for doing so. Every employee thus became a quality control inspector supporting the company's strategic goals of absolutely top quality products. (Contrast this to the U.S. automakers' long-time mentality of punishing any employee found stopping the line.)

2. *Decision-making skills.* These are the abilities needed to choose among options and maximizing benefit while minimizing risk. They entail the wherewithal to separate goals and results from activities and to evaluate a variety of alternatives. The process comprises these steps: establish the goal; establish objectives to be achieved; generate likely alternatives that would meet the objective requirements; evaluate the alternatives and select the most promising ones; evaluate potential risk inherent in each alternative and possible control of it; and select the best-balanced alternative (make a decision). To institutionalize such practices, the organization should:

- Accept only recommendations that conform to this sequence.
- *Always* analyze risk, which is often overlooked.
- Justify and communicate its decisions within this context.
- Insist that meetings and group decisions adhere to this format.

The philosopher George Santayana once said that a fanatic is someone who loses sight of his objective and consequently redoubles his effort. Organizations that are successful in implementing their strategy discourage fanaticism. They support and encourage decision making that is rational and objective and in which the goals are tied into the strategic direction.

3. *Problem avoidance skills.* This is unlike problem solving in that it is a preventive discipline, whereas problem solving is always contingent: It occurs after the trouble has arisen. This skill entails anticipating potential problems and establishing actions to attempt to prevent them from occuring or mitigate their effects if they do occur.

---

[10]For the best and earliest popular description of this technique as applied to business concerns, see *The Rational Manager: A Systematic Approach to Problem Solving and Decision Making,* by Charles H. Kepner and Benjamin B. Tregoe, Kepner-Tregoe, Inc., Princeton, N.J., 1965, especially pages 73–130.

People with this skill receive much less publicity than do problem solvers. It's always more dramatic to put a fire out than to claim you've prevented one from starting. It's the firefighter dashing up the ladder who makes the evening news, not the fire marshall quietly going about his or her job of checking to see that safety procedures are met. ("We interrupt our regularly scheduled programming to tell you that Cindy Adams, Acme Widget Fire Marshall, has today arranged for new "no smoking" signs and had all extinguishers checked for pressure. Film at eleven.")

Potential-problem avoidance is one of the key skills required to be competent in risk management, for example. In mid-1988, Pepsi abandoned its promotional campaign that featured rock star Madonna, writing off a $5 million investment in her contract alone. One of her commercials was shown a single time before an unrelated, controversial rock video she starred in created such protest that Pepsi decided she couldn't be used as its spokeswoman. Unavoidable snarl from an unpredictable celebrity? Or preventable fiasco from someone known for her iconoclasm? Pepsi wanted the fizz of the star without the work of anticipating what could go wrong. Its plan went flat. Some individuals didn't have the skills to raise the right questions of the former people before approving the campaign.

This lack of foresight seems endemic to the soft drink industry. "New Coke," which has created new lives for thousands of business school professors in the general category of fiasco, was supposedly launched with the benefit of substantial market research. The problem, of course, was that the market research was blind, and the subjects who commented strictly on taste didn't realize that the company was contemplating tampering with one of the prime forces of life. Coke never bothered to test the psychological element, and perception *is* reality.[11] In every scientific blind taste test conducted after the uproar, even the most vociferous "old Coke" supporters couldn't tell the difference between it and "new Coke," and most couldn't separate it from Pepsi or RC either, for that matter. Why didn't anyone at Coke, which has jealously guarded its name and repute, bother to raise the risks inherent in messing with an institution?

The problem anticipators and preventers need to be nurtured and rewarded even more carefully than the problem solvers. Whom would you have imbued with additional skills: the guy who designed the *Titanic* or the craftsmen who built the lifeboats?

Problem solving, decision making, and problem avoidance constitute the classic triad of basic management skills because they are time-correlated, as shown in figure 4.7. It has been generally believed that an individual who is proficient in these three areas has mastered the basic skills that will lead to competency with any number of issues. If strategy

---

[11]See *Managing for Peak Performance: A Guide to the Power (and Pitfalls) of Personal Style*, by Alan Weiss, Harper & Row, New York, 1989, pages 2-7, for a discussion of this phenomenon.

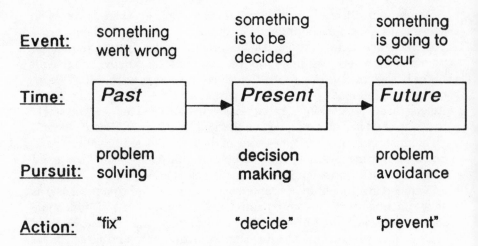

Event:	something went wrong	something is to be decided	something is going to occur
Time:	Past	Present	Future
Pursuit:	problem solving	decision making	problem avoidance
Action:	"fix"	"decide"	"prevent"

Figure 4.7

isn't being implemented as it should be, we must find out why and fix the problem; each day, on a real-time basis, we must make decisions that are compatible with and supportive of the strategy, another key to implementation; and it's incumbent on us all to scan the horizon for problems which might sink the strategy so that we can steer clear of them. Consequently, these three basic critical thinking skills (remember they are not dependent on the *content* of the strategy and they can be applied in any environment) require institutionalization if strategy is to be successfully implemented. However, we believe there are two more to consider, as well.

4. *Creativity.* Philosopher Blaise Pascal once said that there are two equally dangerous extremes: To shut all reason out and to let nothing else in. Good management is a blend of the logical and creative. This is not a matter of right- and left-brain hocus-pocus. (Someday I want to be at the management meeting in which the leader declares, "This is a highly detailed issue. Bring in the left-brainers!") It is a question of art and science, of using judgment and intuition to complement facts and analysis.

I use a technique in my speaking engagements that never fails to prove the importance of being able to blend the two modes. About 30 minutes into my presentation I abruptly call for a volunteer. I never get one readily, whether it's an association meeting of strangers or an in-company conference of colleagues. After some insistence on my part and an awkward silence, someone, reluctantly, finally raises a hand with the fervor of the person opening a letter from the IRS marked "official business." That volunteer receives a round of applause and a free hardcover book. Period.

Why don't more people volunteer? *Intellectually* they realize that I couldn't have anything too awful in mind, because I have a responsibility to my client which doesn't include embarrassing the audience. No speaker benefits by degrading an individual. In fact, the odds are such that the volunteer will probably benefit from the experience—will come out looking good. But *emotionally* the individual is chanting "Let someone else do it!" because of past experiences or irrational fears. So they pass up the applause and the book.

Every day, many of us are passing up the applause and the reward because we are acting strictly on emotions. Others are passing up the joys of the work because they are acting strictly on intellect. We all need to apply both emotion and intellect. We need to raise our hands more, especially to create the continual learning we spoke of earlier as representative of the new organizations. Creativity, and its component techniques, should be fostered and rewarded. It will take strategy from the realm of the cerebral and help it become visceral. You can't implement a strategy that everyone simply *understands*. It must be one that everyone *lives*.

5. *Innovation*. The last of the five critical thinking skills required for institutionalization is innovation. We've spoken in earlier chapters of its importance. Innovation is, simply, the *improvement* of standards. And that improving is best done by employees who make thousands of small, incremental improvements over the course of the year, not by the resident genius who is struck by lightning once a decade.

People are fond of pointing to 3M's Post-it™ Notes as an example of innovation, but it's actually 3M's constant encouragement of innovative skills among its employees, and the daily application of those skills, that leads to the occasional landmark product. It is rare for someone to suddenly come up with "the great idea" who hasn't been coming up with smaller ideas every day. Scientist Linus Pauling once said "The best way to have a good idea is to have a lot of ideas." And Thomas Edison: "Invention is 1 percent inspiration and 99 percent perspiration."

Innovation is different from creativity in that the latter focuses on brainstorming, looking at things in new and unique ways, and generating novel alternatives. Innovation focuses on *implementation*. It is the skill involved in taking an idea (perhaps generated by creativity) and refining it, improving it, managing it, and nurturing it until it becomes a reality. The person who says "What we need is a package delivery service with overnight guarantees. I think the way to do it is by using a common hub to reroute everything. . ." is creative. But the person who *does it*—despite the regulatory hassles, financing problems, public skepticism, and competitive pressures—is the innovator. There are many instances of people like Fred Smith of Federal Express who are both innovators and creators. Innovation is *applied* creativity.

Strategy implementation, by its very nature concerned with altering the status quo, cannot succeed if people focus on making it fit the current system or using procedures that have worked well in the past but may no longer be appropriate. It requires a new look, new standards, and a willingness not to think but to *do* things in a new fashion. New strategies raise new goals. Innovation allows for new techniques to support the quest.

The organizational "house" has been based on selecting the right people, melding them into effective teams, and institutionalizing the beliefs, feedback, and skills that will serve to support the implementation of the strategic direction. It's time to determine what the inside of the house will look like.

5

Every Employee a Champion of Change: "If You Ever Really Want to Understand Something, Try to Change It"

That quote about change comes from consultant and psychologist Edgar Schein.[1] In changing a strategy, senior management should come to understand the nature and dynamic of its organization and thereby become better equipped to shape it and mold it. The operative word, of course, is "should." Doug Bray, one of the founders of The Forum, the Boston-based consulting group, notes that the result of successful strategic change should be manifest in "a common vision, common beliefs, and a palpable sense of intent, with everyone working in support of the chosen direction. What's required to effect change is executive persistence, management courage, careful preparation, constant communication and high-quality, specific training."[2]

The literature is replete with examples and models of what should be done to implement strategic change, but there are very few guidelines for how to do it. Even when the how is believed to be understood, its execution is often deficient. For example, Leonard Johnson and Alan Frohman report that "we can see that attempts in many organizations to improve organizational effectiveness by giving more responsibility to people at middle levels are not working. Vertical channels are still clogged; decisions are not being made any faster; and foreign competitors are still able to introduce new products faster than U.S. firms can."[3]

What seems to be missing is a process, a methodology, for implementing strategic change. The *process* of implementation should, after all, be constant, irrespective of the content, direction, or antecedents of the strategy. Moreover, it should not be industry-specific. In the preceding chapter we discussed some specific skills that should be institutionalized regardless of the nature and direction of the business. The skills are required in *any* business at *any* time. Strategic change skills are no different

---

[1]As heard by the author during a speech by Dr. Schein.
[2]From an address made at the Annual Conference of the American Society for Training and Development, June 5, 1989, reporting on Forum's experience with clients attempting to implement strategic change.
[3]"Identifying and Closing the Gap in the Middle of Organizations," by Leonard W. Johnson and Alan L. Frohman, The Academy of Management *EXECUTIVE*, Vol. III, No. 2, May 1989, page 107.

and, although certain elements of the process might not be employed on a daily basis—strategy doesn't change on a daily basis, one would fervently hope—other elements should be continual, for example, monitoring progress, assessing the environment, and providing reinforcement.

One such "change model" is shown in figure 5.1. The model is a continuous flow, and it must be appreciated in that holistic manner. Its component parts comprise the following:

Vision

At the outset, the chief executive officer and top people must decide why the organization exists. What is the business *concept?* Is it to make a minimum of 10 percent net-after-tax profit, or to improve the human condition? (Surprisingly, very few organizations are in the former category as representing their *raison d'etre.*) Vision is the very first thing to be determined, and it should serve to guide the remainder of the process. At the conclusion of the final step in the model, the tactics should have moved the organization to the vision, and the test of the success of the implementation is whether the organization has arrived at the destination created for it. Has the ship, no matter what its speed or condition, arrived at the current coordinates?

As discussed earlier, vision must come from the top and precede any organizational diagnosis or feedback. Because of its delimiting influence, planning is the particular nemesis of such visioning. "The future," says management expert and *Harvard Business Review* editor Ted Levitt, "is not the linear extrapolation of the present. The world does not move on perfectly parallel railroad tracks laid down by rational social engineers. Humankind intervenes...."[4] That intervention might as well be deliberate and be controlled by the people responsible for the success of the organization.

The visioning process includes a determination of the organization's mission, the energy with which the vision will be pursued, the values that will guide its behavior, the focus (or priorities) for its decisions, and the principles to which it will adhere and which it will utilize as standards of performance: its self-monitoring devices. The vision is an expansive view of the future performed by those who, presumably, are ultimately responsible for shaping that future.

Gap Analysis

The first transition step from one model component to the next is gap analysis. It is an assessment of the dissonance that exists between the vision of the future and the reality of today. (Planning and projective processes would tend to start with the following step, diagnosis, and determine that the vision should be based on today's reality. Consequently,

---

[4]Writing in an editorial titled "Convictions," *Harvard Business Review,* July–August 1989, page 8.

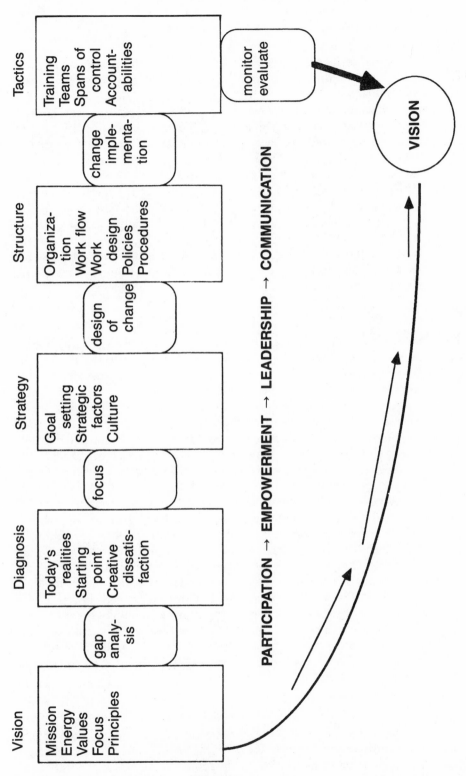

Figure 5.1

there would be no gap, merely a linear flow.) Gap analysis is neither good nor bad. It should not make judgments; it should only provide comparisons. In many organizations, depending on the vision and the reality, a large gap would be favorable because it would represent dramatic change, which might be consistent with top management's intent. In others, a small gap might be distressing because it would signify that the strategy was invoking only moderate change when a significant course correction was desired.

The gap analysis should inform management of the distance between its vision and the current operation, which is useful *not* in terms of whether the vision is achievable, but rather in terms of how profound a change the vision provides. There is probably not much of a gap between the vision and the reality of Mercedes-Benz, for example, but one suspects that there is a significant gap in the parent, Daimler-Benz, as it expands its nonautomotive interests.

Diagnosis

The diagnosis step provides the starting point for strategy implementation in that it defines the jumping-off place. Besides an assessment of the current operation and its strengths, weaknesses, and complexion, the diagnosis should include an evaluation of the current dissatisfaction with the operation. No strategy should be predicated on correcting weaknesses. That would be a fix-it approach that, at best, would make you as good as you used to be—hardly adequate for future strength and the management of change. However, current unhappiness can be marshalled into a creative and positive force to implement change in that it is a motivator to create a better reality.

Employees who have complained about the compensation system or bemoaned the work flow procedures that result in needless duplication can now work from within the system to improve it. Joseph Schumpter once labeled innovation as "creative destruction." After all, we would hardly seek to innovate if we were satisfied with the old order. Similarly, the diagnosis step involves the capture of dissatisfaction and its molding into a positive force for change within the parameters of the vision established in the prior step. It is the opportunity for employees at all levels to light candles rather than continue to curse the darkness. It is our belief that this harnassing of current sentiment is one of the critical steps overlooked in the attempts to involve people in the process of strategic change.

Focus

Once the diagnosis of the current organization is complete, the strategic change process can begin to focus on the specifics of strategy. Management should be in a position to determine the specific goals that the strategy should develop. The focusing is accomplished only *after* the vision has been established and the current realities have been understood. Trying to set strategy before these steps are accomplished is like trying to hit a target in the fog. You might hit it, but it would clearly rely on luck; you might hit something unintended, which could be catastrophic; or, more likely, you wouldn't hit anything at all, which would be wasteful and demoralizing. Note that the end result of the tactical step, down the road, isn't to reach the organization's strategy; it is to reach the organization's *vision*. Strategy is a means to that end, not an end in itself, yet there is great confusion at all echelons of management about these very relationships. That is why focus is so critical.

Strategy, to cite an earlier reference, establishes the nature and direction of the organization—*but only after its vision has been established and an evaluation has been made of the distance that needs to be traveled* (the gap analysis) *in order to reach it.* Some years ago I was working with the top-management team of a major household products company. The leadership was engaged in all kinds of sophistry and intellectual manipulation about the process of strategy. "Does strategy precede objectives, or do objectives set the strategy?" they demanded with the haughtiness of the self-righteous. "What about the mission? Is it a mission to implement strategy, or does the strategy implement the mission?" And on and on it went. They were intent on the words, but they refused to consider a model. They wanted relationships, but they wouldn't focus. What emerged was a continual barrage of "gotchas!" as they debated terms, but with no coherent vision. It was small wonder that the employees couldn't understand what was to be implemented—their senior managers weren't about to take the time to focus on it themselves.

Strategy

The strategy component of the change model includes the goals to be set in order to achieve the vision—to achieve the organization's envisioned future. Cultural consideration begins to emerge in terms of assessing what the implications of change might be. Generally, there are ten strategic areas which should be assessed:

- Products and/or services offered
- Customers and/or user groups
- Markets served
- Technologies utilized
- Methods of distribution
- Methods of sale
- Natural resources utilized
- Production capabilities
- Size and/or growth goals
- Return and/or profit goals

Not all of these strategic areas may apply, although most typically will. There may be additional areas in certain industries or organizations. For example, some organizations consider "human resources" to be a separate category and others consider "financial strengths" to be one.

Appropriately, the strategy step is in the middle of the process, the linch-pin around which hinges the successful implementation of the organiza-tion's vision. It is the strategy implementation which will ultimately achieve that vision.

Designed Change

The notion of "designed change" is the critical result of the strategic pro-cess. (And another example of why planning is so premature at that stage: It can produce only "projected change," not designed change.) The process now allows the structural aspects of the organization to be approached with a predetermined game plan in mind. It is a question of what must be done to implement the strategy, not what we can do with what we have.

The popular rubric these days is that change manages us before we can manage it. The proactive nature of the change model provides for change to be designed and implemented on the basis of the organization's goals and not external demands.

Structure

The organization's structure includes the tangible and the intangible. It is the physical layout, the written policies and procedures, as well as the work flow, informal policies, and unwritten procedures. Earlier we pro-vided examples of the differences between structures that are task-oriented and those that are work output–oriented. No aspect of the organization's design is exempt from potential change in view of strategy implementa-tion. In fact, implementation often suffers from attempts to force-fit it into existing structures which are considered sacrosanct and immovable.

In the 1970s, Exxon decided to enter the office equipment business, which was then very hot. The organization had a luxury of riches to sup-port the strategy, and an organization named Qxt was created. It was a disaster of near epic proportions, and Exxon departed from the office equipment business licking its wounds. The problem was neither the market nor the strategy itself, and certainly not the financial or human resources. The difficulty was that Exxon tried to run the business as it would the oil business, as a part of its existing culture. The fit couldn't have been made even if a corporate sledge hammer had been available.

In the mid-80s, several publishers acquired training firms on the premises that training was a growing business (true), that it had some affinity with the publishing business (true, but minor), and that it could be readily incorporated into the publishing business (absolutely false). By 1982, McGraw-Hill, for example, had acquired three moderately successful training firms as the core of its plans to build a substantial training business within McGraw-Hill. I remember a particularly ominous conversation in which I attempted to explain to the president of the McGraw-Hill book division, who was responsible for the new venture, that the training companies he had acquired required unique compensation systems, far greater latitude of operation, specific promotional approaches, and so on. He was astonished at my naïvete. "Don't be silly," he scoffed, "they'll operate as part of McGraw-Hill and be strengthened by our procedures and experience." By 1988 all three firms had been divested, a substantial amount of money had been lost, and McGraw-Hill was out of the training business. The question that remains is whether or not anything was learned in the process.

For strategic purposes, form follows structure, not vice versa. And the structure must be considered before change can be implemented successfully.

Change Implementation

Implementing strategic change occurs rather late in this overall process. Its proper perspective is seldom understood. Management is in a hurry to get to it. And changes are often a reaction to nonstrategic events, meaning that management actually enters the process at this point and acts as though a coherent strategy implementation were underway.

Implementing change follows the analysis of structural changes needed to implement the strategy and prior to the development of the specific tactics that will serve as vehicles for the implementation. Implementing change before the structure is ready for it is futile.

Tactics

Tactics include the training and preparation of individuals to implement strategic change, the creation (or reinforcement) of the teamwork required to achieve it, and establishment of accountabilities, spans of control, relationships, and so on. The tactics must be evaluated in terms of the organizational direction that will result: Are they consistent with the vision as established, or will they result in a different destination? At times, even when the prior steps in the model have been adhered to, tactics can take the form of what's convenient and not what's necessary. Or they can be personality-dependent rather than issue-dictated. Or they can be activities for their own sake, and not actions aimed at a specific end result.

This may be the juncture at which most management confusion occurs because a set strategy isn't being successfully implemented, although the precursor for the failure can be found in one of the prior steps. "Why aren't they doing what we've told them" can usually be answered by "What on earth are you telling us?"

Some years ago we were retained by a training firm which had been consistently unable to implement its strategy of changing its image. Its vision was to become a well-rounded, comprehensive consulting firm. Its promotion, advertising, product development, and investment had been oriented toward that end, but to no avail. What we found was a sales force—the key, and often sole, interface with clients and prospects—still being hired, trained, compensated, and rewarded on the basis of sales of prepackaged training materials.

"It has worked for us to this point," we were told, "and we see no reason to change a successful formula." "These sales people will sell whatever they're given," we were admonished, "and once we get consulting services, we'll sell them, too." As we've established earlier, behavior has to change before attitudes and values can change, and the organization had done nothing to change behavior among its key implementors. Tactics must be commensurate with vision, no matter how painful or how much of a departure *from current strengths.*

Monitoring and Evaluation

Finally, the tactics must be monitored and evaluated for their progress in achieving the vision. The feedback loop must be constant and direct so that midcourse correction can be readily implemented. This is another key area in which breakdowns occur. Just because actions have been implemented— and have even enjoyed early success—doesn't mean they will continue to be successfully pursued. People, motivations, and conditions can change abruptly.

Several years ago a United Airlines 747 with nearly 400 people on board was flying on course for Los Angeles from New York. Unfortunately, all three cockpit officers fell asleep with the plane on automatic pilot, with the result that West Coast air traffic controllers spent a frantic evening trying to rouse the pilots as the plane flew over the Pacific, with passengers and cabin crew enjoying a presumably pleasant and undisturbed flight. The pilots finally received their wake-up call, and the plane reached its intended destination, but without the air traffic system and its radar and flight plans, that smoothly operating flight might have wound up in a considerably different destination, and almost guaranteed to be an unpleasant one.[5]

The sequence that underlies this change model might seem to some to be out of synch:

Participation → Empowerment → Leadership → Communication

Many would assume that leadership precedes all else, but we are not referring to executive leadership. We are alluding to *leadership of the process of implementing strategic change.* And this must be a joint leadership, one which involves all employees.

1. *Participation.* This is the active involvement of management and all other key individuals in the model depicted above. It is more than receptiveness, more than responsiveness, even more than commitment. We

[5]*Psychology and Industry Today: An Introduction to Industrial and Organizational Psychology,* 5th edition, by Duane P. Schultz and Sydney Ellen Schultz, Macmillan, New York, 1990.

can define participation for our purposes as the enthusiastic support of those involved. That is what is meant by active involvement.

2. *Empowerment.* This comprises the vested trust, authority, and responsibility necessary for employees to feel they can control their destiny. When conjoined to the implementation of strategy, it provides for the self-perpetuating change agents that the organization must rely upon. Change is implemented by those who interact with the customer, those who are directly responsible for product and service. It is not implemented by management, nor is it implemented by fiat or directive. Empowered employees are those who believe their self-interests are entwined with organizational success. There is a mutuality of objectives (what Vroom and Yetton call "goal congruence"[6]).

3. *Leadership.* The collective leadership required for strategy implementation spreads responsibility to all individuals. Such leadership is possible only when employees are empowered. It means that, every day, employees are directly or indirectly taking responsibility for implementation. And it means that innovation—required for strategic change—will become an operating reality on a daily basis. "Ideas are not good enough," says Ted Levitt, "Ideas are rarely converted into action unless proselytized with zeal, carried with passion, sustained by conviction, and fortified by faith. They need authentic champions. Above all, ideas need people who are doers, not talkers."[7]

4. *Communication.* The essence of the strategic implementation process can be characterized by continuous, accurate, and honest communications. One can assess communications rapidly by determining if management is told what is actually happening or what is perceived to be what management wants to hear, by determining if employees are told everything they might need to know to implement strategy or only what "they can be trusted with," and by determining if the grapevine and rumor mills are more accurate channels of communication than regular meetings and reporting. Without the highest standards of communication, monitoring and evaluation are impossible.

Before we examine each of these components of the change model in some detail, we should focus on one particular role: that of the general manager and his or her responsibility in creating linkages between executive vision and middle-management implementation.

The general manager (or division head, or top local operating person) is the "point person" for strategy implementation. He or she sets the local tone, is usually the most critical local exemplar, and is the prime source of feedback. The excellent general managers are those willing to make the key—and often difficult—decisions that are required to make strategy happen.

---

[6]*Leadership and Decision Making,* by Victor H. Vroom and Philip W. Yetton, University of Pittsburgh Press, Pittsburgh, 1973, pages 218–220.
[7]Levitt, "Convictions."

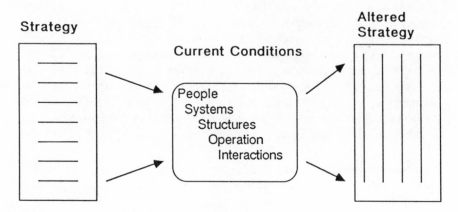

Figure 5.2

In many cases, figure 5.2 prevails: The GM, faced with conditions substantially different from those called for by the strategy, explicitly or implicitly transforms the strategy. This may occur while the GM is giving the strategic direction the strongest possible lip service to executives, but it occurs none the less. A GM, faced with a strategy calling for improved customer service, finds himself in command of a sales and service force heavily leveraged toward commission sales and minimum time with existing customers. Rather than take the difficult path of changing the reward and feedback systems, the GM (who probably grew up in the old system) bows to the pressure of the existing nature of the business. At best, superficial moves are undertaken. We've all seen them: handbooks that advocate greater customer service ("I'm on the customer's side"), buttons, statistics on repeat business. But these are the *easy* options. The tough ones—changing the new business commission ratio, forcing sales managers into customer operations, conducting surveys of customer attitudes—are not considered and certainly are not implemented. Superiors are put off with warnings of "We have to get through our current studies before we can begin to change the operation," or warned that "There's no way we can make those changes now if you want us to meet current quotas."

Conversely, the excellent GMs follow the sequence in figure 5.3. They alter the current conditions—beginning with their own behaviors and styles—in order to ensure that the strategy can be successfully implemented. GMs who make these tough decisions are usually readily identifiable because there is steady and visible progress toward organizational strategy in their areas. Each year, they are not only closer to the strategy already but have in place people and systems that are better equipped than the year before to implement and realize the strategy.

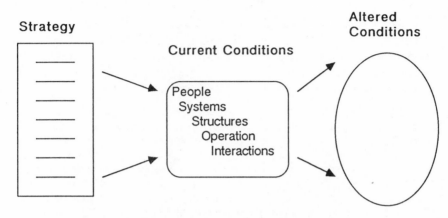

Figure 5.3

What must excellent GMs accomplish if they are to serve as the leaders of strategy implementation?

1. *They must be visible.* It is impossible to be an exemplar *in absentia.* This is where "management by wandering around" actually makes some sense. The GM must be seen to "walk the company's talk" by demonstrating the behaviors, priorities, and focus that are required. If customer service is the key, the GM should be out visiting customers and spending time in the customer service unit listening to the phones and reading the mail. If the focus is innovation in product application, the GM should be holding meetings with all levels of employees to hear ideas and should take pains to congratulate those whose ideas *didn't* work—and thereby create the freedom-to-fail atmosphere required for this strategy. The top person must be seen. Underlings reporting that "Ms. Smith is wholeheartedly behind this" leave employees to fill in the rest of the sentence: "wherever she is."

2. *The GM must personally be the leader of the performance evaluation process.* All individuals must be crystal clear on the importance of their job requirements to the implementation of strategy. Hence, the GM should make certain that his or her direct reports have emphasis areas that reflect the strategy, progress checkpoints to assess results, and evaluations which are based on that performance. And then he or she should ensure that his or her direct reports perform the exact same process with their reports, until everyone in the division is intimately connected to the strategy through performance emphasis areas and resultant rewards. This may mean high differentiation in rewards—top performers against the strategy receive considerably more than others, even if it means disappointing the "average" performers. The message sent out here should be unequivocal.

3. *Every facet of the organization should reflect strategy.* Meeting agendas should be based on it. Incentive programs should serve to support it.

Promotions should support the people who are best able to implement it. There should be no exceptions. The guidelines must be "We are going in this direction, and everything we do must support that direction."

4. *The GM must keep the entire process focused and simple.* Employees need to be able to keep the strategic direction in their heads, not in three-ring binders with complex cross-indexing. And he or she needs to take liberties with the organization chart. The strategy must be the determinant of the organization's processes, not enslaved by them:

> The best GMs seem to look for the simplest ways to do things, which usually means fewer layers, bigger jobs, and broader responsibilities. They also get personally involved in solving important problems, regardless of what the organization chart says. . . .[The best GMs] organize around people rather than concepts or principles. When they have a strategy or business problem or a big opportunity, they turn to the individual who has the right skills and style for that job. Then, having made the match, they delegate responsibility without hemming the person in with a tight job description or organizational constraints. Then managers feel more responsible for results simply because they are more responsible.[8]

Tregoe and Zimmerman[9] suggest that senior managers serve as "alter egos" for the strategy and provide these responsibilities:

- Helping to articulate the vision, serving as devil's advocate before their people do
- Maintaining ongoing commitment and support and providing the structure, plans, and budgets to make it work in their areas
- Setting strategic priorities and managing strategically and driving strategy home in the face of competing operational demands for resources and time

They quote John D. Milliken, vice president for Logistics at the J. M. Smucker Company, on his techniques for managing strategically:

> I keep a calendar in which I note the strategic issues I'm responsible for during a particular year. I don't have to wonder. They're right in front of me. These issues are my strategic performance objectives. Where appropriate, I translate them further for my subordinates. We all know what priorities are—both strategic and operational. My subordinates will challenge me *if I give them a task that does not support our strategy.* [Author's italics.] They'll tell me, "That's not strategic. It's off course. It's not on plan." So I know they're managing their people and their own time like that as well.

GMs, despite the guidelines and examples of those performing well, do face substantial obstacles in serving as the leading strategy advocates. There are seven of significant proportion that we've identified:

---

[8]"Six Basics for General Managers," by Andrall E. Pearson, *Harvard Business Review,* July–August 1989, page 99.
[9]*Top Management Strategy: What It Is and How It Works,* by Benjamin B. Tregoe and John W. Zimmerman, Simon and Schuster, New York, 1980, pages 143–145.

1. *Breaking with the past.* The GM, as noted above, is usually a product of the old systems and procedures and, in fact, has been rewarded and promoted for adherence to values and pursuits that the new strategy is trying to change. The first set of behaviors that the GM must change is his or her own, and that often must be accomplished without the desired supportiveness of the top executives. As the pivotal role between the troops and the generals, the GM must exhibit all the qualifications of bold leadership that may be absent from his or her own circumstances.

2. *Increasing complexity of organizational life.* The GM is less and less the ruler of all he or she surveys. Departments and divisions seldom operate in a vacuum. Interactions with other organizational units, suppliers, customers, and the community (not to mention regulators, lawyers, and banks) force the GM to be more of a persuader and less of a dictator. The implications for strategy implementation is that it simply can't be commanded and is often reliant on influence exerted with others not under anyone's direct control.

3. *People skills.* People skills have become paramount, and many GMs are in their positions by dint of content expertise, not people management skills. The dynamic in Smucker's cited by Tregoe is one that demands that Mr. Milliken exhibit substantial people skills—handling conflict, accepting feedback, developing consensus, allowing for group decision making, and so on. These are not naturally acquired capacities in most cases, yet few organizations appreciate the value of developing such interpersonal skills among those leading the strategy implementation.

4. *Information explosion.* All of us, for better or for worse, are dealing with increasingly detailed data and avalanches of information, yet strategy implementation is only tangentially dependent on reports, statistics, and numeric comparisons. It is most dependent on values, attitudes, and behaviors, precisely the things which can't be so easily quantified. Frankly, the organization making progress toward its strategy should look, sound, and even feel different from the way it did before. GMs can be lulled into false senses of security by making strategy implementation one more statistic to be tracked and ignoring the human and cultural elements.

5. *Resource allocation.* For close to a decade now, we've been in a general downsizing environment. If strategy implementation is seen as "an extra job" to be undertaken, resources will be stretched even thinner than they already are, and the strategy will be blamed for operational goals being undone. Employees should not view strategy as another accretion to their jobs. GMs must view strategy as outlined earlier: as a direction that must be reflected in every aspect of their operation, and not as *an addition to their operation* which demands separate attention, division of resources, and so on.

6. *The buffeting of change.* Accelerating change is a challenge to any strategy. But implementation plans must accommodate the inevitable,

unexpected changes that will occur and neither ignore them nor try to be impervious to them. The GM must allow for the flexibility needed to accept changes *within* the strategy implementation plan and provide the support and encouragement to subordinates who may feel that "everything is against us" as the unexpected threatens to thwart their plans.

7. *The burden of short-term operational goals.* This is the most insidious of the GM's obstacles, and it is often a problem that he or she must resolve alone. "Make the adjustment to a more customer service–oriented operation, but don't allow our productivity indices to slip" is the *bête noir* of more than a few GMs. This kind of conflict often places the GM in an untenable position, and the remedy here is upward, not downward. The excellent GMs overcome this obstacle by demonstrating to the top people that neither their strategy's implementation nor their short-term goals will be met through such organizational schizophrenia.

To implement strategy effectively, *every* employee must be a champion of change. And although the GM serves as the local leader in word and deed, ultimately everyone must feel responsible for attainment of the new strategic direction. Employees can be skeptical about such things, of course, which is why the environment must be changed in order to reward the desired behavior and provide examples of what such behavior is.

One restaurant industry CEO[10] cites a new strategy of "absolutely guaranteeing customers' enjoyment," no matter what it took. In so doing, he empowered employees to do whatever was necessary to make diners happy. Never having had this authority, his people were wary. What would the *actual* organizational response (consequences) be when a free drink or meal was offered? Once company management unequivocally backed up every such decision, employees' motivation was strengthened to provide that service guarantee and—as is essential to the implementation of any new strategy—they began to develop innovative methods to accomplish it.

> Once our employees overcame their skepticism, they quickly grew creative and aggressive in their approach to the guarantee. In one case, a customer wanted a margarita made the way a competitor made its. So our bartender called the bartender at the other restaurant, and bartender-to-bartender, learned the special recipe. In another case, an elderly woman who had not been in our restaurant for years ordered breakfast, which we no longer served. The waiter and the chef sent someone to the market for bacon and eggs and served the breakfast she wanted.

These are not isolated examples resulting from enlightened and inspired management. They are the rule in organizations in which every employee is made responsible for implementing the strategy. It is why a Mazda

---

[10]Timothy W. Firnstahl, CEO of Satisfaction Guaranteed Eateries, Inc., writing in *Harvard Business Review*, "My Employees Are My Service Guarantee," July–August 1989, pages 28–34. The following examples are from his article.

engineer, participating in what is probably the most dramatic new car introduction since the Mustang, the Miata, listened to over 200 recorded sounds of car exhausts before deciding on the one that best fit the image of the car as Mazda wanted it to appear. It's why a clerk in a local pharmacy stocking shelves goes to retrieve a product because he noticed a customer holding a coupon for it and knew she was standing in the wrong aisle. He didn't wait to be asked, and he didn't direct her—he took the time to get the item because he doesn't see his job as stocking shelves; he sees it as helping customers. The name of the drug chain is CVS, which stands for "customer, value, service."

Here's what Richard J. Loughlin, president and CEO of Century 21 Real Estate, says about employee involvement:[11]

> Without a strong degree of ownership in the development of corporate goals and strategies, one cannot expect any level of management to implement a strategy with maximum enthusiasm and commitment. When all levels...are an integral part of the development of corporate strategies, it is more reasonable and equitable to expect them to commit to, and be held accountable for, its successful conclusions. Without this corporate philosophy, an organization is likely to be managed by directives and fear...rather than by pride and the commitment of authorship.

Before we conclude this chapter, let's take a look at a case exercise. How would you expect your employees to handle this situation:

A family has booked an airline vacation overseas. They must leave from New York, and they have booked an early connecting flight on the airline's commuter partner to arrive in plenty of time to make their connection. On the morning of their departure, they call the local airport to verify that the connecting flight is on time and find, to their horror, that it's been canceled. The family places an irate and threatening call to the parent carrier, then decides to rent a car to drive to New York (3 hours away) to catch their plane. The family informs the carrier that they will call back after they check in at the gate in New York.

While the family is traveling to New York, your customer service manager finds out that the commuter canceled the flight because of a serious equipment problem, and was unable to secure an alternate aircraft. The commuter's staff successfully called every passenger to arrange alternative transportation, but this family couldn't be reached because the travel agent who booked their flight recorded the agency phone number and not the family's home phone number. Apparently, the family will make their New York departure without further difficulty.

What actions, based on this situation, would you like your customer service manager to take, knowing that she'll have the opportunity to talk to the family prior to departure?

Responses vary on this exercise among groups with which we've used it. Obviously, there are no "correct answers," though the exercise is based on an actual occurrence. Here is the range of alternatives usually suggested:

---

[11]Correspondence with the author.

1. Do nothing except to explain why the cancellation was unavoidable and how the travel agent caused the failure to communicate the problem expeditiously.
2. The above, plus an upgrade to first class on the flight, if available, or the offer of an upgrade on a future flight.
3. The above, plus repaying any difference between the unused ticket value and the cost of the rental car.
4. The above, but instead of an upgrade, reimbursing the price of one or more of the family's entire tickets.
5. The above, but instead of the reimbursement, a free trip for one to be taken in the future on any domestic flight.

Which did you choose? If you were to poll your people, would they choose a similar response or vastly differing ones? In this actual case, the airline was American, and the initial response of the customer service representative was to do nothing except to guarantee a later flight in case the original were missed from New York. However, slightly later the customer service supervisor called back, on her own volition, with this offer: The rental car would be paid for if it exceeded the price of the unused tickets (which were refundable), and a $100 travel voucher was provided for use on any future American flight. The supervisor went on to explain that they were working with the commuter's personnel so that home phone numbers were demanded from agents, and she also pointed out that the local phone directory probably would have produced the number as well if someone had thought to consult it.

In my book, this response got a "B+." It should have been the *first* response, but it was adequate because it proved that the airline not only intended to make a financial commitment, but wanted to change the *system* that failed in the first place. It is important to note that: Such responses to customer problems are invariably more effective when offered by the initial contact at the lowest practical level in the organization. No matter how significant the ameliorating actions, they lose impact when they are the result of the customer having to go up the line. Executives who solve customer complaints should not be patting themselves on the back; they should be asking why the complaint wasn't solved at the point of contact. The answer is usually that someone didn't realize that he or she had the power to resolve it, and only infrequently that the employee didn't care.

Somewhat paradoxically, every time you are spending money to resolve a customer complaint (or a vendor, agent, salesperson, or other complaint), you are investing money if determining why your strategy implementation is weak and you have created the opportunity to correct it.

Finally, if every employee is to be a strategist, this simple sequence is essential:

1. The strategy must be clear to everyone.
2. It must be practical and applicable to everyone's job.
3. Employees must have the tools and abilities to make it happen.

4. Employees must have the responsibility and authority to make it happen.
5. Exemplars in senior management must live the strategy every day.
6. The organization's rewards and feedback should reflect the strategy.
7. Feedback should be regularly solicited and *used* to improve implementation.

We'll now examine some of the specifics of products and markets as they relate to these needs.

6

The Realities of the Marketplace:
How to Avoid Turning Gold into Lead

Every organization, public or private, provides either a product or a service that fills a need in the marketplace. There is a well-documented trend that we are moving toward a knowledge, and therefore service, economy in the United States. After all, there are more people employed in U.S. universities than there are in U.S. agriculture, more people working in McDonald's than in the U.S. steel industry. And we're not alone in that transition. Hong Kong, once known for cheap goods and toys, has become a financial services center as cheaper manufacturing conditions have come to be provided in Korea, Indonesia, and the Philippines.

But the trend is not as clear-cut as some experts would have us believe. There are some who say that no nation can maintain a world power status through an economy based on the flipping of hamburgers. There are others who claim that the technologically advanced nations will lead the way in specialty manufacture that cheap labor can't handle. There is certainly evidence of this in the smaller but rejuvenated sections of the American steel and rubber industries.

Yet I think the connection between product and service is more basic than world economies or technological advance. I think it is a question of customer need. American Airlines provides a service. Yet it also does its best to sell passengers products through a catalog in every seat pocket, offering everything from swimming pool accessories to fine wine. (It's always been of interest that there seems to be more than one catalog available per seat, but there's never more than one flight safety card available per seat! I know the catalogs are meant to be taken, but the safety cards are often liberated as book marks or scratch pads, as well.)

What turns up in your American Express and Texaco bills? If you're at all like me, you get offers to buy products such as jewelry and calendars from that giant financial services company, American Express, and services such as insurance and automobile club membership from that petroleum products company, Texaco. My telephone answering service recently sent me an offer to purchase (I did) a device that automatically forwards calls to my office phone and provides an indicator of whether any messages were received while the office was closed, and the local discount store which sold me a television of impeccable reputation offered me the purchase (I didn't) of a 5-year service warranty. I am told by many of my retail clients that there is often more profit in service contracts than in the original product sale and that in most cases the contract is not cost-effective for the consumer.

What does your local computer store offer? Probably classes and tutoring as well as hardware and software. The local deli offers catering along with its cold cuts. Fewer and fewer businesses are engaged *solely* in product or service offerings, because the needs of their customers—*and, consequently, the key to their survival, let alone growth*—demand that the organization respond with a comprehensive mixture of complementary products and services.

Any strategy implementation, regardless of its scope or nature, must embrace the organization's present and future mix of products and services. The manner in which the mix is described, communicated, and understood is one of the most critical elements in effective strategy implementation. Here are some examples:

1. As a competitive edge, the mix of product and service has often proved to be the pivotal factor. Years ago, a quality hotel was judged by the comfort of the room and, perhaps, courtesy of the front desk; today, an entire industry is devoted to "room amenities." Room amenities are the shampoos and shoehorns found in the more modest establishments and the thick bathrobes and VCRs found in the more elegant ones. A pitched battle is being waged by amenity suppliers and the hotels to provide guests with room products that will provide guest loyalty in a viciously competitive market. Years ago, it was tough to get a newspaper delivered. Today, if you ask the desk for a hair dryer, you'll be asked what wattage you prefer.

2. As an escape from a saturated market, introducing a product or service has become an effective tactic. Local TV repair shops now offer video cassette rentals. Computer software retailers offer applications classes. Gas stations are transforming into minimarts in which you can purchase food, cosmetics, reading material, and even plants. The local pharmacy has become the American casbah with prescription drugs relegated to a distant corner so as not to impede the traffic. And on a much broader basis, answer this: What organization is the largest financial institution of any type in the United States? (The answer is at the bottom of the page—it will win a lot of bar bets.)* So, introducing an allied product or service has helped organizations large and small escape the confines of an overly competitive marketplace.

---

*General Motors through its credit arm, General Motors Acceptance Corporation. One of my cars is leased through General Electric's GE Capital Corp. which, at this writing, was the most profitable unit in the entire organization. GM, by the way, is also the largest manufacturer of computers in the world.

3. As a transformational vehicle, to lead the organization in radically new directions, a new product or service introduction is virtually a requirement. On a dramatic scale, the old, bankrupt Penn Central Company that operated railroads is now a highly profitable real estate investment firm utilizing the valuable land that happened to be under and around the tracks.[1] (This is not to be confused with the *perception* of changed service or product, which may be called "usage adaptation." For example, baking soda was an ingredient of foods until Arm & Hammer ingeniously capitalized on what many of its users already knew and promoted it as a refrigerator deodorant, putting a calendar on the package to aid in replacement. More about this later.) Transformation is often forced upon an organization by changing technology or changing mores. Frieden was driven from the calculator business because it didn't embrace electronics. Tobacco companies rushed to diversify in the face of a societal backlash to smoking. Health clubs have proliferated because of a frenzy for fitness. (There is no empirical evidence that jogging physically helps those who engage in it, though it seems clear that the psychological payback is significant.)

The organization that is unable to utilize new products and/or services to reach new markets or to adapt to changing times can, literally, disappear. In his book on innovation,[2] Richard Foster talks about an S-curve that reflects the ability to remain abreast of technological change (figure 6.1). Very few organizations successfully bridge the gap formed when one curve flattens (products and services are mature and no longer unique or unchallenged) and the next one begins (through technological breakthrough, perception change, and so on). For example, no vacuum tube manufacturer became a major player in transistors, and the entire Swiss watch industry came to digitalization only after the Japanese had virtually usurped the market. Although Foster concentrates on the manufacturing and product side, I believe that his thesis is no less true for services. Fred Smith at Federal Express has obviously been searching for the next breakthrough after the saturated small package delivery market flattens (Zap-Mail wasn't the answer, although fax machines are) and has purchased Flying Tiger Airlines to enter the heavy-cargo market. Insurance agents have tried to become financial planners. The vast majority of products and services will hit the top of their respective S-curves because:

- They become obsolete—we no longer need buggy whips.
- They are improved—why would I want a rotary phone?
- They become old hat—a hula hoop is not lifetime entertainment.
- They lose cost-effectiveness—this was the demise of U.S.-flag cruise ships.
- They suffer perception change—muscle cars come and go, as do clothes styles.
- They lose their demographic strength—farm products for the small farmer.

[1]See "Centennial Journal: Merger on the Occident Express," *The Wall Street Journal*, Sept. 6, 1989, page B1.
[2]*Innovation: The Attacker's Advantage*, by Richard N. Foster, Summit Books, New York, 1986.

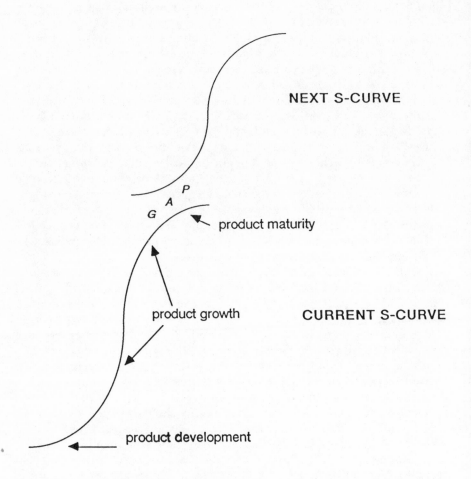

NEXT S-CURVE

P
A
G
product maturity

product growth

CURRENT S-CURVE

product development

Figure 6.1

Given these realities, every organization must include a comprehensive assessment and application of present and future products and services into its strategy implementation plans. This is important because every employee must be able to:

- Understand the roles and relationships of future products and services
- Become trained in their uses and applications
- Plan for the proper resources and support of them
- Interact with customers in support of the product/service directions
- Provide feedback to management appropriate to those directions
- Seek opportunities commensurate with those directions

If your organization has introduced new products and/or services over the last 5 years, you might gain some insight from this test. Choose any single new product or service (or new user application) and answer the following questions:

New Product/Service/Application: _____

1. In retrospect, did it fit with our projected strategy at that time? ☐ yes ☐ no
2. Were people thoroughly trained in its role in our strategy? ☐ yes ☐ no
3. Were the proper resources made available to support it, in launch *and* subsequently? ☐ yes ☐ no
4. Was feedback actively solicited relative to its use, acceptance, successes, and failures? ☐ yes ☐ no
5. Did key members of management serve as exemplars and champion its cause? ☐ yes ☐ no
6. Were employees encouraged to innovate in its use and promotion? ☐ yes ☐ no
7. Was it toward the bottom, rather than toward the top, of the S-curve? ☐ yes ☐ no
8. Was the organization culture (rewards, feedback, and so on) modified to support it? ☐ yes ☐ no

Tally the yes and no responses; then answer these additional questions:

9. Is it still a part of the organization's products and services today? ☐ yes ☐ no
10. Would most reasonable observers consider it a success today? ☐ yes ☐ no ☐ too soon to tell

Our experience is that *all* eight questions must be answered "yes" to ensure success. Here are four possible interpretations:

1. If you answered yes in 10 but checked some no responses among 1 to 8, then your organization engaged in some effective contingent actions to maximize the chance for success as the obstacles were encountered. (Of course, some new products/services/applications are so earthshaking that they can't miss no matter what—sliced bread comes to mind—but they are few and far between.)
2. If you answered no in 10, yet checked only yes responses in 1 to 8, it's probable that the failure is due to the list of factors above explaining why the top of the S-curve is invariably reached. Your offering simply began its life there as a result of poor market analysis.
3. If you answered "too soon to tell" to 10, then you have the opportunity to review 1 to 8 to ensure that all those factors are being properly managed.

4. If you answered no to 9, understand which factors among 1 to 8 were mismanaged and make sure that the mistake isn't repeated for future launches.

A simple yet elegant way to consider product and market mix is shown in figure 6.2. The choices are limited and clear for any strategy:

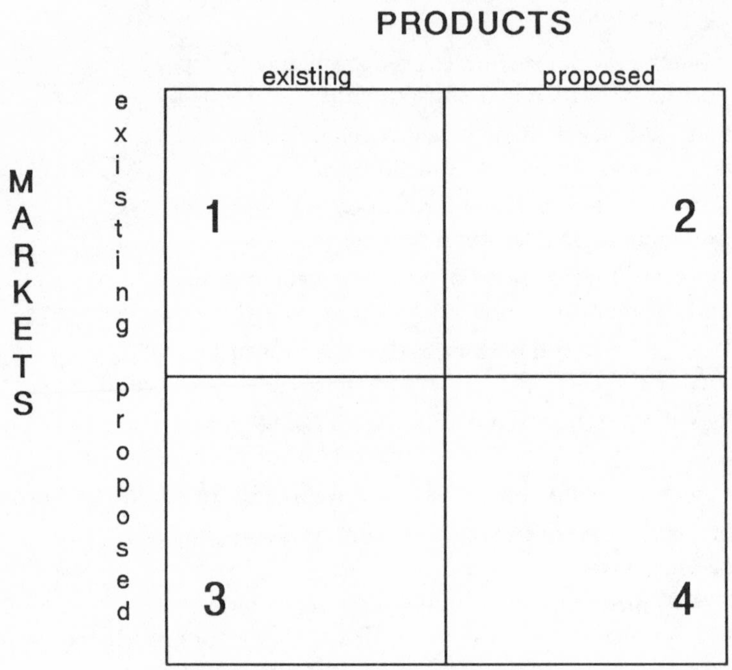

PRODUCTS

	existing	proposed
M A R K E T S existing	1	2
proposed	3	4

Figure 6.2

1. Focus on existing products in existing markets. In other words, don't change strategy to any significant degree.
2. Develop new products and services for existing markets. The strength here is that the customer base is known and developed. The risk is the developmental process for the new product or service. Can the strategy be met through incremental additions, for example, pay-per-view programming introduced into a cable system, or are radical additions required, such as, providing custom furniture to house cable "home entertainment centers"?
3. Take current products and services to new markets. The strength is in the knowledge and application experience of existing products and

services. The risk is in the unfamiliarity of new markets, perhaps influenced by potential competitors. (If dominated by competitors, one can make the case to avoid it unless you have a *new* product or service to introduce.) Can the strategy be met incrementally, for example, expanding travel agencies from the northeastern to the southeastern United States, or is a more substantial change required by the strategy, for example, opening up offices overseas?

4. Develop new products and services for new markets. This, of course, is usually the riskiest position of all, and it must be justified by a strategy that can only be met by such aggressive actions.

The segment 1 product/service/market combination in figure 6.2 is exemplified by Boeing. It builds airplanes, and only a small number of models, for the relatively few major airlines in the world. Boeing doesn't consider itself a "transportation company," for example. It's an airplane builder, pure and simple.

Segment 2 is exemplified by Gillette. That company has introduced a succession of products into its traditional men's toiletry market. Playboy has attempted the same strategy by developing book clubs, clothing, accessories, videos, and a cable offering for its market. Gillette has been consistently successful; Playboy, erratic at best.

Cellular phone organizations belong in segment 3, bringing their technology into new geographic markets with expansion and new demographic markets with increasingly lower prices.

Finally, DuPont is a good example of segment 4; it has introduced new products, e.g., Kevlar-inspired offerings as diverse as bulletproof garments and superstrong bindings, to any market in which that product can be applied.

Go back to the test above. In which segment was your organization's offering? Did the organization acknowledge that relationship and support it accordingly?

In figure 6.3 is a slightly extended relationship with which to view the product/market mix. As the figure illustrates, there can be three possibilities for markets and products. Existing products are those being manufactured at this time. Improved products are those that can be easily produced within the abilities of the existing organization—making a different size or color, for example. And new products are those that require design, resource, and promotion investments to launch them—you produce pencils and you've decided to introduce ballpoint pens (note that this is a new product but it is sold in your traditional marketplace).

Existing markets are those in which you now comfortably operate. They may be geographic or demographic. Expanded markets are those readily moved into—you may be moving from one state to the next or from doctors to attorneys. New markets are the ones that require an investment in sales, promotion, and analysis to enter—moving from domestic sales to overseas or from adults' attire to children's.

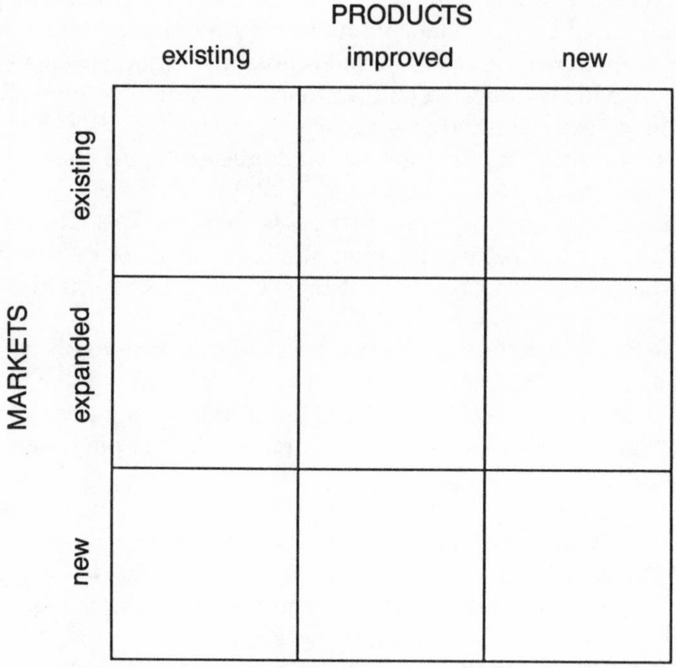

PRODUCTS

Figure 6.3

The problems with these types of views are that:

- They assume that services can be "substituted" for products in the equation.
- They ignore the increasing interconnection between products and services.
- They really restrict an organization to implementing more of the same.
- They ignore the intangible aspects of strategic change: relationships.

Consequently, while such traditional matrices can be useful for examining differences between where you are and where you want to be, they are subliminally restrictive in their viewpoint. Moveover, they are overly simplistic as communication tools in trying to create a sense of direction for the implementation of the strategy. They produce black-and-white issues:

- "We're launching a new product."
- "We're moving into a new territory."
- "We're modifying our approach to the market."
- "We're making some improvements."

This is hardly the stuff of new directions. Because of the intertwining of an organization's activities in terms of its *relationships* with its customers and because of the increasing service orientation of *every* business, we would suggest the figure 6.4 view of the organization in terms of its current

	IMPROVEMENT (maintains competitiveness)	ADVANCE (gains competitive edge)	BREAKTHROUGH (achieves dominance)
PRODUCT (tangible purchase)	multiuse razor blades / collapsable umbrellas / cordless tools		
SERVICE (intangible purchase)	multiplex cinemas / 24-hour supermarkets / adjustable mortagages		
RELATIONSHIP (intangible nonpurchase)	casino room comps / bank-by-mail / store charge accounts		

Figure 6.4

and projected view of itself, and what is needed to implement change. In this model, we attempt to consider all of the elements that interact in the current dynamic and in any projected change. Our definitions:

1. *Product.* Any tangible produced for sale. The utility is in the use of the items itself—in other words, a book is used in its own physicality, whereas an insurance policy is only representative of an abstract benefit that has been acquired.

2. *Service.* Any intangible assistance for which the customer pays. We differentiate here from the often-cited free service. The bus company performs a service for a fee. The town van for senior citizens isn't really free, since it's supported by tax dollars that are earmarked for it.

3. *Relationship.* This is any service or assistance that is provided for no perceived fee, and it may differ in its substance and form from customer to customer. Products and services are generally covered by explicit or implicit warranty; relationships are not. One may usually seek redress for poor performance in the first two areas, but not in the third.

4. *Improvement.* This is an advance that maintains one's position in the marketplace. We are operating under the assumption that virtually no organization can survive without reacting to (or instigating) change. Consequently, improvements are the "minor" things that must be done simply to tread water.

5. *Advance.* These are managed changes that gain a competitive edge. They are creative and innovative solutions to existing problems, and they represent marked enhancements to the customer. They are usually emulatable by the competition, so their timing is the key to their utility.

6. *Breakthroughs.* These are landmark events which can spawn industries, change the vernacular ("Make a Xerox copy of this"), and produce temporary or prolonged market dominance, depending on the effectiveness of their implementation. Disposable diapers changed the industry permanently.[3]

This model, we believe, is more accurate in reflecting the multifarious interactions between today's organization and its customers, and it's even of greater use in examining what the *future* interactions ought to be. That's because no strategy can be implemented if it is based on a singularity such as a product produced or a service offered. Moreover, we believe that this dynamic *determines* markets.

In the examples we've chosen, the multiuse razor blade, collapsible umbrella, and cordless tool all represent product improvements that maintained competitive edge. They were quickly copyable (although short-term market inroads may have been created) and are a staple of any organization in that product area that wants to remain competitive. Similarly, multi-screen movies, all-night supermarkets, and adjustable mortgages are examples of services that were improved, often in imitation of others, to remain as viable alternatives for the consumer. Note how quickly "improvements" become the status quo, which is why we recognize them as essential parts of the daily business. Can you imagine a bank *not* offering ATMs and remaining a serious competitor in the marketplace?

Now, however, let's examine the relationships. Casinos extend room, food, and drink comps to key players. This practice varies from casino to casino and from player to player. It even varies within the casino *as the organization's strategy changes.* Until the mid-80s, the Golden Nugget Casino in Atlantic City was the self-defined high-roller casino in the city. It actively sought out high-end players and awarded lavish complimentary benefits on them. This was also reflected in the average higher-amount limits on its tables, for example. However, when acquired by rival Bally's, the strategy was changed. And just as services changed—lower-limit tables in higher numbers, more focus on slot machine players, and so on—so did the relationship. There are now far fewer comps given to far fewer people. Previously, floor supervisors actively searched for players whose volume and time could be rated. Now, such rating is often done only at the request of a player.

---

[3]They currently account for 80–85% of the $3 billion diaper market. See "This Market Didn't Bottom Out," the Centennial Journal: 100 Years in Business, *The Wall Street Journal,* Aug. 30, 1989, page B1.

Store charge accounts at the local community level are good examples of a relationship aspect of strategy. The customer doesn't pay for the service *per se*, although there may be a finance charge for late payments. The store feels that it will maintain its competitiveness by offering its customers the option of paying later. Note that this is quite different from providing and charging for a clear service, such as dress alterations or assembly. (If one store charges $15 for an item and $2 for delivery, the latter is a service. If it does not overtly charge for delivery but charges $17 for the product delivered—vs. $15 for competitors—it is still providing a paid service. But if the product is $15 in-store or delivered, then delivery is part of the relationship that the store is engaged in.) Bank-by-mail is another such relationship. Many people might not use it, but it is there and is promoted by the bank as an aspect of its relationship with customers, as are automatic tellers. Some banks are now considering assessing a charge for bank-by-mail, bank-by-phone, and even ATM use. These features will then become services, and not aspects of the bank's relationship with its customers.

By now, you've probably noted several features of this breakdown:

- Some organizations offer no relationship beyond product and service.
- The customer may or may not avail himself of the relationship opportunities.
- Services and relationships can move between categories.

You may also be thinking that *all* relationships are really services, since they are paid for or subsidized in some manner, not unlike the senior citizen's van. However, the key distinctions are these:

- The customer perceives no direct charge for the relationship.
- The organization does not earmark the relationship as a line budget item.
- The relationship is situational, and it can differ in quality by customer.
- The relationship is measured in terms of *quality* impact, not quantity.
- The relationship is intended for long-term goodwill, not short-term profit or revenues.
- The customer must choose to avail himself of it—it is a contingency.

Our casino can offer more comps to its higher-volume players; the bank may offer self-mailers or automatic bill payments to its largest depositors; and the store may choose not to charge interest on any outstanding balances for its biggest purchasers. (This last point is worth a brief example. I frequent a men's clothing store which is farther from my home and more expensive than most. But its feature of allowing me to pay whatever I wish a month without any interest charge encourages me not only to use it exclusively but to purchase more than I otherwise would. How much business is it gaining in return for sacrificing the interest charges?)

Take a look at the next column in figure 6.4, "advance." Now list three examples of product, service, and relationships that you think illustrate the "gaining of a competitive edge."

Product (tangible purchase)   _____

Service (intangible purchase)   _____

Relationship (intangible nonpurchase) _____

Was it easy or difficult to think in these terms? Were you able to come up with examples from your own organization or did you find it easier to use those from others? Did you easily recognize competitors' examples? (This is an excellent technique for analyzing competitive actions, by the way.) Compare your examples to those in figure 6.5. Under products, the quick-brewing and easy-to-use Mr. Coffee machines gained a clear competitive edge, and the machines are now ubiquitous in American homes. They didn't quite transform coffee making (a breakthrough), but they did create clear marketplace superiority. And, of course, they were quickly copyable by competitors. Similarly, the rolling-ball marker provided a market that could be used in carbon or NCR paper (one could argue that the original Flair markers were a breakthrough). And NCR paper brought a new dimension to copies.

In the service area, time-sharing created an innovative new way to sell property: on a pooled basis. Discount brokerages created clear market advantages for those selling to smaller investors. And call-forwarding is a clear competitive edge for the traditional phone companies (or whatever their postdivestiture parts are). Competitors like MCI counter with dedicated fax services, for example.

	IMPROVEMENT (maintains competitiveness) ↓	ADVANCE (gains competitive edge) ↓	BREAKTHROUGH (achieves dominance) ↓
PRODUCT (tangible purchase)		Mr. Coffee rolling-ball markers NCR paper	
SERVICE (intangible purchase)		time-sharing discount brokerages call-forward	
RELATIONSHIP (intangible nonpurchase)		frequent-flyer program roadside assistance affinity credit cards	

Figure 6.5

Now let's look at relationships. In a classic example, over a decade ago someone in the marketing department of American Airlines developed the idea of the frequent-flyer Advantage Program, and none of us has been the same since. Note that the mileage points in such programs accrue *automatically.* No fees are assessed for the program, and whether the traveler wants to use them or not, the points pile up (today they are all computer-tracked). The only necessity for the consumer is to join, which is painless and free. Polls have shown that many flyers choose their airline for this relationship, and entire industries have been spawned to try to exploit it (for example, free-ticket brokers). In addition, every competitor and most allied businesses (rental cars, hotels) were forced into similar relationships in order to merely remain competitive, so that the original program would not fit under "improvement." The advances of today are the incessant tie-ins with others—MCI, for example, offers points in the American program based on monthly phone charges. And both Mercedes-Benz and BMW offer roadside assistance programs to their customers.

I fondly remember a rainy Sunday morning when my car broke down 50 miles from home. My first reaction was, "This is *not* supposed to happen to a Mercedes!" (Movie mogul George Lucas of *Star Wars* fame said that "If your Mercedes-Benz has a dead battery, it's even worse than a dead battery in your Chevy. When you're rich, everything is supposed to work.") However, my second reaction was to call the toll-free roadside assistance number, and 40 minutes later two mechanics arrived (in a Mercedes station wagon, no less), replaced a broken hose, and got me on my way. Mercedes' pledge is to at least get your car roadworthy until permanent repairs can be made, and they charge only for parts. My remembrance, of course, isn't that a high-priced car broke down, but that the company unequivocally stands behind its product for me and cares about how I perceive that backing. That is the essence of relationships, especially in the competitive edge category. I don't pay for that relationship; I don't even have to use it. But it's there if I want it, and it's a unique relationship at that.

Affinity credit cards are one more example of such advances. They are provided, usually free of any charge, to members of certain groups or patrons of certain organizations. So United Airlines may have an affiliation with Visa, and your professional association may have one with MasterCard. These are relationship competitive edges meant to establish special bonds with the customer or member. (Examples abound: Many travel agencies offer flight insurance coverage, charge cards used for air travel offer lost baggage insurance, and so on.)

So now we've seen some categories that an organization must examine in attempting to advance beyond the merely competitive position and gain an edge. The implementation must reflect those advances and support and reward employees engaged in them. Most importantly, their roles must be communicated effectively and consistently so that the implementors don't just understand their roles but also understand the rationales of their roles in terms of the strategy. It is easier to do this in terms of such categories, rather than in general. Compare, for example, the admonition "Let's make sure we're one step better than our competitors in service quality" with "Emphasize the flexibility of call-forwarding and the decreased likelihood that an important call will be missed."

Finally, let's examine the third column in figure 6.5, "breakthrough." This should be fairly easy for product, but what about service and relationship? Try to cite three examples for each.

Product   _____

Service   _____

Relationship   _____

This time, were you able to use familiar examples from your own experience, or did you have to rely on external ones? Did the relationships come easier, or are they still difficult to visualize? In figure 6.6 we offer some examples of breakthroughs.

The product breakthroughs are well known, and any number are available to add. The original Mustang was a product breakthrough, as is the more recent minivan. The dramatic product breakthroughs are big news, but their fame belies the fact that they are relatively few and far between in both time and investment. And although a few organizations make their daily living at it—Merck, DuPont, 3M, Bell Labs—most don't and can't. The big-hit product is always a gamble, and even when it works, there's no pattern established to create a succession of such hits. Several years ago we had the opportunity to work with Case Communications in England. The two founders had produced a breakthrough communications device in 1972, and the firm had lived off its success ever since. However, 15 years later the owners were edgy. "The primary product has lived its life in all its variations," we were told. "How can we create an organization that continues to pursue new product breakthroughs?"

Under the best of conditions it's tough, and when your hiring, incentives, and overall culture reward those who can rework the old and punish those who dare to suggest the new, the prognosis for shifting a strategy isn't good. We suggested that a more innovative organization that accommodated customer services and relationships might be a viable path, but it would require substantial changes in the owners' management style to achieve the necessary changes. The owners didn't want to invest that kind of energy. In 1988 Case was sold under pressure. One of my colleagues put the episode into perspective: "Actually," he observed, "they lasted longer than most on a single-product breakthrough."

Service breakthroughs are the current state of the art. Note that they are not necessarily based on radically new *ideas*, but they are based on

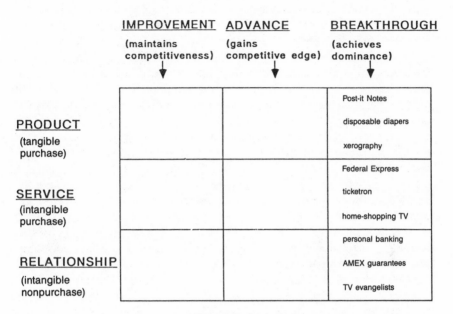

Figure 6.6

radically new *applications*. This is a fundamental distinction that any management must come to terms with. In many respects, there *is* nothing new under the sun. However, application of what's already known is the royal road to success. Earlier we noted that innovation is applied creativity. Genius in the abstract is relatively abundant; idea people abound. But practical genius, which is the difference between the Dick Tracy wrist radio and the Walkman, is a much rarer quantity.

Fred Smith took a hub-and-spoke method of delivery that had been posited for years and *applied* it to small-package transportation. Ticketron simply combined the phone and the computer to provide widespread access to entertainment, sporting, and cultural admissions. And home-shopping TV services combined the computer, telephone, and television to create the ultimate consumer couch potato. Service breakthroughs are more valuable than product breakthroughs to most organizations because:

- We are evolving toward an increasing knowledge and service economy.
- Concern for the quality of our time prompts interest in time-saving services.
- The electronic and communications requirements are already in place.
- Services constitute repeatable, not one-time, sales.
- Services augment both existing products *and* existing services.
- Services tend to build customer-loyalties that surmount price.

In the last few years airport van services have developed in San Francisco, Los Angeles, and other cities. The vans will generally pick up the passenger at his or her door, guarantee a maximum of four stops, and take the passenger to any particular airline terminal for under $12. The services work in reverse from the airport. Compare that with a taxi ride for $25 or an airport bus that demands that you utilize a common location. This is a primary example of a service breakthrough that is based on existing technology and ideas but had never been applied in this particular way.

If service breakthroughs are current state of the art, let's now look at the future, because relationship breakthroughs might well be a core part of most organization's implementation strategies in the coming years. A superb example of such a breakthrough is the American Express extended guarantee. Buy a product with an American Express card, and the company will double the provisions of the product's own guarantee. So, if your coffee pot has a 90-day guarantee and it breaks down in 5 months, American Express will pay for the repair, no questions asked. Does the consumer have to pay extra? Nope. Does the consumer have to be a new card member, or renew before a certain date? Nope. Just use the card already in your pocket. Simple as that.

Many banks have instituted personal banking privileges for their major depositors. This means that there are no more lines to stand in for mundane deposits and withdrawals, there are preferred rates for loans, brokerage services, and financial planning advice, and, most important, there is someone to appeal to when the checkbook doesn't balance or the escrow accounts seem out of whack. Although this relationship can serve as a lure to attract new business, it is extended without fee to those already on board.

Finally, it has always seemed to me that the television evangelists are prime examples of relationships at their ultimate. Their products are relatively minor in terms of their endeavors—some books and tracts, perhaps. Some offer services for contributions, such as prayers. But most people watch and contribute on a regular basis because of the relationships. The evangelist is bringing comfort and solace, interpretation of the Bible, and a general sense of well-being to those who watch. And watching, of course, is free. Anyone can watch without investment or donation. Many are moved to contribute solely on the basis of the comfort and perceived value on that electronic relationship. Jim and Tammy Bakker built an organization of immense size and complexity based on such relationships. Virtually no one who donated large amounts to qualify for guaranteed stays at their resort for life bothered to analytically and objectively calculate that there couldn't be enough rooms to accommodate everyone.

Relationships, you see, are built on trust. That's why they are the key to the interaction with any customer. Trust is self-perpetuating and long term. It isn't based on "what have you done for me lately?" or "what is the cost vs. the competition?" If it weren't for such relationships and the intrinsic trust underlying them, why would anyone:

- Buy a Mercedes-Benz?
- Base your choice of a doctor on repute and not price?
- Buy from the local butcher instead of the lower-priced supermarket?

It is our contention that successful strategy implementation is based on the successful accommodation of as many of the three elements—product, service, and relationship—as pertain. There will be instances of organizations that engage solely in services and develop relationships and those that deal only in products and relationships. The latter should be somewhat rarer (we illustrated earlier in this chapter that every producer of products is or should be considering attendant services), and many service producers are finding the benefit of providing products. And both need to develop relationships.

So the effective strategy implementation needs to consider all three (or at least two). American Express Platinum Card members receive services (the ability to charge purchases, travel assistance, gift-buying help, and so on), products (year-end financial summaries, personal diaries, and so on), and a relationship (special toll-free numbers, cash availability worldwide, and so on). The Platinum Card division of American Express, one would assume, has understood and contributed to the following:

- What is distinct about its customer base?
- What is distinct about its marketplace?
- The perception customers should have of the organization and its assistance.
- The innovation that is to be used in resolving customer (and organizational) issues.
- The feedback required to sustain and improve the organization.
- What each individual role means to the end result.

On a daily basis, every organization should be examining its operation in the three basic areas of product, service, and relationship to determine whether improvements are underway to remain competitive. That is the antidote to complacency. Federal Express seems to do this quite well. It is constantly improving its product (it enhances its packaging and provides preprinted computer forms), its service (it experiments with lower-cost afternoon delivery, local drop-off boxes, automated phone service, and so on), and its relationships (on my desk is a lovely paperweight commemorating its sponsoring of the 1988 Olympics). Strategy implementation works best when these are ongoing activities to begin with. And when implementation calls for a continuation of or only minor modifications to existing strategy, improvement is crucial. One might liken it to the lookouts aboard the ship, sensitive to the ship itself and its environment. Here is a checklist that is useful for determining if your organization is effectively managing daily improvement demands and, consequently, is capable of implementing current strategy:

Improvement Checklist

Product

We continually seek new applications for our products.   ☐ yes   ☐ no

We regularly solicit customer feedback about our products.   ☐ yes   ☐ no

We regularly purchase and analyze competitor's products.   ☐ yes   ☐ no

We buy our own products as customers and use them.   ☐ yes   ☐ no

We actively examine how current events may affect our products.   ☐ yes   ☐ no

We seek to establish attendant services in support of our products.   ☐ yes   ☐ no

We seek to provide services attractive to users of competitive products.   ☐ yes   ☐ no

We examine the causes that result in long-term product loyalty.   ☐ yes   ☐ no

We are constantly trying to make our products as user-friendly as possible.   ☐ yes   ☐ no

Service

We continually seek new applications for our services.   ☐ yes   ☐ no

We regularly solicit customer feedback about our services.   ☐ yes   ☐ no

We regularly purchase and analyze competitor's services.   ☐ yes   ☐ no

We buy our own services as customers and use them.   ☐ yes   ☐ no

We actively examine how current events may affect our services.   ☐ yes   ☐ no

We seek to establish attendant services in support of our services.   ☐ yes   ☐ no

We seek to provide services attractive to users of competitive services.   ☐ yes   ☐ no

We examine the causes that result in long-term service loyalty.   ☐ yes   ☐ no

We are constantly trying to make our services as user-friendly as possible.   ☐ yes   ☐ no

Relationships

We actively attempt to build strong relationships with customers.   ☐ yes   ☐ no

We examine the strengths and weaknesses of current relationships.	☐ yes	☐ no
We examine the strengths and weaknesses of competitors' relationships.	☐ yes	☐ no
We attempt to offer some assistance and support at no real or perceived fee.	☐ yes	☐ no
We encourage our people to go the extra mile for a customer request.	☐ yes	☐ no
We make a tangible investment in developing customer loyalty.	☐ yes	☐ no
We establish strong relationships with our employees as an example.	☐ yes	☐ no
We conduct customer surveys and/or focus groups *and act on the feedback.*	☐ yes	☐ no
We ensure that our highest level management is accessible to customers.	☐ yes	☐ no

The more of these to which you are forced to answer no, the more work you face in preparing your organization to be an effective implementation tool for current strategy or modest change. The questions on the list reflect what the best organizations do on a daily basis just to maintain their current level of competitiveness and to achieve healthy, ongoing, incremental change.

Superior organizations pursue the elements that will enable them to achieve a competitive edge. They are examining the elements, in tandem, in the second column of figure 6.6, advance. These are organizations whose strategies are more dynamic, more change-oriented, and more of a departure from the present. Check your organization against a profile of this nature:

Advance Checklist

Product

We aggressively attempt to develop new products based on customer needs.	☐ yes	☐ no
We use our basic technology as a base for developing new product ideas.	☐ yes	☐ no
We project changing demographics to develop new product ideas.	☐ yes	☐ no
We assess unexpected external events in light of new product ideas.	☐ yes	☐ no
We provide champions for new products so that the products are subordinated.	☐ yes	☐ no

We are willing to substantially change our products to fit new uses. □ yes □ no

We produce products that create their own standards for excellence. □ yes □ no

We examine industry and market structural changes for product ideas. □ yes □ no

We attempt to influence perceptions in terms of product and applications. □ yes □ no

Service

We aggressively attempt to develop new services based on customer needs. □ yes □ no

We use our basic technology as a base for developing new service ideas. □ yes □ no

We project changing demographics to develop new service ideas. □ yes □ no

We assess unexpected external events in light of new service ideas. □ yes □ no

We provide champions for new services so that the services are not subordinated. □ yes □ no

We are willing to substantially change our services to fit new uses. □ yes □ no

We produce services that create their own standards for excellence. □ yes □ no

We examine industry and market structural changes for service ideas. □ yes □ no

We attempt to influence perceptions in terms of service and applications. □ yes □ no

Relationships

We strive to create unique relationships, not copy others. □ yes □ no

We create relationships that support both product and service applications. □ yes □ no

We dedicate personnel and resources to relationship goals. □ yes □ no

We assign equally high priority to relationships and to products and services. □ yes □ no

We seek to be among the leaders in our relationships with employees. □ yes □ no

We respond to relationship breeches severely, even
though they are "free." ☐ yes ☐ no

We will readily take a loss on acquisition of a customer. ☐ yes ☐ no

We believe that image and perception are keys to our
success. ☐ yes ☐ no

We evaluate relationships to reward our people and
manage our system. ☐ yes ☐ no

The more yes responses, the more likely it is that your organization is
equipped to seek out competitive advantage on a daily operating basis.
These organizations aren't constantly producing such an edge—that's an
impossibility—but they are on the leading edge more often than not.
American Airlines is here, not TWA. In the past few years Chrysler has
been here more often than GM. You'll find American Express there, but
not Carte Blanche. It is Baltimore and Pittsburgh, but not Newark or Los
Angeles.

Finally, we have the organizations of outstanding nature: the truly excellent innovators which seek dramatic change in order to dominate in their
fields. They are examining the third column of figure 6.6, breakthrough,
in terms of all three elements. These organizations tend to pursue the most
dynamically changing strategies of all, and they must be prepared to implement and support them. Here are their guidelines:

Breakthrough Checklist

Product

We allow people to pursue virtually any product idea
on organization time. ☐ yes ☐ no

We encourage freedom to fail in product development
research. ☐ yes ☐ no

We continually scan the environment for new application ideas for products. ☐ yes ☐ no

We experiment with new combinations of technologies
to create products. ☐ yes ☐ no

We examine user groups to develop demographically
specified products. ☐ yes ☐ no

We try to anticipate future events and needs in our
product development. ☐ yes ☐ no

We do not demand instant product success; we invest
for the long term. ☐ yes ☐ no

We support a value of being first in the market with
a product. ☐ yes ☐ no

We stress unique product applications and quality, not price. ☐ yes ☐ no

Service

We allow people to pursue virtually any service idea on organization time. ☐ yes ☐ no

We encourage freedom to fail in service development research. ☐ yes ☐ no

We continually scan the environment for new application ideas for services. ☐ yes ☐ no

We experiment with new combinations of technologies to create services. ☐ yes ☐ no

We examine user groups to develop demographically specified services. ☐ yes ☐ no

We try to anticipate future events and needs in our service development. ☐ yes ☐ no

We do not demand instant service success; we invest for the long term. ☐ yes ☐ no

We support a value of being first in the market with a service. ☐ yes ☐ no

We stress unique service applications and quality, not price. ☐ yes ☐ no

Relationships

We actively invest in relationships that will set the standard. ☐ yes ☐ no

We establish relationships that transcend price, fees, and costs. ☐ yes ☐ no

We are known for taking a loss if we must to preserve a relationship. ☐ yes ☐ no

We distinctively train our people in building and maintaining relationships. ☐ yes ☐ no

We create unique relationships from our own executive level on down. ☐ yes ☐ no

We set the pattern through unique relationships with our own people. ☐ yes ☐ no

We do not associate relationships with cost or profit center management. ☐ yes ☐ no

We dedicate time, money, and other resources to innovative relationships. ☐ yes ☐ no

We surprise our customers, clients, and employees with our relationships. ☐ yes ☐ no

Organizations that can respond with a predominance of yes reactions to the breakthrough checklist are those that don't accidentally set the standards; instead, they deliberately set out to establish them. Federal Express has developed the hub-and-spoke delivery system, attempted (albeit unsuccessfully) to anticipate the fax with Zap Mail, and has purchased Flying Tiger Airlines to enter the heavy-cargo business. No doubt it will continue to pursue such ventures.

American Express introduced the Gold Card, the Platinum Card, and an assortment of worldwide supports and enhancements. The very concept of membership as opposed to anything so mundane as being a cardholder or customer is a superb example of relationship pioneering. "Membership has its privileges" is worth its weight in, well, platinum.[4] The high-end personal banking relationship evolved from free checks to special lines at the bank (each of which could be justified with specific benefits to the organization) to today's broad scope of personal relationships that aren't justified by any individual transaction or account. It is the long-term, overall relationship that is important. The benefits to the consumer are enormous. My bank recently told me, when a certificate of deposit matured, that although its stated rates were not the best around, it would match the best in the area for my rollover. This was accomplished by an assistant branch manager without a phone call or authorization of any kind. The transaction took 90 seconds, and the bank had its rollover and, more important, a customer who remains very loyal. (If, next time, that individual says, "I'm sorry, but we can only offer a rate 0.2 percent below the best in the area," I'm certainly not going to move my business. And therein is a moral: Build relationships ferociously during good times, because they will serve you well during bad.) Not long ago I called my personal banking officer to ask her for directions to an event to which the bank was a peripheral sponsor, though I was invited through other channels. Within the hour directions were sent by fax to my office. If they only did windows.

Breakthrough organizations are noted for their fierce devotion to their pursuits, exemplified by management and borne out by every employee. DuPont is a good example of a product breakthrough organization whose strategy and implementation demonstrate these qualities. DuPont's strategy would indicate an organization dedicated to using its research and technological capabilities to produce *any* type of product (e.g., Kevlar), and its implementation includes the implicit or explicit directive to its researchers to develop anything that their capabilities allow without regard to potential market, distribution, or customer. The organization will worry about that later. Mercedes develops the finest state-of-the-art car it can and worries about the price later (or doesn't worry at all). 3M provides

---

[4]There are some fascinating examples of such innovation. One of the best and most basic is the name itself of Simplicity Patterns. The organization's entire philosophy and intended relationship are really conveyed in its name.

for its researchers to spend 20 percent of their company time on private research avenues that interest them. From such implementation tactics, in support of a breakthrough product strategy, are Scotchguard™ and Post-it™ Notes born.[5] At this writing, two manufacturers are on the verge of marketing a car battery with a safety reserve to provide for self-jumping if the main charge is dissipated.[6]

The finest organizations are those that create excellent strategies *and* the implementation tactics that will support and realize those goals. My contention in this book is that a great many organizations do the former—that's the area that receives the predominant emphasis in the boardrooms—but then subvert their own plans through poor performance in the latter area. They figuratively turn gold into lead, a perverse, reverse alchemy of sorts. Through the synthesis of the product, service, and relationship factors detailed above, an organization can examine its strategy:

- Is it seeking to maintain its competitiveness through incremental improvement?
- Is it trying to gain a competitive edge through outright advances?
- Is it attempting to dominate through breakthrough accomplishments?

Ideally, these strategies are best accomplished (implemented) through *all three* of the organization-customer interfaces described: product, service, and relationships. Heavily product-oriented organizations must consider supporting services, and heavily service-oriented organizations must consider supporting products. And any kind of organization must be sensitive to its relationships.

The checklists above provide not only the clues to what kind of organization you currently encourage but also provide the direction to reorient along the lines that would best support your strategy. No value judgment is implied as you proceed left to right, improvement through breakthrough. Nor is there a requirement that an organization stay strictly within those bounds, although every one will have a home base. For example, the organizations that consciously choose to pursue the improvement level of strategy might occasionally produce an advance or breakthrough, and the breakthrough organizations certainly must maintain their everyday competitiveness while pursuing their landmark events and relationships. And, as you may have anticipated, an organization may pursue an improvement-oriented product-service strategy while concurrently pursuing an advance-relationship strategy. This will have fundamental implications for the resources and focus of the organization—in other words, its implementation plans.

---

[5]The 3M strategy calls for 25 percent of current revenues to come from products developed during the prior 5 years. Put it another way: 25 percent of revenues 5 years hence will come from products that don't yet exist! Source: "Intrapreneurs" (video), McGraw-Hill Training Systems, Del Mar, California, 1986.
[6]See "Two Firms Making Auto Batteries That Self-Jump in Emergencies," *Providence Journal Bulletin* (AP), Aug. 30, 1989, page B1.

American Airlines may be said to be pursuing an improvement-level service strategy (it's vying to be better than others in traditional indices—on-time performance, baggage delivery, and so on) but an advanced relationship strategy, as seen in its initiation of the Advantage Program, its Sabre reservations system for travel agent relationships, and so on. The banks attempting to create breakthrough relationships in personal banking may well be at the improvement level in product and advance level in services (or any combination thereof). The point is that few organizations can or should pursue breakthrough strategies in all three customer interface areas. The keys are to:

1. Determine which customer interface areas merit which level of pursuit.
2. Assign and allot resources and implementation abilities accordingly.

Finally, it's important to comprehend the full dimension of the service economy that we speak of. *Even the organizations that can legitimately make a case that their customer interfaces are only around product nevertheless provide services internally.* An organization that makes only widgets and sells those widgets to retail widget stores is still alive with services. Functions such as personnel, accounting, planning, and transportation provide essential services to the rest of the organization. (And even the retail clients must be supported with billing, product support, and delivery.) There are no "pure" product organizations. And there will be more and more integrated ones, with admixtures of products and services, as the competitive realities drive organizations in that direction. In 1989, according to the Bureau of Labor Statistics, 75 percent of all U.S. employees were engaged in what is officially designated as the "service sector."[7] This raises some interesting questions in terms of strategy implementation.

We hear of product development and product management and product support functions. Are enough organizations creating and sustaining *service* development and *service* management and *service* support functions? Don't take the language too lightly. We've found that organizations that assume that product development includes service development are far less effective in developing new services than are those that deliberately create a service development function. If you are serious about service and relationships, then these customer interfaces deserve serious treatment within the organization's implementation tactics. "Customer service manager" was once a breakthrough title. Now it's commonplace. Today we are beginning to see functions such as "relationship manager" and "vice president for customer relations." These are logical advances.

Here's a mythical organization—we'll call it Foresight, Inc. Foresight manufactures lawn supplies and provides a variety of services (lawn evaluation, soil analysis, and so on) and relationships (hot line for lawn problems, chemical applications, and so on) through its company-owned chain

---

[7]As cited in "A 'Mickey Mouse' Class—for Real," by Douglas C. McGill, in *The New York Times,* Aug. 27, 1989, section 3, page 4.

of stores. So Foresight's strategy calls for competitive products that feature state-of-the-art offerings, services that are meant to gain a competitive edge (such as soil samples analyzed on premises and leased-plant programs), and breakthrough relationships (such as unqualified money-back guarantees for 2 years—"Green lawns for greenbacks"—and lawn mower "loaners" with no questions asked). Foresight's implementation would include, but not be limited to, the following considerations and tactics:

- Buyers trained to identify and acquire the latest in lawn care products.
  But not research into new product creation.
- Staff knowledgeable in all existing product applications and interactions.
  But not experimentation with new combinations of product applications.
- Promotion vehicles that proclaim the full range of customer interactions.
  But not promotion of single products or claims to be the unique supplier.
- Analysis of competing services to determine how to go them one better.
  But not attempts to simply copy and replicate other services.
- A store environment conducive to the amateur who needs direction and assistance.
  But not the launch of a mail-order garden supply catalog.
- Hours of high accessibility, including evenings and weekends.
  But not a toll-free number.
- Staff encouraged to spend as much time with customers as possible.
  But not compensation based on personal volume of sales.
- No-questions-asked policy, even if a return can't be supported by a store receipt.
  But not 10-day, store-credit-only policies.
- On-site visits to customers with problems.
  But not hourly call rates.

Foresight will be planning its future and acquiring and assigning resources based on this mix of these dos and don'ts as they emerge from their profile. The floor salesperson whom Foresight hires will tend to be consultative in approach, not an assertive seller. The store managers will be compensated on measures such as quantity of repeat business and product-service mix, not simply sheer volume. Stores will be attractive, clean, and scrupulously maintained; if there is local contractor business, it will be handled in a separate area or in the rear of the store.

One can watch the better organizations, large or small, public or private, manufacturing or service, and identify how they are investing in and supporting each of these three primary customer interface categories commensurate with their overall strategy. This is the detail work that enables excellent strategies to realize their potential and to maintain their glow rather than sink like stones. Despite what the alchemists experienced, it's easier than anyone suspected for a modern organization to turn gold into lead.

7

Finger on the Pulse, Eye on the Road, Ear to the Ground: Keeping the Organization Whole While Tearing It Apart

Strategy implementation is a dynamic process. Psychologists are fond of pointing out that the mere act of observing human dynamics has an effect on those dynamics, so the impact of the observer has to be accounted for in the conclusions or the analyses. In implementing a strategy, the very act of implementation will influence, affect, and alter the implementation process.

For example, a tactic that calls for reorganizing the customer service unit will have fallout on the attitudes and behaviors of the individuals involved (pro and con), the manner in which they interact with the public, and their relative cooperation with the overall strategy. (This last element might have been vastly different if there were no need to reorganize the customer service unit.)

How can an organization and its management be continually sensitive to the implications of its implementation, and keep implementation in its proper perspective, so that problems are resolved, opportunities are exploited, and overreaction is avoided at all costs? A variety of monitoring and temperature-taking techniques are available, and many of them may be already in place but not be utilized to those ends.

In figure 7.1 is a simple grid that can be used to evaluate virtually any organizational issue in terms of its strategic fit and the organization's current ability to implement.[1] In the grid, any issue may be quickly analyzed in terms of its strategic fit *and* the organization's ability to implement it. Bear in mind that this analysis is like a "snapshot," and it records conditions as they exist when the snapshot was taken. Conditions soften change, especially when, as a result of such analysis, the organization deliberately sets about changing them.

---

[1] Adapted from *The Innovation Formula: How Organizations Turn Change into Opportunity*, by Michel Robert and Alan Weiss, Harper & Row, New York, 1988, pages 69-79.

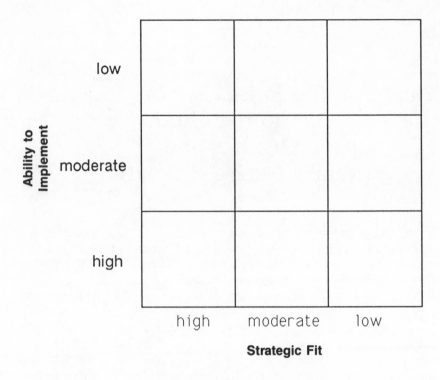

Figure 7.1.

So, for the purposes of our grid, we will assume that the strategy is known and clear (and that it includes the customer interaction factors discussed in chapter 6), and that the evaluators are in a position to accurately judge implementation requirements. With those givens in mind, let's look at three examples.

Example 1: The Regional Airline

Flying High Airlines (FHA) is a regional carrier in the northeast connecting secondary cities with each other and with hub airports in major cities. It has 25 turboprop planes of various ages, an excellent safety record, and average profitability for the industry, and it was voted "Regional Carrier of the Year" 2 years ago. It is privately held and is determined not to become a captive feeder of one of the trunk carriers.

FHA could be classified as improvement-oriented in its products and services, though advanced in its relationships. It is one of the very few regionals to offer comfortable, attractive boarding lounges, free coffee and newspapers, and a local frequent-commuter program. It has allied itself with a major airline's reservations system, so the busy numbers and inaccurate information often found among smaller carriers are not a problem for FHA customers.

FHA is facing three issues:

1. The airline has the opportunity to lease employees from a local firm. Such leasing is increasingly the rage, since more flexible hours are easily arranged, benefits are much lower, layoffs don't exact a morale cost, and it is easy to adjust staffing for high and low volume.
2. As part of the airport expansion in FHA's home base (a major hub city), the airline has been offered new gates that can incorporate boarding ramps in the event that FHA ever wants to use them for jet aircraft—its own acquisitions or those of others. At the moment, passengers must walk on the tarmac to board the turboprops.
3. A limousine service that has franchises in most of FHA's cities has suggested an affinity program whereby for a slight extra cost on an FHA ticket—but for less than the cost of hiring a private limo—passengers can order limo pickup at time of flight. This might have to be handled by a local line, since the current major reservation system might not be willing to handle these requests on such relatively small volume.

Place a 1, 2, and 3 in the grid of figure 7.1 to correspond to your assessment of where each issue fits in the considerations of strategy and implementation for FHA's situation. Obviously, you'd like much more information about FHA and its specific strategy. But evaluating where they may be at this point is, nevertheless, a useful pursuit. If you were a rival of FHA, you wouldn't have much more information about its strategy than what we've given. (You'd have more past experience regarding FHA's actions, but that doesn't necessarily dictate future actions, especially if FHA's strategy is changing.) In figure 7.2 is one way to look at FHA in the matrix. Your responses may well differ, because, given our perspectives and experiences, we all interpret "facts" about an artificial case in different ways. The key is whether or not your responses can be justified by your analysis within the parameters of the matrix.

For example, our analysis is that the leased employees would be an idea that is moderately difficult to implement. It's a departure from what we're doing now, and it could cause some employee ill-will if the move is perceived as a device to cut benefits and overtime (which it is). Leased employees would require ongoing and repetitive training as they came and went with business volume, and even previously trained people would need a refresher when they returned. Strategically, we consider the fit to be poor. These leased employees would not be as motivated to apply the relationship skills that we feel are our competitive edge. They have no long-term stake in the organization, and they would probably be both unwilling (attitude) and unable (comprehensive skills base) to go the extra mile for passengers. On balance, this is an idea whose cost benefits are outweighed by the poor fit with FHA's present and future strategy. It should not be implemented.

FHA ASSESSMENT

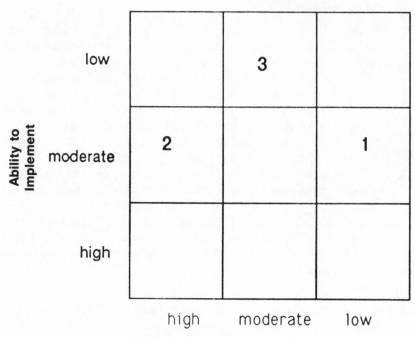

Issue #1: leased employees
Issue #2: new gates
Issue #3: limo service

Figure 7.2

The new gates being offered also present moderate implementation difficulty. There would be inconvenience at FHA's home base during installation, and they would require investment that would not demonstrably reflect a return in products, services, or relationships. The benefit of using a jetway ramp is small because FHA cannot use jets profitably on its short-hop business, and another airline would probably not make the effort to use FHA's just for connecting passengers. This idea, however, is very consistent with FHA's relationship strategy, in that the gates, if practical, would enhance the relationship edge that FHA seeks to maintain. Yet the benefits seem pale compared to the difficulties, and this idea should not be implemented either.

The limo service would seem to be very difficult to implement. Coordination would be required for each city involved, and the added costs might not be recouped from FHA's part of the relationship. The strategic fit is only moderate because, despite the edge it presents over the competition, the possibilities of missed limo pickups, accidents, traffic tie-ups, and so forth present a serious threat to FHA's relationships. In fact, the limo service would probably benefit from the idea much more than FHA. Recommendation: Don't do it.

Issues that fit neatly into the bottom left of the matrix are not all that common, nor should they be. After all, we are faced with hundreds of decisions, issues, and opportunities each day, and it's easy to see that only a few would represent "ideal" fits with our strategy and implementation abilities. In the FHA case, you might disagree with some of our assessments, or you might feel that the risks are controllable and the implementation difficulties surmountable. These are areas in which management judgment must prevail. The models and matrices shouldn't run organizations; managers should. However, those managers require some objective framework within which they can evaluate, communicate, justify, and document issues as they pertain to strategy.

Now that we've worked through the model, let's look at the second case.

Example 2: The Insurance Company

Reliable Insurance is a multiline, publicly traded insurer. It is number 9 in volume in the United States, employs 30,000 people, and has a captive sales force. It has recently purchased two financial subsidiaries, a brokerage house, and a mortgage company, and it finds itself in a very competitive position within the financial services industry.

Reliable sees itself as advanced in the service category. It provides services that are always close to the leading edge. The company was among the first to offer universal life, for example, and it provides an assortment of flexible investment vehicles to its policyholders. It makes sure, for example, that the interest it charges on loans against cash value is below the industry average and within the bottom 10 percent of interest rates. Reliable invests heavily in customer service people and sells only through its field sales force, not through independent brokers or agents. The company is seeking to move from advanced to breakthrough in its relationships, since management believes that the organization's perception on the part of customers is the key to larger market share. Its advertising has stressed "Be a part of a Reliable family," and it carefully trains its field and home office personnel to treat policyholders with great care (for example, they are called "clients" instead of "insureds" or "customers").

Here are three issues currently confronting management:

1. Middle managers have suggested a toll-free number for clients to use in contacting customer service; at the moment the number is a normal toll call to headquarters in Topeka, Kansas. The toll-free number would probably cost $100,000 a year in incoming charges and, although there is no budgeted money, contingency funds are sufficient to cover both installation and first-year expenses.
2. In a radical departure from conventional wisdom, there is a recommendation from marketing to keep the new subsidiaries as strictly separate ventures with their own identities. The intent is to keep the name "Reliable" strictly associated with insurance and make the point to potential customers that "insurance is our only business" as a state-

ment about the company's commitment to family protection. Virtually no cost is associated with taking this approach, since the subsidiaries have not yet been reconfigured.

3. The sales director has asked permission to initiate a sales incentive program in which anyone can win. In order to spur new sales, she is seeking a volume award for regions surpassing last year's totals by 20 percent. She is careful to point out that it is not a win/lose proposition, and literally every one of the six regions can win, which would be an enormous boost to company profits. She also sees the incentive as service to incorporate the products of the subsidiaries into the sales presentations the field force.

Where on the grid (figure 7.1) do the three issues fit in terms of Reliable's competitive edge position in service and its pursuit of a breakthrough position in relationships? We won't go into as much detail as we did when we first went through the matrix. In figure 7.3 are our assessments with a brief explanation. The toll-free number looks like a sure winner. It is relatively easy to implement—the funds and the technology are readily available, and disruption would be minimal—and it constitutes a genuine coup in terms

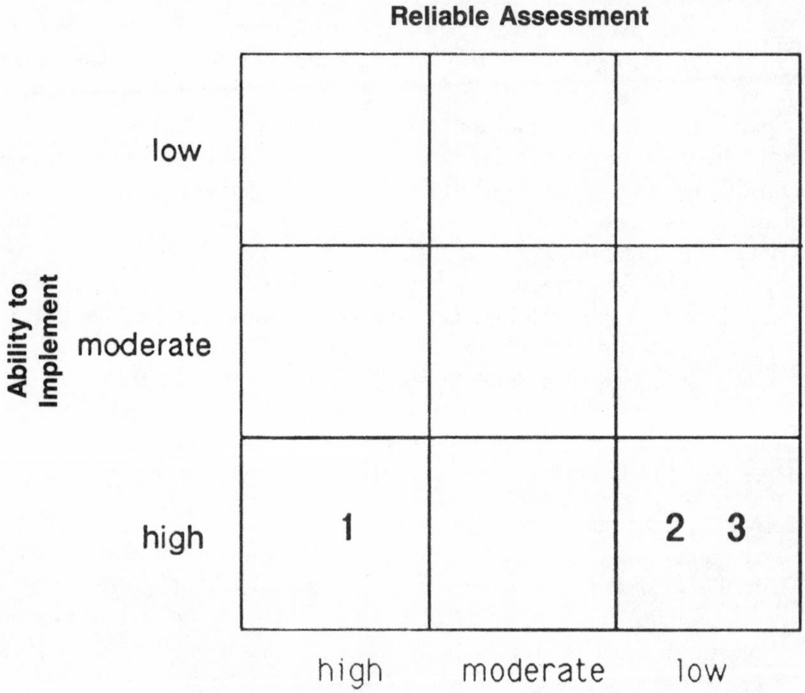

Reliable Assessment

Issue #1: Toll-free number
Issue #2: Subsidiaries separate
Issue #3: Sales incentive

Figure 7.3

of customer service relationships. Generally, few insurers have toll-free numbers and virtually none of the majors have, except in some cases for claims service. The free call fits in perfectly with the family concept, and it raises Reliable beyond simply competitive edge, at least in this area.

The separate subsidiaries are something else, however. Implementation is not at all difficult, since the companies are currently separate anyway. But the strategy to achieve breakthrough dominance is not met by a variety of loosely connected individual entities. A good family should present any and all viable financial options under one roof, given the same trust and guarantee as are extended with more traditional products and services. The separation would fragment, not strengthen, the family image. Despite the lure of ease of implementation, this is not a sound idea in terms of the strategy's thrust for the future. (Note that the suggestion to incorporate the subsidiaries fully would probably be reflected in the chart as high strategic fit and low ease of implementation.)

Finally, the sales incentive contest has the same ramifications as the subsidiary issue. It is easy to do—the costs would be borne through the sales increases—but the emphasis would clearly encourage sales people to spend less time servicing existing clients and selling small-volume products and more time on the less frequent but more rewarding big hits. This is contrary to any kind of breakthrough relationship strategy, and it is a means for the wrong ends. The program shouldn't be implemented.

We spoke earlier of an incentive system that gave away two luxury cars to achieve the same results as the prior year. In this last example, we have the traditional call for more sales incentives in order to boost volume, which is almost always a parochial viewpoint of the sales and marketing functions. One could make a case that Reliable's salespeople shouldn't be on commission at all; they should be on a bonus basis comprising sales and service (low turnover, few client complaints, avoidance of insurance commissioner interventions, and so on). Most insurers pay hefty commissions for first-year policy premiums and drastically lower commissions on renewals. Perhaps they should be reversed to encourage long-term relationships and ongoing service when they are components of the strategy?

Here's our final example.

Example 3: The High-Tech Company

Andromeda is a five-year-old firm producing enhancements for Apple Computer hardware. Among its most popular items are chips that increase memory, hard drives to increase storage, large screens that allow for entire pages to be viewed, and accelerators that speed up the processing. It is a $300 million business that had grown at 20 percent a year. This year's growth will be only 12 percent, which is due in part to increasing competition and in part to Andromeda's heretofore singular concentration on product design and quality.

The organization can be said to be in the breakthrough position with its products—it's one of the three firms that control about 70 percent of Apple's after-market purchases—and in the improvement position in terms of its service and relationships. It currently sells direct to consumers through direct mail and advertising in a wide variety of technical and popular literature. The company stands unequivocally behind its products, as does virtually every company of its type. Andromeda wants to retain its breakthrough product position, but its new strategy calls for improving the service and relationship positions at least to advanced in order to regain its growth momentum.

Given that scenario, rate these three options facing Andromeda:

1. There is an opportunity to approach retail sales chains such as The Computer Factory and Computers R Us with the intent of setting up retail distribution through such outlets. Andromeda's profits would be less on such sales to allow for the store markup, but volume should increase dramatically. In such environments, Andromeda's products would be in direct competitive situations right on the sales floor. These outlets provide local servicing, so training of local technicians to handle rudimentary repairs would be required.

2. Catalog houses such as The Sharper Image and New Dimensions have requested relationships whereby Andromeda products are included in the catalog. This would require virtually no work on the company's part, since the catalog distributor would take their orders and simply forward them to Andromeda for filling, taking a cut of the price. Prices would be established in collaboration. Andromeda would handle any subsequent returns, repairs, and service requests.

3. A software producer has proposed creating software that explains Andromeda's products to the purchaser and provides tutorials and tours on screen to help the customer learn what the product's exact capabilities are. These would replace the need to read through lengthy technical literature, although such an option would still be available. The software house offers a one-time design charge and then a set fee on each piece of software required—one for each new product sold.

Now assess these issues on the matrix (see figures 7.1 to 7.3).

Andromeda is facing two different distribution alternatives, neither mutually exclusive, and a value-added product enhancement. In figure 7.4 is one assessment of these issues. In this case, retail distribution represents a high strategic fit. It provides for additional exposure of Andromeda products in direct competition with others which are generally inferior. The local servicing and product support are ideal for increasing Andromeda's service and relationship positions. Implementation challenges of training and supporting the retailer are moderate—they are added tasks for the operation, but not ones that are beyond its ability to assume. This is a valuable idea, especially if implementation problems can be ameliorated (for example, technicians come to Andromeda's headquarters for training).

Andromeda Assessment

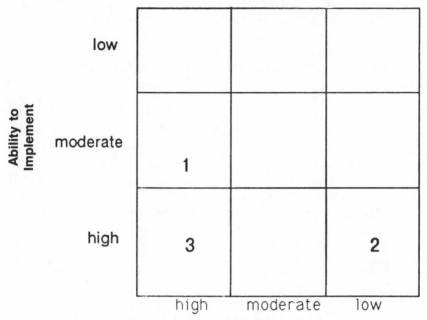

Issue #1: Retail distribution
Issue #2: Catalog distribution
Issue #3: Software instructions

Figure 7.4

The catalog distribution is not so attractive. Although infinitely easier to implement than the retail distribution, it presents probabilities contrary to Andromeda's strategy. For example, customers might call the catalog distributor with technical questions only to be answered incorrectly or referred to another number. Also, the potential confusion between Andromeda's print ads and direct mail and catalog mailing may create the perception that it's less expensive to buy Andromeda products through one source than another. This alternative really provides no benefit in seeking to improve service and relationship positions. (Note that two alternative distribution options can have radically different effects on strategy implementation when viewed in light of specific positioning.)

Finally, the software seems like an ideal alternative. It is a clear relationship gain, and it would set Andromeda apart in trying to create a user-friendly atmosphere. It should enhance service by allowing the customer to be "self-servicing" via the tutorials to a significant degree. And its implementation is largely one of investment—the software house will undertake the actual work and production responsibilities. This is the kind of innovation that would help set Andromeda's relationships apart and augment its strong product position.

How does your organization analyze issues and opportunities in relation to their strategic fit and potential for implementation? Most organizations fall somewhere between "not at all" and "we make a stab at it." Yet
we've found that one of the primary reasons why strategies never make
it off the corporate drawing board into organizational reality is that their
components are never subject to such a reality check. *Note that such a reality
check needn't be made solely on the basis of the* existing *operation, it may be
made on the basis of the strategy's* projected *organization*. The point is that
it must at some point be made against whatever your vision of the
organization is. We have found some managers who are able to make such
comparisons intuitively and naturally, especially if they have been participants in the creation of the strategy. But most managers, and especially those who were not privy to the creation of the strategy—which in most
organizations would be most of the management—require some yardstick
or criterion against which to measure operational issues.

The grid can become that yardstick, and its gradations the criteria. Here
are the definitions we generally use:

Implementation Ability

High. The organization can implement the idea, solution, decision, or innovation with a minimum of disruption. Resources are in place and available;
the existing sets of processes and procedures can handle the issue; and
there is some precedent for the approach.

Medium. Implementation will require some steps or actions that are not
common to the organization. The issue will have to be shepherded
through, not simply trusted to existing avenues and channels. Extra
resources and special circumstances and/or deviations from the norm will
be required on occasion.

Low. There is virtually no internal precedent for the action. A champion
will probably be needed to blaze a path for the idea, and entirely separate
units and dedicated resources must be acquired or identified to ensure
success. There is the highest risk of failure of the three categories because
this one involves the novel, the untried, and the poorest cultural fit.

Strategic Fit

High. The issue fits ideally into the organization's strategic direction
(whether that direction is an extension of today or a marked departure
from today). In terms of products, services, and relationships, it takes the
organization to the level of performance, image, and management vision
that constitute the organization's goals.

Medium. The issue does not quite fit perfectly into the strategy. It may
be slightly more advanced in the area of product, for example, or not advanced enough in forging relationships relative to the organization's

strategy. The idea may still be useful, but it will require some fine-tuning and testing before being acceptable.

Low. The idea clearly does not fit with the organization's direction and business vision. These may be "good ideas whose time has not come," but they are nonetheless diversions from the strategy that will not take the organization in the direction it has planned for itself.

It should be apparent that it is more productive to choose an issue from moderate implementation ability that has a high strategic fit (A in figure 7.5) than it is to choose one that is easy to implement but not as good a strategic fit (B). It is always better to pursue issues that may require some fine-tuning—or even major rennovation—than it is to pursue issues that don't quite fit the strategic goals. Yet, without this type of grid on which to plot issues, where do most organizations usually go? That's right, with issues that are easy to implement because they are the least disruptive, even though they may be light years away from the strategic goals of the organization. That is akin to a football team running plays toward its own goal line because the defense doesn't get in the way!

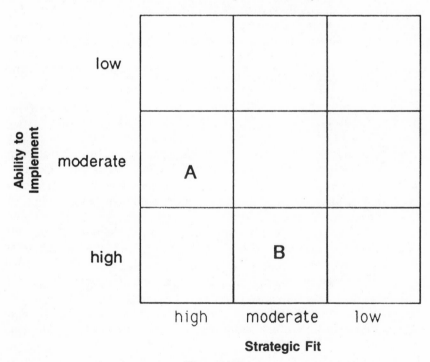

Figure 7.5.

Why do organizations pursue such foolish and costly directions in spite of the best of strategies? We've seen these forces at work:

- It's easier to change (or ignore) strategy, which is on paper, than it is to disrupt people.

- The failure to implement carries a higher punishment than the failure to be consistent with a strategic need.
- Many managers are simply ignorant of all or parts of the strategy and cannot make the assessment along the horizontal scale. Consequently, they give all their attention to the vertical scale.
- The organization provides no such yardsticks or measurements for its middle-level managers.
- The organization fails to reward and punish based on the importance of the less visible horizontal scale, which reinforces total attention to the vertical.
- The more difficult the implementation (according to the definition above), the more a manager finds him or herself in conflict with others over resource allocation, priorities, and risks.
- The emphasis on "today's numbers" and the current quarter's performance forces managers to regard *any* disruption to the operation as too difficult or too threatening to undertake.

Ultimately, virtually no one is held accountable for strategic goals in such organizations. The reasons may stem from a variety of problems we discussed in the opening chapters, but the results for our purposes here are always the same: Management will accept issues and ideas and solutions that are in the middle and right-hand vertical ranks—which is precisely what they should *not* do if strategic goals are to be met—and will readily reject any which are in the top or middle horizontal rows—which they should be willing to undertake in order to meet strategic goals—because they are too risky.

Hence, in most organizations, we have a topsy-turvy approach to those daily management decisions which affect the ability to implement strategy. That is often the reason behind the great mystery surrounding why the strategy that took weeks of executive time (and often hundreds of thousands of dollars) hasn't moved off square 1. The organization is its own worst enemy, in that it rejects the ideas and issues that are trying to change it precisely when such change is required, and it safeguards the issues and ideas that protect the status quo precisely when it is the status quo which must be abandoned. Yet rather than try to use the grid of figure 7.5 or a similar measurement device to gauge what's happening, more often than not management will call into question its own strategy, or hire another consultant, or determine that some conspiracy is undermining its efforts. What we need is management by parameters, not management by paranoia.

In figure 7.6 is an example of the polar extremes of the grid as a final example of the relationships of strategy and implementation. We've tried to use examples that we can all relate to.

A. This is a case of very high strategic fit but very low ease of implementation. A good example occurred when Hertz initiated its gold program, which provided its best customers with the ability to go directly to its bus, be directed to the car by a lighted marquee with the customer's name on

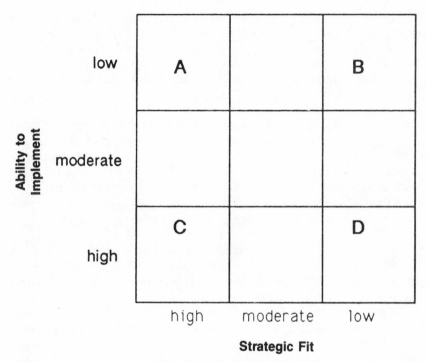

Strategic Fit

Figure 7.6

it, and find a car with the motor running, air conditioner or heater already on, and contract completed. To accomplish this, Hertz had to rebuild existing facilities, retrain personnel, and promote the program. As would be expected in this category, the organization experienced some delays and problems in getting the system on line. But the approach was consistent with Hertz's strategy to provide breakthrough service and relationships in its competitive business.[2] The organization didn't choose the easy road, just the correct one.

B. This is the black hole of strategy. It is the idea that not only is inconsistent with strategic direction but is also difficult to implement. Even if you struggle successfully to the finish line, you're told that you've just run the wrong race. Exxon's futile venture into the office equipment market and GE's debacle with computers come to mind. But even more vivid was the purchase of Frontier Airlines in the mid-80s by the then low-frills carrier People Express. Frontier was everything that People wasn't; it was a

---

[2]Here's a contrast with category C that also pertains to Hertz. In the late 1970s IBM was a client of the consulting firm I worked for. In a test of strategic intent, the European president was asked why he didn't suggest that his organization buy Hertz, which was up for sale at the time and was very profitable. "Why, I'd be laughed right out of the boardroom if I ever suggested anything so crazy!" he said. IBM could have easily purchased Hertz and run it as a separate entity with little problem. But such an acquisition had nothing to do with IBM's strategy at the time. Our assessment is that most acquisitions today suffer from a similarly poor fit, but few organizations bother to make the evaluation.

traditional carrier that was unionized and was headquartered 2,000 miles away from People. But Fred Burr, CEO and founder of People, insisted on the acquisition, which, itself, was extraordinarily difficult to digest. More than any other element, that acquisition doomed People and the idea (strategic direction) it had stood for, and both airlines were swallowed by the Lorenzo air empire. Among the losers were management, employees, stockholders, and passengers.

C. These are the ideas we all wish we had every day—strong reinforcers of strategic direction and relatively easy to implement. These are Post-it™ Notes at 3M, fax machines from Sharp, extended warranties from auto dealers, the extended product guarantees from American Express. Note that we've chosen rather "grand" public examples because we can't know the thousands of *internal* ideas that are pursued daily by these organizations but never come to our attention and nonetheless faithfully support strategic direction on a constant, incremental basis.[3] When Arm & Hammer Baking Soda began advertising itself as a refrigerator deodorant, it probably exemplified this category. There was no product change whatsoever, merely a public perception change, but the strategy of increasing the product's uses was more than met.

D. This is the easy-to-do-but-why-do-it? category. It is the low road that middle managers readily pursue in the absence of guidelines or reinforcement to the contrary. After all, you'll look good for the short term, and is anyone really paying attention to the long term? These are the sales promotions that reward the wrong kind of business, the product promotions that push the wrong products. It would be Mercedes offering rebates. It is our earlier example of implementing a wide variety of pricing and promotions that ultimately confused its clientele as to its position in the market—was it an alternative to K-Mart or Bloomingdale's? One-price policy is an attempt to create an image consistent with its strategy. In doing so, it is attempting to move from D to A, in my judgment.

Any organization can create its own checklist or guidelines to assess issues in the manner we've demonstrated. Here's an example of a generic set:[4]

Strategic Fit

Questions to ask:

- Does the issue/solution/opportunity fit our present and/or projected strategy?
- How well does it support the direction of our business?
- How well does it fulfill our business vision and perceptions of ourselves?

---

[3] If you judge some of these examples to be moderate in implementation difficulty, fair enough—outside the respective organizations, such determinations are in the eye of the beholder. Our local video store implementing a computerized inventory and ordering system is our idea of moderate implementation difficulty with high strategic fit, for example.
[4] See Robert and Weiss, *The Innovation Formula*, pages 66–67.

Areas to examine:

- Technology
- Products
- Services
- Relationships
- Customer base
- Market segments
- Production requirements
- Distribution requirements

- Methods of sale
- Resources needed
- Size demands
- Growth results
- Profit potential
- Return potential
- Resultant directions

Implementation Ability

Questions to ask:

- Will the organization accept or reject this idea/solution/opportunity?
- Do we understand the technology and configuration needs?
- Is there a track record or precedent in this area?
- Are we dependent on outsiders for key resources or expertise?
- What are the chances of uncontrollable disruptions?
- How many new and novel approaches are required?

Areas to examine:

- Current production
- Current people
- Degree of control/influence over the process
- Current culture
- Current informal leadership
- Acceptance of change
- Need for a champion

- Financing requirements
- Image fallout
- Access to external needs
- Legal ramifications
- Regulatory requirements
- Precedent
- Risk-taking reward/punishment perceptions

This final factor, risk and reward, has a rather profound impact on the overall assessment, and we will examine it separately in the next section of this chapter.

To conclude this section, however, it's important to understand and apply the concepts of strategic fit and implementation ability on a daily basis, mainly through middle management, so that the organizational strategy is a *daily* guide to operational decision making. Consequently, managers at all organizational levels must be conversant with the strategy, aware of the measuring devices for issues (whether the ones we suggest or any others), and actively reviewed and rewarded for their integration of these factors. That applies to line and staff equally. Issues of compensation, investment, and inventory control (to name a sampling) are no less applicable than those of price, customer service, and quality. Decisions as basic as how to respond to a customer complaint and what to do about a vendor's late deliveries can and should be made in light of these criteria.

For example, we encountered an assistant operations supervisor in a utility field station who routinely faced this decision: When calls came in from customers requesting assistance (for example, power was out, a line was down) in the later afternoon, the choices were to extend the on-duty troubleshooter's hours into overtime and respond immediately or to delay responding by about an hour or two to wait for the next shift's troubleshooter to handle the problem on normal time. The man we talked to always extended the on-duty person's hours to handle the call. We asked why.

"We've been told by management that customer service is paramount, since we're going to have to ask the [public utilities] commission for a rate increase, and we want our customer's support for it. The extra overtime is a drop in the bucket compared to the larger goal."

Could there be an easier decision? The supervisor's actions fit the strategy perfectly, and the implementation difficulty was, at most, moderate: increase in expense. Yet we found other supervisors in other districts opting to wait for the next shift because, in the absence of their involvement in the strategy and the use of any evaluation criteria, they chose the course of safest and most immediate reward: keep expenses down. This kind of dichotomy is reflected in any organization in which there is not a uniform approach by senior managers to the issues of strategy involvement and evaluation criteria. And it is these daily decisions that, over the course of a month, quarter, or year, will determine whether organizational strategy will be realized.

Let's take a look at the hazards of risks and rewards for these decision makers.

Risk is generally a relative term. "Don't skate on thin ice," for example, is a common admonition, but to some skaters 5 inches is not thin, to others 2 inches is not thin, and to still others the ice isn't too thin unless water is sloshing around their ankles. Similarly, one manager may feel it's too risky to raise prices at all, another may feel that raising prices 15 percent and losing the lower 10 percent of the market is justifiable, and a third may be comfortable raising prices by 20 percent and waiting to determine the degrees of adverse reaction.

We use our own judgments about risk, and those collective judgments often become the organizational yardstick. Yet the risks we are willing to assume will directly determine our ability to implement strategy—the more change involved in the strategy, the higher the perceived risk and the more difficulty associated with implementation. So how can we quantify risk? How can we assess it objectively and not emotionally? That is especially important given normal human reaction to change.

Consider this scenario: You are addressing colleagues and have announced that you are going to implement some major changes. What are the immediate reactions, spoken or unspoken, of your colleagues? Write the words or phrases that would describe them below:

_____   _____

_____   _____

_____   _____

_____   _____

_____   _____

Was that difficult? For most people it's easy to write the anticipated responses because they've been through this situation so often. Here are typical statements:

- What does this mean for us?
- Why do we need to do this?
- How will this affect our daily operating needs?
- Do we *really* have to go through with this?
- This sounds like someone's bright idea that we got stuck with.
- This is going to be another classic boondoggle.
- What genius who never interacted with a customer thought this up?
- You must be kidding!
- I'm just not going to do it.
- When I see you do it, I'll do it.

And here are the typical emotions and feelings in the room:

- Fear
- Skepticism
- Conservatism
- Uncertainty
- Cynicism
- Resentment
- Dread
- Protectiveness
- Confusion

Maybe you were able to list more positive statements and emotions because your organization and people are more accommodating of change. But most of the time, the reaction is negative. Just look at the phrases and words we've written and you've written. Are they conducive to change, innovation (a major component of strategy implementation), and the exploration of new territory and technique? Not by a long shot. They are indicative of people who want to preserve the status quo at any cost, and those emotions will overwhelm any positive intellectual reactions to new strategies.

The major importance in recognizing and managing risk in strategy implementation is to prevent the "normal" negative reactions to change from undermining the implementation process. No matter how successful the communication process, and no matter how tight and rational the reasoning behind the strategic changes, the emotions will overcome the intellect unless they are considered. And that consideration revolves around the need to place risk—the basic cause of the fear created by change—in perspective. Here's what George A. Schaefer, CEO of Caterpillar Tractor—which has adjusted to a vastly changed business perhaps as well as any organization in the world—has to say about facilitating change.[5] "Have the right individual as part of the decision process. A good

_____
[5]Interview with the author, Peoria, Ill., Sept. 7, 1989.

business head at the top of the unit is a key. You have a lot of leadership putting in a lot of hours to get buy-in, or else change the people. Human nature simply doesn't like change."

There are three factors that tend to influence reactions to change and the ensuing risk:

1. *Degree of personal acceptance of risk.* Many of us have had more exposure to risk in our work and lives than others. It may have been forced on us by circumstances or provided for us by a risk-taking boss or associate (or, trauma of traumas, a family member!). The experiences will color our current view of risk and its acceptability to us.

If a salesperson watches the sales manager acquire a tough sale by promising delivery 2 weeks prior to the organization's stated ability to deliver and then sees the boss manipulate the system (and manipulate his or her boss) to meet the client's deadline, that will influence future sales technique. If, however, the sales manager is upbraided by the sales director and the business is lost with hard feelings, *that* will influence future technique. We've seen instances in which children, aware that parents are gambling, are told by their parents that they almost always win, a common reaction of many chronic gamblers. The children adapt a much different attitude about gambling than do kids raised in environments, as were several of my friends, in which charging merchandise on a credit card was considered a bad gamble by the parents. Cash was the only way to buy if you were to stay out of trouble. Such experiences generally form influences for us very early in our lives and careers and once formed, are difficult to change.

2. *Degree of organizational acceptance of risk.* Every organization has an attitude about risk taking. It may be explicit and stated in its strategy and encouraged or discouraged by formal company policy. Or it may be implicit, not readily identifiable as a policy, but reflected in promotions, rewards, punishments, perquisites, recognition, and other signs.

An organization like 3M, which provides company time for its researchers to pursue private ideas, is making a clear statement about its acceptance of risk. It states this boldly in the strategy we discussed earlier, which requires 25 percent of revenues to be generated by products created in the prior 5 years. An insurance company, in its underwriting policies, sets clear standards about the acceptance of risk with potential insureds, and underwriters who stray from those standards can expect to be questionned—strongly—about their straying. Yet insurance companies *will* accept higher risk in return for higher premium rates. Smokers, for example, or those with prior medical problems can be insured but will pay more for the privilege. This process is called rating, and we'll see its relevance to risk taking in a few minutes.

Organizations can create a *cognitive dissonance* in their approach to risk taking by claiming one posture but actually assuming another. This dichotomy can derail any strategy, because managers don't know how to act—in

the manner the company says or in the manner it acts—and consequently they will refrain from any risk because it is the safest course of action.
We interviewed managers in one firm which consistently promoted risk
taking and innovation yet was experiencing conservatism and cynicism
from its management. We asked why there was such a discrepancy.

"The organization doesn't mean what it says," we were consistently told.
"You can take risks only if they prove successful. If they fail, you've had
it." As evidence, managers cited promotions to general manager positions.
They were inevitably made to directors who had consistent, unblemished
track records which, of course, are achieved only by very conservative,
low-risk means. Key emphasis areas said nothing about innovation and
the application of new ideas. And managers who occasionally did take
risks were singled out for talks with superiors if there were no short-term
successes. Finally, the approval process for new ideas and techniques included four levels of management and was a cumbersome, time-
consuming process. By the time approval did come, the opportunity was
often lost.

No amount of suggestion boxes or rah-rah articles in house organs will
overcome organizational reality, which is much more visible than senior
management realizes. The organization has to "walk its talk" or, inevitably,
managers will take the safest perceived course of action when mixed
signals are given relative to risk.

3. *Degree of perceived actions available to manage risk.* Personally or organizationally, managers will discount risk by the amount of perceived control
they feel they have over it. That control is a function of the actions available
to deal with risk. The greatest influence will be actions that are known
to work and have been used in the past. For example, the risk of rain is
usually well handled by an umbrella. That takes care of *seriousness.* In
scheduling an event in the future, it's generally assumed that it won't rain,
because usually it doesn't. That's an assessment of *probability.* Risk is a
function of:

Probability of an event	PE
Less preventive actions	−PA
Equals residual probability	RP
Plus seriousness of an event	SE
Less mitigating actions	−MA
Equals residual seriousness	RS

Residual probability times residual seriousness
equals residual risk: $RP \times RS = RR$

Most managers don't understand that risk is a function of the likelihood
of an event occurring *and* the seriousness of the event if it does, indeed,
occur. The sales manager mentioned above knew the seriousness of not
meeting the client's date was very high—a lost sale and a lost client—but
was confident that the probability could be lowered by manipulating his

or her own delivery system. He placed all the emphasis on reducing or eliminating probability and was willing to live with the seriousness. If the sales manager had offered a price reduction if the delivery was late, the seriousness of the lost client would have been reduced as well (although the seriousness of the lower revenue and superiors' reactions would have to be evaluated).

Sometimes probability can't be reduced. One takes one's chances with the weather, for instance. Less frequently, one takes one's chances with seriousness, as did our sales manager, although this is rarely a wise course. Probability is the lesser threat of the two, because:

1. A high probability of occurrence coupled with a negligible seriousness is usually not a high-risk situation. There's a high probability I'll get a parking ticket by staying at this meter for more than one hour, but the ticket is less than the local parking lot! Compare that with parking overtime in a tow-away zone.

2. Sometimes no legitimate preventive action is conceivable. You can't prevent rain on the date your daughter has chosen for her wedding. (But you can provide a tent if it's to be an outdoor affair.)

3. Some preventive actions are unacceptably expensive or impractical. Passengers on airplanes will not be equipped with parachutes or private escape modules no matter how many air disasters we experience. Building a dome on most existing sports areas is not cost-justified.

4. Resources aren't always available. For that very reason, preventive maintenance often receives a low priority and only what is actually broken receives attention.

It's incumbent on the organization to actively demonstrate to its management the tools, techniques, resources, and authority available to reduce risk. Only *residual* risk is important, which is the risk which remains *after* appropriate preventive and mitigating actions have been taken. No one I know of refuses to attend ball games because of the probability of rain a month from now. They know it's unlikely, and they can always take an umbrella. At worst, the game will be canceled, which is not terribly serious. Similarly, good managers don't refrain from action because of perceived risk. They don't fall prey to the emotions and reactions listed above. That's because they have techniques and support available to separate initial risk from residual risk and are able to differentiate between probability and seriousness. If this separation weren't the key to risk analysis, no one would ever fly on an airplane (probability of a crash is remote, but seriousness is astronomical) or try anything new at work.

Various "formal" techniques are available to evaluate risk. We've found that virtually all managers make at least one implicit calculation in evaluating risk: they compare it to the status quo. In other words, they know what the current situation is, so what will the new idea or change do in terms of current security? The status quo is the one constant we've observed in managerial risk taking. Thus, no matter what techniques are utilized for risk analysis, the current situation must be accommodated as a yardstick.

I suggest the device shown in figure 7.7. It's simple and consistent, and it can apply to any organization.[6] The calibrations on the chart are unimportant. We like to keep things simple, but any numbers and graduations will work. The midpoint, 0, represents the status quo. Anything to the left is a deterioration of current conditions; anything to the right is an improvement.

RISK/REWARD COMPARISON

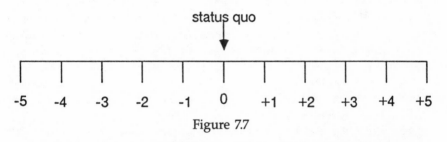

Figure 7.7

For those unaccustomed to dealing with residual risk and the difference between it and risk as first perceived, it's a useful exercise to use the scale to measure risk as initially perceived and then use it again after applicable preventive and mitigating actions have been considered. More about that after we explain the scale.

−5: *Potentially disastrous risk.* Business, morale, image, reputation, and so on, suffer tremendous damage. This could be a catastrophe for a small business and a major setback for a large one. Example: People Express purchasing Frontier Airlines.

−4: *This is a major disruption.* Money is lost, and the organization must perform substantial damage control in order to return to normal operations. Example: An organization invests its financial surplus in the stock market rather than treasury bills just prior to the 1987 crash.

−3: *Significant problems result.* Remedial actions must be undertaken and progress toward overall business goals is disrupted temporarily. The effects will be remembered. Example: Federal Express's Zap Mail.

---

[6]Robert and Weiss, *The Innovation Formula*, pages 89–95.

−2: *Controllable risk at the local level.* Comes under the freedom-to-fail axiom of many organizations. Only those directly affected will be involved in correction. Example: An account is lost when a deliberately higher price than competitors' was used, although justified by the promise of better service.

−1: *Negligible risk.* A minor snag easily accommodated in the normal course of doing business. Few are even aware of it. Example: Protection is slightly delayed as a result of a decision to cross-train assembly personnel.

0: *Status quo.* This is the situation as it exists today. (Not as it's *supposed* to exist, but as it *actually* exists.)

+1: *Slight improvement.* Most will not even realize it has occurred, and it will quickly disappear into normal operating status. Example: The decision to save all courier packages until one agreed-upon time so that only one pickup is required.

+2: *A clear advance.* Those directly involved will be appreciative of the result; it is tangible and repeatable. Example: A switch on the phone that allows calls to be forwarded to a secretary without ringing on your desk.

+3: *Significant improvements.* The effects will be known widely, perhaps throughout the organization. Does not quickly become second nature, and there will be clear attempts to exploit the opportunity. Example: Technology that affords call-forwarding and call-waiting options.

+4: *Dramatic gain.* Clear competitive inroads and long-term benefit results. A major event for the organization that will be noted on the outside as well. Example: Antilock brake technology.

+5: *Landmark event.* A turning point or watershed occurrence for a large organization or a breakthrough for a smaller one. A profound change in the culture and/or operations. Example: Steel-belted radial tires, frequent traveler programs, local copy and printing franchises.

By utilizing a scale such as figure 7.9, managers are able to judge *both* best and worst case outcomes for any change, opportunity, idea, or issue. Seldom is there simply one prospective result. Depending on the foresight in evaluating the probability and seriousness of risk and the actions available to deal with them, outcomes can and will vary. Residual risk should generally be lower than the original risk, but even residual risk will depend on management's ability to devise safeguards—preventive and mitigating actions. The assessment on this risk/reward scale should demonstrate how effective the safeguards are deemed to be.

So the manager should ask: After taking all appropriate actions we can think of to reasonably manage the risk, what are the best- and worst-case outcomes? What are the potential risk and reward, and am I willing to endure them in view of my personal responsibilities and organization's culture?

The three possible outcomes of such an examination are graphed in figure 7.8. In figure 7.8, you can't afford *not* to pursue the issue. Both best- and worst-cases represent improvements over the status quo. In figure 7.9,

RISK/REWARD COMPARISON

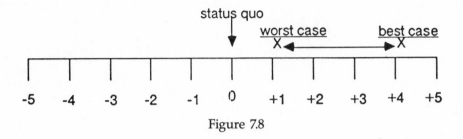

Figure 7.8

RISK/REWARD COMPARISON

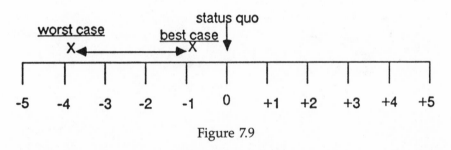

Figure 7.9

we have an example of the situation we should all run from. No matter what we do, the result will leave us worse off than we are today (yet many of us seriously examine such situations in the absence of a yardstick). In figure 7.10 we have the most common example of the real world, especially in major issues: The best case represents significant improvement, and the worst represents significant risk.

Most bold changes, as required by strategic change, involve potential which spans the status quo in either direction. "No risk, no reward" or, as William Penn said, "No cross, no crown." Hence, a system for risk evaluation is mandatory if the organization wishes to implement strategic change. Only through a systematic evaluation—whether you use my system or any other—can the true degree of implementation difficulty be

RISK/REWARD COMPARISON

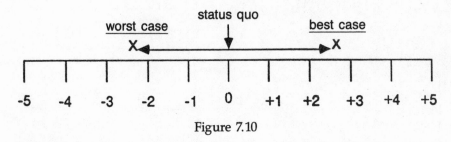

Figure 7.10

determined. And, as we discussed earlier in this chapter, the implementation difficulty is the key axis on the matrix which determines the appropriateness of actions in strategy implementation. (The other axis, strategic fit, is generally obvious and is not maneuverable in any case.)

It's now time to see how everything tends to fit together.

8

Turning On and Tuning Up Strategy: Why Mechanics Get $65 an Hour

We said at the outset that a strategy requires a discrete and focused implementation plan if it is to be successfully implemented. You could say that the strategy needs a strategy, but if you began to explain that to your colleagues, many of them would begin to mysteriously start to spin in place. Fortunately, there are subtler ways to convey the point, because it's a key to making strategy work.

Before beginning the process, it's absolutely critical to understand that what the CEO (who should be the chief strategist) *says* is generally not what others *hear*. We discussed the importance of communication in chapter 3, but in table 8.1 is some additional proof of the power of communication for those who need it.[1] The study concludes that "No wonder so many chief executives complain that it's lonely at the top. Isolated in executive suites, they not only are unaware of what other managers think, but they also aren't being heard themselves." There appears to be a chasm between what senior people believe are extremely important and what subordinates think. Table 8.1 is taken from the study.

Table 8.1

| | Priorities, % | | |
	CEO	COO	VP
Quality of customer service	92	87	83
Long-term growth	85	79	78
Employee productivity	79	77	70
Immediate financial results	51	69	70
Employee satisfaction	65	61	54

While reviewing this table, bear in mind that *82 percent* of CEOs polled stated that they believed their strategy is "clearly understood to a great extent by everyone who needs to know." Yet only 68 percent of COOs and 76 percent of VPs concurred with that belief. What would be the percentage of middle-level managers? The poll doesn't tell us, but my experience tells me it's well below 50 percent.

[1]The following points are cited in "CEOs Are Out of Touch with Subordinates," *The Wall Street Journal*, Sept. 8, 1989, page B1, reporting on a survey undertaken by the Forum Corporation of Boston involving 611 executives at Fortune 500 organizations.

For example, if only 51 percent of CEOs see immediate financial results as a priority but 70 percent of VPs do, then there is a very strong probability that:

- The lower you descend in the organization, the more emphasis in the reward and recognition systems there is on short-term results. After all, short-term results are tangible and measurable, and they provide an easy mechanism with which to manage daily performance.
- The CEO's vision—his or her true priorities—are probably unknown to most of the rank and file and can't be supported even by those who do know them because the organization's culture and reinforcers are pushing in other directions.
- The CEO will be handcuffed by the inevitable results of this wayward orientation. That is, the organization will find that its strategy has crafted an excellent, piston-driven aircraft that can make reliable short hops in great comfort, even though the top person envisioned a daring rocket that moves the company uncomfortably but rapidly into the future. Once the prop job is built, it's the only transportation available. You have to make the best of it.

This need for clarity and buy-in in strategic communications is not synonymous with executive visibility or charisma, although all elements may certainly be present in one individual. We've consistently cited Merck & Co. as one of the finest-managed organizations we've seen, as its results and its admiration by peers would attest. However, even the excellent firms are constantly battling with the problem. (Note that the poll referred to above comprised Fortune 500 companies, all large and, presumably, fairly successful. If an inability to communicate strategy is hampering them, that inability is virtually killing others.)

In working with managers in Merck's manufacturing area over a 6-month period, sample groups expressed confusion over "what Roy [P. Roy Vagelos, CEO] really wants." Merck is sensitive to employee communication, and virtually every one of its 33,000 employees can cite the organization's values and beliefs. Yet the intent of the top man is sometimes distorted despite face-to-face discussion groups conducted by management, an open and free communication system, and a variety of other efforts. And, of course, some parts of the organization communicate the intent better than others. Now, Merck is "America's Most Admired Company" and it's constantly battling these problems. What about those that aren't at its level of excellence?

In a poll undertaken for the American Press Institute of 21 major news organizations,[2] we obtained the following responses to the question "How would you describe communications and interchange of ideas among people at all levels in your organization?"

[2]"Survey of Participant Organizations: Customer Service and Quality," for the J. Montgomery Curtis Memorial Seminar, conducted by Summit Consulting Group, Inc., July–August 1989, page 11.

Everyone communicates openly and well	6%
Some communicate well; others do not	73%
In general, communications are not good	16%
We are mostly in the dark	5%

Don't forget, these results are from organizations that specialize in communication!

There needs to be a *process* of strategy implementation that ensures both communication at the outset and communication throughout the implementation. That process must begin between the top executive and his or her direct reports and then be carried through between the direct reports and *their* direct reports, and so on, to every person in the organization. I hope we've demonstrated earlier why every person is important to strategy implementation, so the model has to encompass everyone. The *process* of communicating and implementing strategy is as important as the *content* of the strategy itself. The lawyers call this form and substance. Excellent strategies simply and unequivocally require excellent implementation processes.

One way to look at that process is shown in figure 8.1. There are eight generic steps that constitute the strategy for implementing strategy. In your organization, there might be three more that are critical to the scheme— perhaps examining specific demographic changes, or new knowledge, or technological advance. These eight are certainly not mutually exclusive of other factors. On the contrary, they are highly plug-compatible, as the high-tech people would say of complementary elements. Each of these elements must be communicated carefully and be continually evaluated for the clarity with which they are received.

One of our newspaper clients asked us how he (as publisher) could *really* determine if people were all hearing the same message he was trying to deliver, in the midst of deadlines, scarce resources, competitive pressures, and the general organized chaos of his industry. It was a good question, and one every top person should be asking. The techniques for evaluating the effectiveness of the message are discussed below:

1. *Hold focus groups with customers.* Are customers receiving the kind of product, service, and relationship that you envision? This is a far more telling indicator than asking your own people. After all, the customer is the end user we're all concerned about. Note that the intent isn't merely to ascertain whether or not the customer is satisfied or happy. The intent is to determine whether or not the customer is receiving the treatment you envision. (One executive who engaged in a sampling found that the customer was receiving attention that was *too lavish*. The CEO's message had been exaggerated to the point of neglecting pragmatic business considerations in order to satisfy the customer at any cost.)

2. *Hold focus groups with employees.* Lest you fear that employees won't tell you what's really on their minds, structure the focus groups on the premise that you want to know what's getting in the way of their jobs,

Eight Steps: Strategic Vision to Organization Reality

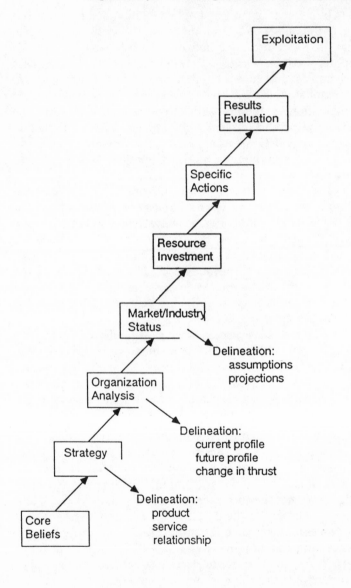

Figure 8.1

so that you can remove the obstacles. In so doing, you'll find out what they perceive the end products of their jobs to be, and you can compare that with your goals. The more the discrepancy (for example, an employee needs to process more phone requests per hour when you're placing a premium on comprehensive response, not speed), the more the communication has faltered. (When you find that to be the case, it is almost never the employee's fault. It is his or her manager's fault, or the manager's manager's fault. A senior vice president of Merck once told me that whenever he sees an employee performing poorly, he immediately seeks out the manager to find out why the situation has been allowed to exist.)

3. *Get informal feedback.* It is simply amazing how rarely key executives even walk through their areas of responsibility. I find that many aren't even recognized on sight. That isn't so much management by wandering around as it is mobile listening. Eat in the cafeteria. Listen to conversations in the hallway. Chat informally. Are the concerns and issues on people's minds commensurate with the destination you've chosen for the organization (or you're responsible for fulfilling)?

4. *Demand that formal management time every month be dedicated to small, informal meetings to test the waters.* As these meetings take on a regular stature in people's perceptions, participants will feel freer and freer to speak out during them.

5. *Shop your business.* Buy your products; utilize your services; test your relationships. Visit your stores (hire an outsider to do it if you are known); call your phone lines; complain to customer service. I know of precious few executives who take even an hour a month to do this. The results, I'm both encouraged and alarmed to report, usually make a consultant unnecessary and employee surveys irrelevant. You must be where the rubber hits the road in your particular business. That is absolutely *never* in the executive suite. It's fashionable to visit the competition, and to analyze their products and services, but that does you little good unless you are evaluating how well the competition is doing in meeting *their* strategy.

6. *Communicate each of the eight steps continually by comparing current status to anticipated goals.* Note progress in the house organ, videotapes, orientations, memos, and meetings. Use every forum possible to drive these points home. For example, if an assumption in the market/industry structure step was that "cellular phone technology will cover 95 percent of our business area by the end of 1991," then reflect what the actual coverage is as 1990 progresses. If assumptions have not been borne out, indicate the adjustments that are being made to the strategy to accommodate the latest assumptions or reality. (If your question is "What if we haven't any contingent actions to deal with a changed environment?" then you're reading the wrong book.) Note how this communication process forces senior management to examine these issues and stay on top of them. If you're responsible for ensuring that people are clear and informed, then you had better be clear and informed first.

Here we are advocating neither thick, three-ring binders of strategic documents that even actuaries would find tedious nor concise strategies that only the inner circle is privy to (remember my client who proudly proclaimed "All seven of us have read it"!). We are suggesting a simple, eight-step sequence that people are continually aware of and to which they can relate their jobs. Let's briefly examine what each step entails.

Core Beliefs

Core beliefs are the guiding values of the organization. They should be short, simple, realistic, and practical—the kinds of things an employee can keep in his or her head. Examples:

- Conduct all business with the highest standards of honesty and integrity.
- Fulfill our societal and environmental responsibilities to the utmost.
- Provide benefit to society that will generate value for our shareholders.
- Be the perceived and actual leaders in the technology of our business.
- Treat our fellow employees with respect on all occasions.

I've heard managers question a new compensation system in terms of the organization's basic beliefs and supervisors wonder if a value is being abrogated by a performance review procedure. Those events take place in healthy organizations, in which the core beliefs are a part of people's business reality.

Strategy

Your strategic approach may vary considerably from what we've proposed as we've touched on the formulation process. After all, this book is about implementation, not formulation. But whatever your process is, its major components should be summarized and communicated. We call this process delineation. To use an example we've provided earlier, it may be as simple as figure 8.2. No matter what format you choose, the simpler—and more vivid—the better. A graphic which illustrates each major component of the strategy *as it relates to employees* and the progress being made toward it is a wonderfully basic communication device. Of course, as in any such visible yardstick, top management must be held accountable to it equally with everyone else. If this presents a problem, then your strategy process is deeply flawed.

Organizational Analysis

This is a basic comparison between where you are now and where you want to be. The result provides a measurement of the change in thrust required to get the organization to the desired destination. For example:

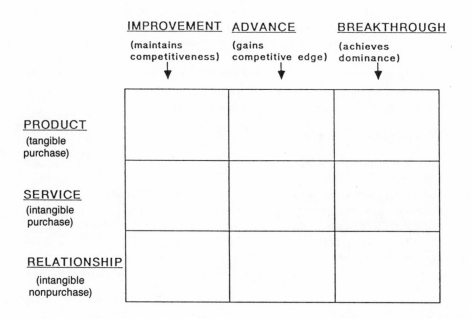

Figure 8.2

Current Relationships	Desired Relationships	Change Required
We respond if contacted	We encourage contact	Toll-free number Added staff Technical training
We provide a 30-day guarantee	We provide unconditional guarantee	Better QC inspection Alternate return number Improved vendor responsiveness

It's important for people to achieve consensus about where their performance is now (it will vary from area to area, but the perception shouldn't vary *among* workers in any one area) and buy into where they are going. It's vital to communicate the changes in thrust required so it will become apparent that the organization is not in the just-do-more-work or you've-got-to-be-more-productive modes. In fact, changes that are called for— different agreements with vendors, an education process with consumers, equipment requirements—support the direction. This is a "holistic" approach that everyone can be a part of on the basis that everyone—senior management on down—is pulling his or her share.

Generally, the more radical or substantial the change in thrust, the more support is required. If employees are merely expected to do more or to do things differently without that support, then management has probably not formulated its strategy implementation plans with the care that it should have. Another way to look at it: If senior people are embarrassed to make visible who's responsible for doing what in order to achieve the strategic intent, then they have probably dumped too much work on the employees and done too little thinking themselves.

Market/Industry Status

This is where assumptions and projections which underlie the strategy are made. Obviously, not everything about the future is easy to foretell, or strategy would be a day at the beach. But less obviously, those projections often become givens which are seldom challenged or scrutinized after their formulation. By communicating these assumptions, management not only demands that they be constantly challenged but enables and empowers the entire organization to gather and analyze data that support or reject the conclusions. So we have the wonderful double benefit of ongoing analysis of the projections coupled with incremental input as to their strengths and weaknesses.

For example, an assumption about competitive actions can be constantly compared with information gathered by the field force in visiting customers, vendors, and prospects. Has the competition begun using direct mail, hired additional salespeople, offered dealer incentives? But these are quantitative assessments. What about the qualitative ones? How have dealers reacted to the incentives; how well trained are the new recruits; what has been the response to the direct mail?

It's difficult for people to provide feedback when they aren't sure what they are looking for. By broadcasting the strategic projections, assumptions, and extrapolations, top management can recruit its own work force in guiding the quality of the strategy implementation. No matter what strategic formulation process you've utilized, it will contain these assumptions. (Many clients are fairly sophisticated at this. For example, if an economic downturn is among the projections, the organization will sample its own employees on the nature of purchases they are making and trips they are planning.)

Resource Investments

The resource investments are the "assets" that the organization will dedicate to ensuring that the strategy is implemented successfully. There is no need to reveal budgets or line items here, since such funding generates manifestations that are much more important than any confidential financial data. Resource investment disclosures should reveal:

- The numbers and levels of people affected and involved
- Any plant and physical equipment required
- "Champions" and top people leading the effort
- Times and deadlines
- Priorities
- Organization image, credibility, and repute on the line

Resource information often also includes research, materials, marketing, promotion and advertising, requirements for a pilot or test, and contingency plans.

Specific Actions

This step is really the heart of the communications process. All else may be somewhat esoteric and abstract, but the specific actions are what hit people where the live: on their particular jobs. The entire action plan need not be revealed in all its glory. It's usually sufficient to specify the steps that people will participate in and/or observe over the next quarter and a general sense of what will happen—if all goes according to plan and feedback on assumptions and projections is supportive—over the ensuing 6 months. If the strategy is short term in nature, then there is added pressure to perform, since the entire implementation is going to be spelled out in some detail. But if it's a longer-term strategy, i.e., it spans fiscal years, then only parts of it will be detailed at a time.

It is against specific actions that people will truly evaluate progress *and* intent. For instance, if a poor financial quarter also results in several actions planned for that time period not being achieved, employees will receive a clear message about the importance of the strategic change vis-a-vis short-term financial performance. Conversely, if the actions are completed irrespective of financial results one quarter to the next, a much different message is being sent. This is the sequence that continually brings middle managers on board or alienates them. It's the difference between "We are serious about getting this done" and "It sure didn't take much for them to forget their grand plans." Note the difference in the pronouns. If you're not willing to share specific actions with employees and allow them to judge the progress, then it's the equivalent of the football coach who refuses to call a passing plan "because only three things can happen when you put the ball in the air and two of them are bad." You're fearful of the impact of the actions on employees, which means they haven't been made owners of the strategy, or you're afraid that the actions will certainly not be met, in which case you probably haven't engaged successfully in steps 1 through 5.

Results Evaluation

This differs from step 6 in that employees are free to judge the efficacy of specific actions and their implementation on their own and at any time. But results evaluation is the "official" organizational assessment of success or lack of it. This communicates management's sense of where things are and what the status is. In this manner, there is no perception gap between what people think, what people think that management thinks, and what management actually thinks!

If people feel that "we're really messed up" and management, when approached, says "we're just fine," then credibility in the proceedings will be diminished. Even worse, when managers' individual assessments vary, credibility suffers all the more. A company position periodically shared with employees and used to encourage comparison and debate will flush these issues into the open. *Most important, such candid communication can utilize a lapse in the plan or goals missed as a learning step that everyone jointly agrees on.* This is the main benefit from management assessing progress and admitting where, how, and why deadlines were not met or actions were not successful. And in *every* instance of strategic implementation, there will be goals unmet and deadlines missed. But they shouldn't cause the plan to founder—which can happen in the absence of communication— they should be occasions of fact (not fault) finding and steps oriented toward improvement. A few *mea culpas* would not be out of place.

Here's how the potentially painful can be transformed into valuable learning. George Schaefer of Caterpillar recalls his organization's venture into paving products:[3]

> Our venture into paving products was particularly painful at first because we critically misjudged—made some incorrect assumptions about—that marketplace. We thought that the market would recognize the Cat name but *not* require or expect our historically high levels of after-sale service and support. We were wrong, on two counts. They both wanted that service *and* they were unwilling to pay for it! As we evaluated our experience, we came to realize that *any* product with the Cat name demands that our high commitment to service and quality accompany it. Consequently, we only belong in markets that are willing to pay for that value.

Exploitation

The final step in our scenario of the strategy of strategy implementation is that of exploitation of success. There is always a need to prepare for setback, if not outright failure, and to have contingency plans ready to deal with misfortune and miscalculation. But too many organizations end their contingency planning at that point—"let's fix it if it goes awry." But what if it doesn't go awry, by and large? What if it goes terribly right?

Football backs are taught to finish off a run to get the last few yards out of the play. Baseball hitters generally roll their wrists at the end of their swing, which is thought to produce more distance when contact has been made with the ball. Follow-through in golf has achieved mythic proportions. Such follow-through is essential, we believe, for two reasons:

---

[3]Interview with the author, Peoria, Ill., Sept. 7, 1989.

1. The mere act of *preparing* for the follow-through improves what precedes it. The golf swing itself and the contact with the ball are better when the player is performing with the follow-through in mind. One could make the case that preparation and follow-through—in any activity—are merely to ensure the quality of what comes in between.

2. Effective follow-through turns small gains into large ones, local victories into widespread ones, and small successes into landmark events. The oft-cited Post-it™ Notes were successful, but it was the follow-through of producing various colors and shapes and preprinted pads that made them into a modern office and home necessity.

Exploitation means that an organization is most capable of embracing change, taking prudent risk, and gaining momentum when dealing from a position of strength. Positions of weakness create desperation and resigned commitment, positions of strength result in excitement and enthusiastic support. Studies of leadership have invariably shown the need to engage the enthusiastic support of the implementors for certain critical interventions.[4] When the action plan has been met and the opinions of both employees and senior management support this belief, it's time to examine how the situation can be exploited. For example:

- Can momentum be gained to execute the more difficult parts of the plan?
- Can prior nonsuccesses now be placed in proper perspective?
- Can key holdouts be recruited into the new strategic approach?
- If sacrifices must be made, is it not the time to explore them?
- Can competitive edge be extended in some manner?
- Can the success be used elsewhere in the organization?
- Is it appropriate to make the strategy more aggressive at this juncture?
- Is it a good time to bestow recognition and reward?
- Should more resources be freed up for implementation?
- Is it safe to reduce the resources and implement change more efficiently?
- Can any of the prior seven steps be immediately improved through this success?

These questions may seem simple, and the answers are generally not complex. But few organizations and few management teams consider them at all! Strategy implementation is not, as Henry James said about life, "a slow reluctant march into enemy territory." It should be an exhilarating adventure. But if all you see around you is alien and enemy territory, your thoughts will be about escape, not building on success. You must see and convey the adventure and be prepared to build on the opportunity that adventure inevitably generates.

---

[4]For example, see *Organizations: Behavior, Structure, Processes*, 6th ed., by James L. Gibson, John M. Ivancevich, and James H. Donnelly, Jr., BPI/Irwin, Homewood, Ill., 1988, pages 392–395. Normative leadership theories, as espoused by Victor Vroom and others, emphasize the need to utilize participative decision making to gain enthusiastic support when quality considerations are high and a "leader-alone" decision is not apt to be accepted.

Those are the eight steps we believe to be vital to effective and successful communication and all that it engenders—vital employee involvement in the strategy implementation process in a constructive and coordinated manner. In taking them, you will also be creating a template for your management team to apply to its own actions and progress. Being forced to communicate with implementors has the magical quality of producing great clarity of thought, economy of action, and honesty of intent! You can fool yourself on paper and you can be fooled by yes-men who seek only to please, but you can't fool the troops who have to go into battle. Communicating your strategic intent and plans may be the kernel of the strategic process as a whole, far more than elaborate matrices, executive retreats, or affectations such as "cash cow" and "dog" can ever be.

The following is a brief example of how the eight steps can be applied and communicated throughout the organization.

Core Beliefs
Our organization holds these values and beliefs as the keys to our ongoing, long-term successes:

1. To invest in innovative approaches to technology and application of our products.
2. Our priorities shall be our customers, employees, shareholders, and management, in that order.
3. We will operate with the highest levels of honest and ethical conduct among all firms.
4. We will seek financial success through products that meet basic human needs.
5. We encourage risk taking and support a freedom-to-fail environment for our people.

Strategy
Our strategy, briefly expressed, is to achieve the configuration in figure 8.2: improvement, advance, or breakthrough in product, service, and relationship.

Organization Analysis
To meet this goal, we see the current organization in comparison to the desired organization, and the changes required, as shown in figure 8.3.

Market/Industry Status
We are making the following basic projections and assumptions about our organization and its environment:

1. There will be no major recession during the next 3 years.
2. The appeal of our products will intensify as baby-boomers begin late families with attendant quality-of-life issues.
3. Subsequent to 1992, the European Economic Community will have significant holdouts which will not accept full-fledged involvement, thereby creating opportunity for niche players in those markets.

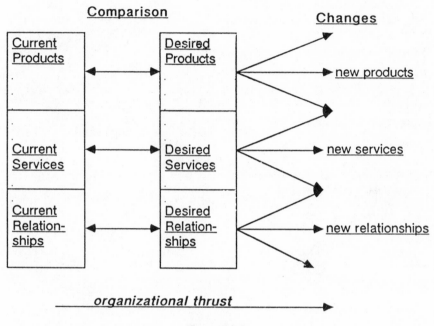

Figure 8.3

4. Our current technology will be copied in cheap labor markets in the Far East and Africa.
5. And so on.

Resource Investments

For our strategy to be successfully implemented, we must commit to the following:

1. About 20 percent of our manufacturing work force will work full time on our changeovers.
2. Customer service will be expanded by 40 people transferred from elsewhere in the firm.
3. The effort will be headed by senior vice president Joan Waters.
4. The first new products should be available to our customers 9 months from today.
5. And so on.

Specific Actions

Our actual plan to implement this strategy will involve:

What	Responsibility	When
Convening of customer focus groups	Director of customer service	June 10
Joint venture proposal to vendors	Vice president of finance	July 15
Assessment of demographic trends	Outside consultants	July 15
New product testing completed	Director of R&D	August 30

And so on.

Results Evaluation

Our quarterly evaluation of plan results is:

What	Responsibility	When
Convening of customer focus groups	Director of customer service	June 10

Result: All groups conducted; feedback circulated; only small-appliance users have expressed concerns. We will assign a task force to look into that product's potential for change.

Joint venture proposal to vendors	Vice president of finance	July 15

Result: Three vendors interested, which is more than we need. We have asked for proposals from all three to ascertain best fit. Decision will be made by September 30.

Assessment of demographic trends	Outside consultants	July 15

Result: Consultant's report is 30 days late because of additional data we requested as a result of focus group feedback. Otherwise, study is proceeding well, and report will be presented to executive committee on August 15 and circulated to employees via newsletter within 10 days of that meeting.

New product testing completed	Director of R&D	August 30

Result: Midway through testing. We will hit deadline or miss it by a week in worst case. Biggest surprise was durability of new configuration, but we have some concern about packaging costs.

And so on.

Anyone having questions or concerns about plan progress should inquire from his or her manager or call our strategy hot line for additional details.

Exploitation

In view of the following successes to date, we are planning to capitalize on them in this manner:

1. The new product availability is far ahead of deadline, although we cannot launch until other plan elements meet their deadlines. However, we are providing new product samples—not prototypes— through our sales force to favored distributors to encourage them to engage in local promotion and start them thinking about allocating

space accordingly. Also, any employee is invited to pick up a personal sample at any time.

2. Our agreement with Acme, our vendor of choice, has been so successful that we are proposing similar arrangements covering our other products that are not involved in the strategic changes. Acme is receptive, and we will propose similar arrangements to other vendors and distributors.

3. The customer focus groups will be incorporated as an ongoing organization procedure and will not end with this strategy step. Customers will be chosen at random by product and will meet onsite to interact with manufacturing, marketing, and design personnel at all levels.

4. Because of the focus we've been able to achieve, Joan Waters has been promoted to executive vice president of the new unit and will be naming her appointments to key positions in the next 30 days.

We strongly encourage these types of communications and documents to achieve active involvement in the strategy implementation process. Whether you use our approach or another, it's vital that the process be *interactive* and that employees have the opportunity not just to hear but to respond. After all, those responses are key in testing the reality of the strategy implementation against the status of the organization at any given time. Some simple techniques:

- Periodic, brief meetings at all levels specifically to discuss strategic progress.
- Dedicated space in the house organ to discuss results.
- Home mailings with results and amended plans.
- Surveys of employees to measure perceptions of progress.
- A strategy hot line which accepts inputs and provides information.
- Emphasis areas keyed into strategic implementation goals.
- Strategy updates preceding any and every company training program.
- Graphics, in the cafeteria and halls, depicting status.

Your organization may favor 6 steps or 16 steps, rather than the 8 we've recommended. There is no magic formula. But there is a discrete process for creating the communications and environment necessary to recruit everyone into the implementation effort. This is the "strategy of strategy implementation," and it is as important as the direction itself. It's very easy to simply step on the gas. But some finesse and careful judgment are required to get the best performance from the car. The designers may create the vehicle, but it's the mechanics who keep it performing.

9

Strategy Implementation and Strategic Alliances: How to Dance with the One Who Brung You

We've tried to make the case throughout this book that relationships are of equal weight with products and services (or technology or method of distribution or any other organizational factor) that have traditionally held sway. That is largely due to another point we've raised: No organization can hold its ground, much less achieve a market edge, by simply standing pat. Continuous improvement is the *least* of what's required in today's marketplace.

Aside from the financial reward, growth has another elemental facet for all organizations, large or small. Only through sustained growth can an organization attract and retain the kinds of people it needs to infuse the operation with vitality and muscle. Complacent organizations grow fat and flabby—middle management often represents its beer belly. Growing organizations are lean and healthy. Their middle management is trim, accustomed to running distance races as well as sprints. Continual growth—in customers, applications, market share, or whatever—and the concomitant change it demands, creates these organizational advantages:

- Less chance for a bureaucracy to take root
- Automatic trimming of dead wood
- An environment conducive to new ideas
- A built-in recruiter for top talent
- A leading-edge image
- Ongoing experimentation and the freedom to fail
- Forced collaborations with customers, vendors, and other key parties

Growth and the intelligent management of change demand certain partnerships. These partnerships—alliances—are win-win relationships in which everyone's self-interest is well served. Several years ago, United Airlines asked me to conduct a session in techniques for running a small business for travel agency owners in the San Antonio market. United was just entering that market, and it felt that the traditional wining, dining, and golfing approach had worn thin. The company asked how it could best recruit those key people to believe in United as an airline genuinely interested in their success. Anyone could wine and dine, since that required only money. But not everyone could or would try to *educate* the agency owners, since that required understanding of and commitment to *their* problems.

At first, the participants were skeptical (as were some United marketing people). But once the session took place, the agency owners and managers found themselves in a forum in which issues such as managing cash flow and hiring new people on limited resources were addressed without any attempt to connect the answers to United. The airline was simply the intermediary which brought us together. Subsequently, the participants told me that they were astounded that United even thought to do such a thing. United has achieved a unique image among the local travel agencies which participated (and probably, by word of mouth, among those which did not) that would have required unheard of wining and dining and golfing in the traditional manner.

Anyone with whom we form such alliances must grow. If that's not the case, there will be little or no growth for anyone. The organization should seek to grow not at others' expense, but rather in conjunction with others. That is the symbiosis that truly opens markets and establishes long-term relationships. The implementation of any strategy must take into account present and potential alliances. No organization can act in a manner that insulates it from its environment, and its actions—no matter how attractive internally—must be examined for their ramifications on partnerships. In a curiously ironic way, this restriction of unbounded freedom is the generator of long-term growth through mutual successes. No farmer who grew crops in type and volume that were not required by the farmer's market would long endure, unless he were the only farmer in town. American automakers found out the hard way that, once they were no longer the only farmers in town, the public could no longer be told what kinds of cars were good for them—they had to be *asked*, and their needs and requirements had to be taken into account.

I recall once asking an unsuccessful salesman what the toughest part of the job was so that we could work on it together. "It's the adversarial nature of the relationship," he said. "I intensely dislike that combative element of the sales process." Small wonder. Imagine your psyche when your perception of your job is that you have to do battle with eight or ten enemies every day. No one would seriously endorse such an approach to selling today, yet we advertently and inadvertently endorse it daily in our relationships with those whose success is vital to our own strategy.

Now think of the salespeople who are seen as partners by their customers. I'm not referring to socializing or weekend tennis. I mean helping customers plan their futures in ways that go far beyond the original product or service that created the meeting. To threaten such relationships requires the establishment of an even stronger partner, something not easily done. To threaten strategic alliances requires the equivalent alliance building by some other organization. This is a time-consuming and delicate process that many organizations will not take the time to initiate, especially when short-term results are too often the order of the day. To usurp or replace an alliance requires that the newcomer develop the level of trust and business at the *current* level of performance, whereas the current partner created the alliance at a much more modest level much earlier. That is part of the beauty of alliances. They take geometric increases in effort to displace them, because the newcomer is vying for the current level of partnership. (Of course, it's much easier for the current partner to displace itself through poor service or breeches of trust, but that's another issue.)

I've had a long-term consulting relationship with Merck & Co., during which I've worked with virtually every division and most of the key management. The issues have ranged from ethics and values to recruitment and succession planning. When they have required something beyond the competence of my firm, I've referred them elsewhere. But they have always felt comfortable asking me how I would approach something because of the *relationship* that has been formed. For example, when Merck was named "America's Most Admired Company" in *Fortune's* annual polls, the organization sent a memento to every one of its 33,000 employees—a coffee mug, a clock, a commemorative plate. And each year the company sent me the memento as well, with a letter thanking me for the contribution I had made to its success. Merck understands that my growth is its growth, and I certainly understand that its growth is my growth. The partnerships I've formed with Merck managers transcend the traditional consultant-client roles. They are mutual explorations of growth and learning.

One final issue from this example is crucial to understanding the role of alliances in implementing strategies. Last year I addressed several groups of manufacturing managers with whom I had never previously worked on the subject of ethics in the workplace. At the conclusion, the manager responsible commented that the sessions were so successful because I had the unique ability to serve as an outsider who could challenge their beliefs *while at the same time having great credibility because I knew the organization and its culture as well as they did.* Well, that was simple—all it had taken was 5 years of working with the client on a wide variety of projects! But how could anyone else replace that? They couldn't replicate the relationship I had begun so many years prior; they would have to duplicate the current, intimate relationship that had been forged, which would be an immense task and would require long-term effort and great patience. And from Merck's point of view, what is projected future loss if it changes resources abruptly? Does it want to lose the growth it has nurtured in my organization, which has significant potential value for future projects? That is the beauty of alliances: they become win-win, lose-lose relationships which all parties generally seek to perpetuate. Everyone becomes a common stakeholder.

Traditional lines between buyer and seller, buyer and supplier, producer and distributor, and so on, must be obliterated if strategic alliances are to be established. These collaborations and cooperations make traditional marketing a much simpler process because the organization is not trying to overcome some opposing force. Nor is the more "modern" approach required, wherein the customer's perception is manipulated until the customer thinks that what you have is what he or she needs. It is, rather, a question of a legitimate partnering based on mutual self-interest. In fact, one can make the case that such mutual fulfillment *is* marketing.

In establishing alliances, it is an immediate danger to think of your organization as a supplier or a vendor or a provider. The danger, assuming these positions are reflected in your core beliefs and strategic processes, is that you are competing with other suppliers and vendors and providers and all you have to bring to market are your products and services. If the customer develops the skills, knowledge, and expertise—increasingly simple these days—to make effective comparisons, you have abdicated your ability to influence the choice. Worse, if the customer knows *more* about the market, the needs, and the products and services than you, then you are at a distinct competitive disadvantage. Yet that is often precisely the case, because the organization chooses to implement its strategy without alliances in the marketplace, and its insulation creates such vulnerability. The fashion industry, long accustomed to dictating style, has suffered continual setbacks in that attempt since the Waterloo of the midiskirt. Indeed, some of the fastest growing businesses in that industry cater to larger-size women, with whom they are constantly interacting to determine comfort, design, and use. *No organization can effectively find and pursue opportunities if it is not in intimate touch with its market and customers. The only opportunities it will otherwise find are internal ones, and they alone are insufficient for competitive edge.*

Vendors and suppliers and providers seek to keep vending, supplying, and providing to customers. The customer must become a larger and larger taker if the providing organization is to grow. Yet all customers, unless *they* grow, have limits to what they can take. Moreover, in the absence of a partnership, the customer is constantly evaluating taking from *other* sources, so that volume can suffer at any given time for any given provider. This is the win-lose aspect of selling, and it's a battle that might be fought with ferocity every day, or it will inevitably be lost. The battle rages around buyer decisions—informed decisions—about price, size, dates, volumes, guarantees, and so forth. It is not based on mutual growth through carefully forged alliances.

I once addressed a large pharmaceutical sales force that was feeling the frustrations of its rapidly changing marketplace in the shape of generic competition, legal issues, regulatory demands, and so on. I asked them these questions:

- Are you paid well? (Yes.)
- Do any of you have all the money you made during the last year? (No.)
- Do the physicians and druggists with whom you deal, and their patients, still have all the benefits of the products you've provided over the past year? (Yes.)

Moral: Take heart in these precious and terribly important alliances you've formed, which are among the most vital of all humankind. These alliances will transcend the understandably frustrating realities we all must deal with. And this is, of course, why so many doctors prescribe and so many patients request brand-name drugs, even though generics are available. As one physician told me, "It's a few major pharmaceutical firms that are conducting the expensive and critical research needed to alleviate human suffering. They must be supported, because their success is all of our success."

We see mundane examples of alliances every day: joint ventures, licensing agreements, consortiums, R&D collaborations, and so on. On a larger scale, such alliances will increase with the advent of post-1992 Europe, the emergence of the Pacific rim economies, and the continued emigration of manufacturing to the Third World. On a smaller scale, the alliances will be crucial for local firms to serve the dual-income, quality-conscious consumer effectively. Supermarkets have begun to attend to the needs of shut-ins and home-ordering and delivery, for example. Local chambers of commerce increasingly sponsor events that enable merchants to reach larger slices of the community.

Six steps are necessary to create effective alliances whose hallmarks are mutual growth and long-term success for all parties.

1. *Establishing trust.* Partners in alliances must believe that each will do the right thing without reliance on rules and procedures. I have to believe that you will act in our mutual self-interest, and you have to believe that I will do likewise. Trust is not a one-time effort; it is a continual manifestation that we are engaged in a win-win relationship.

In the 1970s I worked for a major training firm. One of my account responsibilities was an IBM site. I had painstakingly built a trusting relationship over several years, through abundant service calls, complimentary publications, and recognition of what IBM clients had accomplished by using our techniques. In 1974, near the end of our fiscal year, we needed to accelerate our materials sales if we were to meet our goals. My sales manager said, "Do something with IBM—send them their next year's supplies if necessary, but do something to help us out. You've got the relationship with that client to bail us out." (Note: This is an excellent example of normative pressure: don't let the team down.)

Unfortunately, my colleagues at IBM said that it was against policy to accept materials for which they could not pay until the following fiscal year. But, under pressure, *I shipped the materials anyway.* After all, I had the relationship, right? That's right, I *had.* But not after that pressured and unethical act. IBM accepted the materials and subsequently paid for them—it was easier than returning them—but the relationship was never the same again. One act had undone the results of years of nurturing. Although building trust is the initial step, it is also an unending one. If a client (or supplier, or agent) has to think consciously about it, it's probably not yet there.

2. *Clarifying common objectives.* The specific growth goals of the partners must be explicit. Are we jointly seeking to improve quality, spread the application, reduce complaints, enhance visibility, and so on? United's travel agents wanted to improve the efficiencies of their businesses, and United identified with the benefits of being able to accomplish those efficiencies.

This step is important because it clarifies the real needs of others. No one buys drills to have drills—people buy drills because they need *holes*. Mutually winning relationships are best based on needs being fulfilled, not the joint work necessitated by mutually undertaken *tasks*. This is the difference between collaboration and cooperation. Alliances use the former; brief, arms-length relationships use the latter. We've seen many suppliers provide displays for retailers that are beneficial for the supplier but not very appropriate for the retailer. It's the displays that the retailer finds easy and practical to use—and in which he might have had some input—that receive the best response. It's not support; it's collaboration.

3. *Sharing strategies.* It's difficult to collaborate if the partners are unaware of the others' strategies. If such sharing is threatening, then the alliance is probably doomed from the start. In fact, one good test of potential alliances is the question, "Am I comfortable revealing my strategy to these people?" Sharing strategy is important because it forces the organization to test whether its strategy is coherent and clear enough to be shared and whether it has accommodated the potential alliances. Here are other questions to ask:

- How are our strategies compatible or incompatible?
- Do strengths and weaknesses complement each other or exacerbate problems?
- Are our basic beliefs suportive or in conflict?
- What is the exact relationship projected for products, services, and relationships?
- What are the proper points at which to reassess the alliance?
- What constitutes success for each partner's strategic plan?

Sharing strategies does not mean providing access to confidential financial data or privileged technological information. In fact, such sharing is often done with customers who may not have elaborate strategies at all. The sharing does entail a mutual assessment of beliefs, short- and long-term goals, and specific strategy implementation steps that each partner can build on (or at least not endanger).

4. *Continuing communication.* There must be the opportunity for formal, as well as informal, communication among members of the alliance. Trade associations are good examples of entities whose existence is dependent on their serving as a catalyst for alliances. The American Press Institute or the American Medical Association or the Academy of Motion Picture Arts and Sciences performs these communications activities:

- Interchange among members via newsletters and other publications
- Training programs and educational events

- Self-study opportunities via books and tapes
- Annual conventions and meetings
- Recognition of achievement via awards and publicity
- Independent publication in the general media
- Representing members' interests via lobbying and promotion
- Establishment of commonly approved standards of performance

Most fine service firms I'm familiar with regularly host meetings for clients and/or vendors and/or other interested parties. Focus groups and feedback groups, user surveys, and private interviews are other techniques commonly employed. There is a saying to the effect that "you can't communicate too much." In terms of alliances, that's undoubtedly true.

5. *Recognizing mutual threat and taking action.* Each partner's strategy implementation will be affected to some extent by the alliance and should be modified in light of it. The most important place for such modification is in identifying potential problems and planning to prevent or mitigate them. Marriages may be made in heaven, but they're lived here on earth. Each partner must honestly assess the perils presented by even the most attractive collaboration and make plans to deal with them. Those plans must become part of each organization's strategy implementation plans.

Obviously, this step is impossible if the earlier step of sharing strategies isn't honestly completed, so a good test at this point is whether or not mutual risks can be determined. If they can't be, don't assume that the collaboration is perfect. Assume, much more safely, that you don't know everything you need to know.

6. *Planning to exploit success.* Finally, partners should be in a position to capitalize on the fruits of the alliance. Planning to succeed is diffierent from planning for success. How can the partner's mutual growth goals be better met as the relationship proves successful? What further collaborations are possible? Are there subordinate goals that can be met? This kind of success planning solidifies partnerships and drives them for the long term. The organizations that best achieve success with partners are those that actively and confidently plan for it, as diagrammed in figure 9.1.

Forging alliances that achieve the goals of all parties requires certain organizational traits that don't appear on the organization chart or in the strategy statement (or annual report). These traits are exemplified by the tale of the scorpion and the frog.

A swimming frog was hailed from the bank by a scorpion.

"Would you mind giving me a ride to the opposite shore?" inquired the dangerous creature.

"That would be very foolish of me, wouldn't it?" queried the frog. "You would probably sting me and eat me when I approached you."

"No, no," protested the scorpion. "I give my word that I won't. First, I'm not hungry. Second, I must cross this stream to return home. And third, if I kill you in midstream, we'll both die. Can't we cooperate peacefully?"

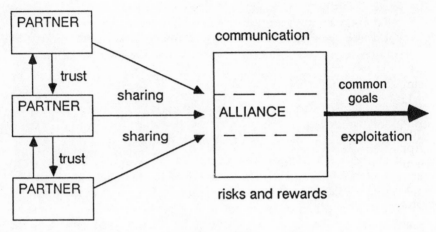

Figure 9.1

"All right," said the frog. "We must make what efforts we can to overcome distrust."

So the frog swam over and the scorpion crawled onto his back. Together, they began the journey across the stream. As the scorpion disembarked on the opposite shore, he was overcome by an uncontrollable passion and stung the frog in the neck.

"But why?" cried the frog as the poison spread. "You said you weren't hungry."

"Ah, but it's not a question of hunger," replied the scorpion, "it's a question of character."

Alliances rely on organizational character. Character is a function of these five traits:

1. *Trust.* The organization must exhibit trust in its partners. Partnerships are not arm's-length relationships; they are arm-in-arm relationships.

Winner: Microsoft will provide upgrades of its software at minimal or no cost with any basic proof of purchase. Moreover, its superb assistance telephone lines are available to anyone who calls, without any proof that the software was purchased on the legitimate market. Even one-time enemies can achieve this level of trust. Cable systems and over-the-air networks, combatants for years, are finding that broadcast alliances, particularly in news operations, are eminently reasonable.[1]

Loser: The local supermarket that refuses to honor a traveler's check—which you were able to use in Singapore—that you happen to have left over from a recent trip.

---

[1]See "Broadcasters, Cable Enter 'Era of Blur,'" by Kevin Goldman, *The Wall Street Journal*, Sept. 28, 1989, page B1.

2. *Tangible cooperation.* The partners must manifest the particular operational changes that reflect the benefits of the alliance. The whole should be tangibly superior to the sum of the parts. "You have to walk your talk."

Winner: The one-time United Airlines–Hertz alliance as represented by United baggage check-in service available at Hertz rental car return locations. This was a brilliant tactic that influenced many travelers in their air and auto plans (and far more tangible and immediately useful than simply adding frequent-flyer points for the car rental).

Loser: The Apple Computer relationship with retail distributors. Apple refers requests for help from consumers to the local dealers where the quality, reliability, speed, and empathy are wildly erratic. As a result, Apple's after-market support is probably its weakest link, and dealer loyalty is usually geared strictly to prices.

3. *Mutual problem solving.* The alliance partners must face the inevitable problems that will arise so as to:

- Find cause, not blame
- Seek improvement not just a "fix"
- Accommodate all partners' objectives
- Strengthen the alliance as a result

Winner: Mercedes-Benz training activities with its dealers. In the United States, about 50 Mercedes corporate trainers constantly visit dealerships to work on problems ranging from mechanical repair to showroom sales. The trainers not only provide instruction but spread lessons learned from one dealership to the next.

Loser: Continental Airlines and travel agents. Continental's huge route system and frequently changing fares and promotions can be the source of tremendous confusion. Agents tend to blame the airline ("They're understaffed in reservations, have too many new people, and don't support us properly") and the airline tends to blame the agents ("We prefer that you deal directly with us, because the agents look for the best commissions and try to steer you to other, more expensive carriers"). The consumer is caught amid the finger-pointing and doesn't come away too pleased with either the airline or the agent.

4. *Perceptual management.* The perception of nonalliance interested parties must be monitored and enhanced (and sometimes created). Alliances can succeed as well-kept secrets, but they generally exploit their synergy when nonalliance customers and prospects appreciate the power of the alliance.

Winner: The legendary Frito-Lay willingness to go to any lengths to service even small, remote retailers. The customer knows that both the supplier and the local store are cooperating to provide the freshest possible product. This alliance has received periodic publicity in the general press (and in books like this one). *USA Today* is virtually always the complimentary newspaper that hotels provide to special guests.

On a more deliberate publicity basis, there is the world of endorsements. Golfers wear attire with manufacturers' names on it; racing cars are plastered with suppliers' logos; and Linda Evans proclaims the wisdom and depth of Clairol for all to hear. Olympics have more official sponsors than athletes.

Loser: Most people are unaware that Amtrak reservations can be made and tickets can be acquired through local travel agents. In San Francisco, a rider can use free transfers to travel on the buses, subways, streetcars, and cable cars but *tourists* seldom learn that, even though they constitute the prime beneficiaries. Rebates and refunds (with the exceptions of supermarkets) are often not obvious or volunteered in many stores, so the consumer, store, and manufacturer are all losers.

5. *Building the alliance.* Finally, partners should seek out and be amenable to making the alliance grow. That can mean extending the alliance to include additional products, services, and relationships, and/or adding new partners to the alliance. Here's an example of growth from a cable television company executive: "Long Island was a perfect market for a local news service because it is underserved by New York television stations. We're wrestling with the question of whether there are other places in the U.S. where there is a concentration of cable subscribers who are underserved by the local news currently available to them."[2] Alliances are merely "super organizations" and, like organizations, must continue to grow to sustain their benefits to constituent parties.

Winner: Filofax (and others) continually develops new forms and inserts for its diaries to embrace a wider and wider range of professions, avocations, and private pursuits. One can purchase forms for wine tasting, golf scores, professional service billings, and so on. (And now there are computer software programs that allow you to create your own, personalized inserts.)[3]

Loser: City University of New York (CUNY) has had long-standing alliances with New York City's Board of Education to try to keep minority students in science and math curricula through high school. The alliance was innovative and constructive, but it never moved beyond its original memberships: CUNY's Office of Special Projects, some junior college faculty, and five of the city high school's selected faculty. Subsequent evaluation of the program showed that its effectiveness was diminished by the alliance's inability to eventually embrace high school principals, parents, and business leaders from the communities.[4]

Those five characteristics—alliance character traits—tend to overcome the irresistible urge of one partner to sting another once the immediate

---

[2]Ibid.

[3]For a lengthy discussion of purely customer-based alliances, see *Growth Partnering: How to Manage Strategic Alliances for Mutual Profit,* by Mack Hanan, AMA Management Briefing, American Management Association, New York, 1986.

[4]Project conducted by Summit Consulting Group, Inc., for City University of New York, "Recommendations for CUNY/OSP Improvements in the CDDP Collaboration," May 1988.

stream has been crossed. It's worth noting, also, that they obtain irrespective of whether the alliance is voluntary, forced, or durational.

Voluntary alliances are those that are formed when the partners see unique mutual advantages independent of any marketplace requirements that they must work together in any manner. Hertz and United weren't required to work together (for either baggage handling or mileage awards) but concluded that such a collaboration was mutually beneficial. Similarly, Toys 'R Us teamed with McDonald's to penetrate the Japanese marketplace.[5]

Compare that to *forced* alliances in which neither partner can expect to succeed without the active collaboration of the other. Pharmaceutical firms and their doctors and pharmacists, soda manufacturers and bottlers, resorts and travel agents, and movie makers and distributors fall into this category. Although the nature of these businesses demands collaboration, the alliance will nonetheless succeed or fail depending on adherence to the five character traits described above. Merck scores high with physicians because it is known for the honesty of its field force in describing competitive products. Doctors can trust Merck information as objective and patient-oriented. Some resorts provide travel agents with superior promotional materials (and commissions) to their competitors.

Durational alliances occur when the situation dictates the depth and duration of the partnerships. An alliance may be quite strong when it is active, but its activity is situational and is geared toward external stimuli and changing market conditions. The successes of durational alliances are most dependent on the character traits because there isn't an ongoing, permanent relationship to bond the partners.

A durational alliance is represented by toy manufacturers and retailers, who are usually in closest collaboration at gift-giving times. Advertising, promotion, pricing, and other market needs will be enhanced or negated depending on the strength of the alliance. If the alliance has to be *reestablished* each year, it will never fulfill its potential. Financial institutions tend to form durational alliances based on prevailing economic conditions (as reflected in lines of credit, auto financing to dealers, consumer products offered, and so on).

Whether voluntary, forced, or durational, alliances must be based on mutual self-interest if they are to be greater than the sum of the parts. Otherwise, they reflect an attitude of "what have you done for me lately?"

Not long ago I was a guest speaker at the American Press Institute along with a former executive of Ford who felt constrained to remind the audience that he had voluntarily left a $1 million position to do "good work" (run a hospice). The participants were top editors and publishers from around the country, and one issue raised was how to work better together with advertisers.

---

[5]See "Toys R Us to Team with McDonald's in Japan," by Nancy Yoshihara, *Los Angeles Times,* Sept. 27, 1989, page 2, part 4.

"I'll tell you how," said the ex-Ford man. "Stop running those ads in your auto sections promoting the guys who will sell a car at $500 over dealer cost. No one wins that way, and you've got to find a way to give the traditional dealers a better break."

The stunned expressions around the room reflected a group who had just heard "we want to be your friends, provided you do what we want, against your interests, and we do nothing in return," viz.:

- Refuse to honor other, legitimate advertisers
- Overcome traditional dealers' inadequate marketing
- Take sides in the marketplace
- Give us free help with nothing promised in return
- Ignore the self-interest of our mutual customers—the consumers

I can only marvel that the compassion of his "good works" in his collaborative view remains so self-centered. It's difficult to provide a service and form an alliance if you're demanding that the other party produce for you as a precondition.

Some alliance alternatives are given in figure 9.2; alliances that provide for mutual growth can take those forms and others. They are applicable to profit and nonprofit, public and private, and large and small organizations. If you are considering alliances or attempting to evaluate one in which you are already engaged, here are some assessment questions:

Products:
- Are our products reaching new customers?
- Are our products gaining new applications?
- Are our products reaching new markets?
- Are our products more efficiently sent to market?
- Are profit margins enhanced?
- Are we meeting growth goals?

Services:
- Are our services reaching new customers?
- Are our services gaining new applications?
- Are our services reaching new markets?
- Are our services sent to market more efficiently?
- Are profit margins enhanced?
- Are we meeting growth goals?

Relationships:
- Are we establishing new and unique customer relationships?
- Are our relationships supporting our product and service goals?
- Are the core beliefs of the organization being supported?
- Is the benefit of the alliance manifest in the marketplace?
- Are we able to gain competitive edge?

Information:
- Is our market intelligence significantly improved?
- Are our mistakes innovative and not fix-oriented?
- Do we gain inputs for our strategic planning purposes?
- Are we able to better fine-tune strategy implementation?

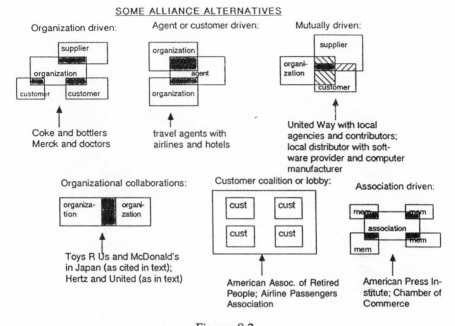

Figure 9.2

- Do we believe we are a leading-edge organization?
- Are we suffering from fewer surprises and unexpected events in the marketplace?

Management:
- Is our management acting with greater confidence and assurance?
- Do we all share the same vision about the alliance and its benefits?
- Do we examine and evaluate the alliance regularly?
- Is there cross-fertilization with partner managers?
- Do we improve management techniques through our partners' experiences?
- Are we rewarding those who build the alliance?

Alliances should be undertaken as catalysts to growth. They are the turbocharge that takes an organization beyond its normal growth arithmetic. The questions above—and others that may fit more specifically into your situation—should reveal whether the nature of the boost is worth the investment in the alliance. We've tried to demonstrate in this chapter that true alliances—true partnerships—require the trust and legitimate investment that one must make in any intimate relationship. The differences between poor and good alliances can be seen by comparing figures 9.3 and 9.4.

POOR ALLIANCE

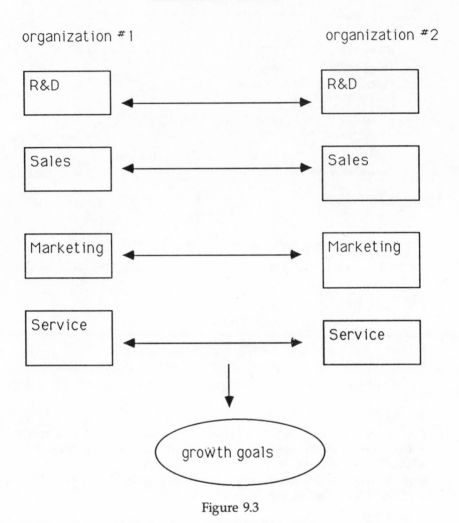

organization #1   organization #2

Figure 9.3

If you can't bring yourself to share with your partners to the extent that you invest in common-alliance managers whose job it is to ensure that the collaboration is an intimate one, then you're either talking to the wrong partners or simply not prepared for an alliance. You're still concerned about matters of character (or not concerned enough). You are preoccupied with the scorpion's sting.

CONSTRUCTIVE ALLIANCE

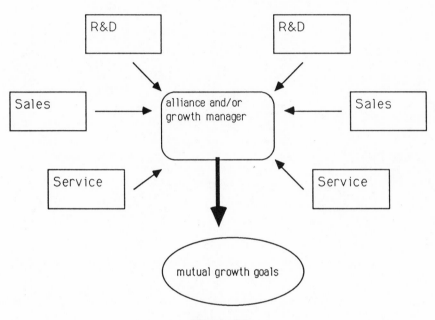

Figure 9.4

10

"Do Good and Good Will Follow" The Profitable World of the Nonprofit Organizations

We tend to segregate for-profit and not-for-profit organizations as though they were cults that follow rival deities. Until this decade, the former was run by "managers" and the latter by "administrators." The phrase, "You don't understand, we are a nonprofit and are, therefore, unique," was intoned in a ritual chant. It was also used to explain away inefficiencies, justify slow responsiveness, and rationalize incompetence.

No more.

In 1989, New York State's Office of Business Permits and Regulatory Affairs, in a budget-pinching year, managed to obtain approval for a strategy project to set its direction for the 90s. Its progressive executive director, Ruth Walters, reported to Governor Mario Cuomo: "We needed to ensure that we are organized in such a way as to maximize the quality and delivery efficiency of our products in the years ahead. This can't be reliant on me or any personality in the director's seat, but must be an ongoing process irrespective of the people involved."[1]

We've found that the priority issues facing nonprofits are essentially the same as those facing everyone else, particularly in the area of strategy formulation and implementation. Here is what William Aramony, President of United Way of America, has to say: "A clear statement of mission and 'buy-in' by implementors of the strategy, i.e., ownership by the implementors, is the major factor for us in successful implementation."[2] And James H. Sammons, M.D., Executive Vice President of the American Medical Association:

> The most important factor for success or failure of strategy implementation for us is the quality of the strategy itself. The ones that succeed are *clearly stated* and unambiguous, and they are *realistic* in the context of the capabilities and circumstances of the organization. Strategies that don't work at the implementation level are usually vague and thus subject to misinterpretation at the operational level, or are unrealistically out of step with either the organization itself or the environment within which it functions....In cases where the

---

[1]Conversation with the author, Oct. 3, 1989, Albany, New York. The strategy project was conducted by Summit Consulting Group, Inc.
[2]Correspondence with the author.

implementation *process* is at fault, it is usually because of poor task definition that allows gaps in the action plan, or poor execution related to communications gaps between the involved parties....Carelessness due to lax attitudes or sloppy management is always a danger.[3]

Nothing in these statements from a state agency, a charity, and a professional association that couldn't be applied with accuracy to a service firm, manufacturer, or small business, is there? Moreover, the statements reflect many of the issues discussed in the preceding nine chapters of this book: issues of communication, ownership, and anticipating change.

Why, then, separate the nonprofits into their own chapter in *this* book? Well, not for the traditional reasons of their being different. My premise is that everything in this approach to strategy implementation applies to nonprofits with only minor variation. The purpose of this chapter is to demonstrate that the lessons that can be learned *from* the nonprofits are clearly applicable to everyone else. This chapter will be more important for the management of the profit-driven firms than for their nonprofit colleagues, and we've chosen to focus on those lessons. And there are more extreme views than ours. Here's Peter Drucker: "The best management practice and most innovative methods now come from the Girl Scouts and the Salvation Army."[4]

For our purposes, nonprofits include *any* organization whose existence is not predicated on generating profit with which to reward ownership or to create increasing value in the entity itself. Its success is derived exclusively from the contribution it makes to the external environment in relation to its basic activities. All of these organizations would be encompassed by our definition:

- Charities, such as the American Cancer Society
- Trade associations, such as the American Press Institute
- Unions, such as the United Auto Workers
- Governmental agencies, such as the division of motor vehicles
- Support groups, such as parent-teacher associations
- Clubs, such as a local social and athletic club
- Interest groups, such as the American Philatelic Society
- Organized activities, such as the 4-H clubs
- Community support groups, such as the Society for Prevention of Cruelty to Animals
- Philanthropic foundations, such as the Ford Foundation
- Self-help groups, such as Alcoholics Anonymous
- Neighborhood affiliations, such as Crime Watch

Obviously, some of these examples may cross categories, but that isn't the point. The point is that there is more employment in voluntary and nonprofit organizations than in any other kind, and more people are engaged in them than in profit-seeking pursuits. According to a Gallup

---

[3]Correspondence with the author. Italics are his.
[4]"What Business Can Learn from Non-profits," by Peter Drucker, *Harvard Business Review*, July–August 1989, page 88.

Poll, volunteerism alone in the United States is now a $150 billion "business" and is growing.[5] John D. Mason, director of volunteer services at William Temple House in Portland, Oregon, who oversees a paid staff of 18 and a volunteer force of over 300, comments that those interested in a job such as his need to be "well versed in management skills, planning, organizing, staffing, evaluating, supervising and controlling."[6]

What can we all learn from nonprofits? Well, for one thing, they have become excellent in fields such as motivation of workers, since they can't depend on the "usual" allures of money and fringe benefits (except for the intangible benefit of gratification in good work). The productivity leaps of nonprofit organizations, in general, have probably outstripped that of all others. Here are eight specific lessons:

Financial Management

By definition, nonprofits must be more sensitive to financial matters than their profitable cousins are. The difference between good and poor financial management in the former is reflected in dividend amounts and stock prices; the difference in the latter can mean existence or nonexistence. Yet the nonprofits virtually never consider themselves financially driven, as too many for-profits do. For-profits often base their thrust on and build their implementation around the singular goal of making x dollars net after tax, or showing y return on assets. Nonprofits, despite the critical nature of funding issues, tend to organize and implement by their perceived *missions*.

Lesson 1. If there isn't a mission—a purpose, a contribution to the environment—underlying implementation, then all actions will simply be focused on the bottom line, and short-term cost expediency will detour the organization from any longer-range objectives.

Clarity of Mission

Because the mission is so important—it represents the very essence of why the organization exists at all—nonprofits tend to be very precise and focused on what the mission should be. Ironically, the missions of nonprofits are often less grandiose and well-intentioned than those of for-profits, because reality and pragmatism are so important. The state Youth Soccer League seeks to provide organized, supervised, and constructive opportunities for youngsters to learn and practice the fundamentals of the game. (We've all observed the win-at-any-price coaches operating under the delusion that they're coaching a professional team. They have lost—or never accepted—the organization's strategy, and they represent true implementation failures.) The New York Zoological Association seeks to enhance

---

[5]As reported by Carol Kleiman, "New Management Posts Arise as Nation's Volunteers Abound," *Providence Journal*, Oct. 9, 1989, page D11.
[6]Ibid.

the public's appreciation of wildlife through the maintenance of its parks and gardens.

Lesson 2. The mission of an organization must start with the *external or outside* reasons for the organization's existence, not the internal rationale of generating a certain profit or return (or, for that matter, improving conditions for management and/or employees). The sequence begins with the end user and the contribution intended for that end user .

User-Friendliness

Not long ago, I tried to have a simple question about my home-owner's insurance coverage answered by Aetna. I had to make seven calls, was put on hold six times for a combined total of 20 minutes, was refused the number of the corporate office by the branch, was icily told by a customer relations person that "we have 24 hours to get back to you," finally had to settle for a call-back, and then received contradictory information ("you're covered," "you're not covered") within 10 minutes. I find this not to be unusual within the insurance industry.

On the local level, when we want to donate clothing to a charity, one phone call results in a truck showing up at an agreed-upon time. On a larger scale, every time I call the library of the American Management Association in New York I receive a prompt and immediate response, no matter how arcane or bizarre my question ("I'm looking for the publisher of a European business journal in London, but I can't recall the exact name"). In the Aetna case, my question was black and white and is probably asked on a regular basis. In the AMA case, my questions are usually peculiar and require specific investigation.

Lesson 3. User-friendly orientation combined with a clear focus on mission provides for easy evaluations of success at even the lowest implementation levels. Aetna employees seem to believe that their jobs are to shield executives from callers despite the policyholder's desire. AMA library staffers seem to believe that the organization wants them to answer questions specifically and immediately, no matter what effort is required. Are you delivering education or running a school? Are you providing transportation or manufacturing cars? Do you recall Kodak's position of providing memories, not making film?

Management of Change

In earlier chapters, we've covered the necessity of successfully anticipating, recognizing, and exploiting change and its treat-opportunity dichotomy. It is often difficult to change thrust and to challenge tradition. Nonprofits tend to experience much less angst in thumbing the organizational nose at tradition. Local baseball and soccer teams, the rare lawsuit notwithstanding, have embraced coeducational membership. The American Dental Association led the way in the profession's change of thrust from tooth restoration to the prevention of periodontal disease. And nonprofit fund-raising has been particularly innovative in generating participative alternatives ranging from auctions to raffles to antique shows.

Lesson 4. If the goal is simple and is easily kept in mind, the organization will more readily anticipate and/or adjust to change as the change is examined in relation to the goal. If the goal is unclear, complicated, or not believed, then protection and self-preservation will hold sway, a position that must fear change and threat to the status quo.

Acceptance of Advice and Guidance

Many for-profit organizations advertently or inadvertently insulate themselves from outside "interference." The problem, of course, is that the "interference" is often in the form of constructive feedback and criticism. The better organizations struggle to accommodate feedback from customers, employees, suppliers, and other interested parties. Yet "communications" is an issue that inevitably surfaces in employee surveys. And at the worst position, the very mechanism designed to guarantee outside feedback— the board—allows itself to be an organic rubber stamp. How else could one explain years of management incompetence at Eastern Airlines under Frank Borman or International Harvester under Archie McDonald?

Not only are nonprofits more sensitive to their ultimate users, they also tend to have boards that play key roles in counsel and advice. In fact, one of the greatest threats to nonprofits' effectiveness is that the board tries to be *too involved* and attempts to run the organization. But that is a more positive extreme than apathy or remoteness. Nonprofit board members tend to have a vested interest in the nature of the organization's work. They may identify closely with the goal, be key sources of resources, or indirectly benefit from that work; members of a board of education, for example, may fit all three. The cases in which an individual serves on a board of education to further political ambitions are rare, and those in which an individual serves are nonexistent.

Lesson 5. Outside advice, beginning at the board level and ending with the final user, must be organized and oriented toward operational realities. Determining *what* the organization is to do—the what of its strategy—is important, but it is no more important than evaluating the implementation —the how of its strategy. Otherwise, boards are forever engaged in the sublime world of abstracts and plans and never in the trenches of current reality. Eastern's strategy was probably extensively thought through and planned while operations, performance, and employee relations were going to hell. John Dewey was commenting on philosophy when he made this observation: "Better it is for philosophy to err in active participation in the living struggles of its own age and times than to maintain an immense monastic impeccability. Saints engage in introspection while burly sinners run the world."[7]

---

[7]From the author's personal collection.

The Involvement and Responsibility of the Work Force

Volunteers are no longer looked upon as "the only people we can get" with commensurate low expectations for performance. Indeed, one way in which nonprofits have handled budget squeezes is by reducing paid management staff and increasing the span of control of the remaining professional staff by delegating more and more responsibility to the volunteer force. Over our 22-year marriage, I've watched my wife's involvement in volunteerism for the various Catholic Churches she's attended grow in sophistication and results in the face of fewer priests and nuns to supervise and organize the activities. A recent fair at the local church raised $40,000 over a single weekend through the efforts of about 100 volunteers nominally managed by two priests and one nun. Lay people run the Sunday School, choir, CYO, and related activities.

Nonprofit staff members have been made *responsible and accountable,* sometimes because of inevitability, sometimes because of foresight. Whatever the reason, people at the implementor level feel intrinsically a part of the mission and its accomplishment and act in a duly constructive and positive manner. My neighbor recently visited me to solicit for the United Way. He enthusiastically detailed his involvement and belief in the organization's activities and asked for—and received—a higher pledge than I would have made had I been contacted by mail, telethon, or phone.

Lesson 6.   The road to growth is marked by the increasing productivity of the work force, not through automation, promotion, or mirrors (e.g., financial manipulation). Workers who are given substantial responsibility and authority, no matter what their level, will respond with generally sound judgment at the operating level and will tend not to create and enforce petty rules that generate artificial power to impede implementation. I've never met a volunteer worker who wasn't anxious to help me help them and would do virtually anything to accomplish that. Unfortunately, that is not the norm in most organizations, particularly among those in customer-contact positions. Even the polite and efficient repair person often must say, "I'd love to take your word that you have a service contract and verify it later, but our policy strictly says that I must see it before I begin work."

Lack of Bias

Nonprofits have readily embraced the young, old, handicapped, minority, and anyone else willing to work for the organization. They have lead the way, and continue to do so, in asking how a person's abilities can best be applied rather than asking how the organization's culture will react to a given person in a given position. For-profits are the weaker for having taken so long to accommodate women and minorities, even to the extent accomplished today. The wisdom and diversity sacrificed have been substantial, all for the name of tradition or the refusal to accept change or because of outright bigotry. Progress to more and more responsibility is based on competence and experience. It's unusual to find a charity manager who has not been a volunteer or a youth athletics director who hasn't served as a coach or official. There is seldom an old boy network to contend with, because every possible contribution is deemed valuable.

Lesson 7. If every employee and potential employee is seen as the provider of a vital and indispensable service, true worth will be better appreciated, developed, and rewarded. Organizational America is still far too bound by school ties, common roots, and xenophobia. It is ironic that in this, the most pluralistic of the world's societies, we have often tried to create and maintain conformist and sere business organizations. If human resource functions aren't in the forefront of this movement to ensure that the organization reflects the society around them, then I'm not sure what their justification for existence really is.

The Importance of Education

Nonprofits have developed career professions to reward ability and the desire for increased responsibility. In addition, they have consistently educated their volunteers not only about the immediate mission but also about the environment and the issues which pertain to that mission. Because of the importance of generally unsupervised individual contribution, such development has been particularly pertinent and effective. My neighbor was an eloquent and forceful spokesperson for the United Way when he visited. The Boy Scout volunteer leaders know the organization's practices and procedures exhaustively. The PTA fund-raisers go out armed with lists of prior contributors and likely new prospects in the community.

Too often, for-profits focus on training and not on education. What's the difference? Well, my dog is trained. He can sit, give me a paw, and even speak. But I can't discuss dogdom with him or find out how Alpo really compares to table scraps. He's trained but not educated. Animals are trained; people should be educated. I still remember the training director at a huge insurance company who showed me his matrix of training courses and managers. The more managers through the more courses, the more successfully he was evaluated. Was anyone being educated? Was anyone making connections between the training and the organization's implementation goals for its strategy? He assured me that such things were not his concern.

Lesson 8. The education of workers is an ongoing process that entails the relationships between one's daily actions and the goals of the company. This needn't be as esoteric as explaining to a bank teller how customer transactions relate to shareholder value, but it should demonstrate to the teller how his or her interactions with the customer create branch loyalty and enhance reputation. If development isn't related to organizational goals, then it is just arbitrary training and your employees will be able to speak but not necessarily make any sense.

The world of the nonprofits has been isolated for too long from traditional organizational America. There is far greater commonality than dissimilarity, but it is overlooked or underappreciated because the IRS doesn't tax it, the Department of Labor doesn't control it, and the Bureau of the Census doesn't count it. Yet about half of our total population is engaged in it.

One estimate calculates an annual worth from this labor of about $150 billion generated from 7.5 million full-time workyears.[8] To a great extent, nonprofit activity constitutes a "second government" in that many social services paid for through taxes and provided by the government in other countries are generated through nonprofit activities here. However, beyond any public service role, the nonprofits have demonstrated surprising—and highly effective—resiliency in the fact of changing times. Drucker[9] cites the Girl Scouts, for example, as an organization that has maintained its membership despite a 20 percent decline in school-age girls by marketing to a new segment: blacks, Hispanics, and Asians. As traditional organization become more involved in the nonprofit world—through their support, community actions, shared executives, and so on—they should make use of the opportunity to learn from the efficiencies of their poor cousins.

A typical organizational hierarchy looks like the top portion of figure 10.1. Even in well-run and well-intentioned organizations, communication suffers from the inevitable distortions of the Roman Legion structure, and the distance of the upper strata from the customers, applications, and relationships is significant (to the extent that special activities have to be devised to bridge the distance, e.g., "We're being visited by the executive vice president next week"). Organizations, cognizant of the drawbacks of such an antediluvian configuration, have tried to remedy the situation in one of two ways. As shown in figure 10.1, some organizations have adapted to their structures by establishing extraordinary channels for managers, workers, and/or customers to communicate directly with senior executives, and vice versa. This is a well-meaning but awkward attempt to retain a structure essentially established to exert strong, centralized control and conservative, multilayered decision making while adjusting to the need for more responsiveness in the marketplace. If it looks jury-rigged, that's because it is, and it might survive a light breeze. But any kind of gale at all will pretty much destroy the superfluous rigging.

The hallmarks of these structures are the periodic focus groups, employee surveys, customer surveys, face-to-face meetings, and the like, which provoke the employee response, *"Here we go again. . . . Why do they keep wasting money on these polls when they never listen to the feedback?"* The giveaway, of course, is "they." In a survey conducted for one client, the results were praised as "highly consistent," in that "poor communications"

---

[8]Cited in "The Culture of Competence," by Peter Drucker, *Success*, Sept. 1989, page 16.
[9]Ibid.

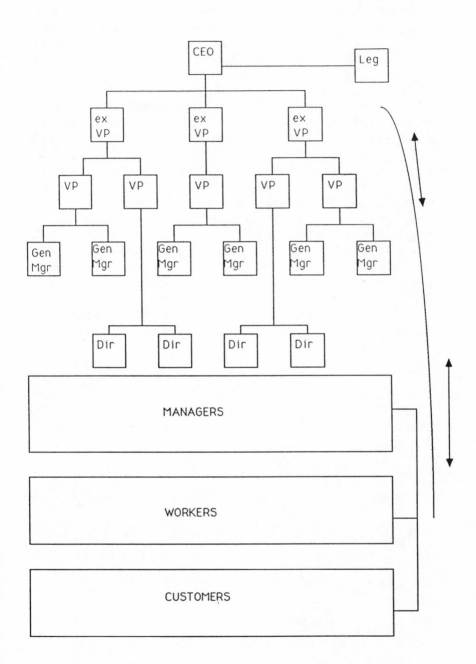

Figure 10.1

was cited as the area in need of greatest improvement. The client was quite content that nothing new had arisen to claim that spot and felt that things were under control because the results were about the same for the prior 3 years running! Of course, the client assured us that the communications issue was being "examined." Others have said "Communications will *always* be cited as a problem." (That is generally true, but it doesn't mean that attempts at improvement will be futile.)

Other organizations have tried a more radical approach, in that they've willingly abandoned the traditional hierarchy and adapted a variant of a matrix-type management structure shown in figure 10.2. Here the customers and workers are much closer to the upper echelon of the organization and the key operating managers are in touch with all the units requisite for meeting their responsibilities. However, matrix management creates its own headaches such as conflicting reporting obligations, conflicting interests, and competition over resources and priorities. In many cases, the same customer is called upon (by a salesperson, an advertisement, or some other promotion) by different representatives and entities of the same organization. A supermarket manager may see four or five different Procter & Gamble product salespeople; a physician might be asked for his or her time by two or three different field representatives of Squibb; and the consumer is regularly deluged with competing brands from one source.

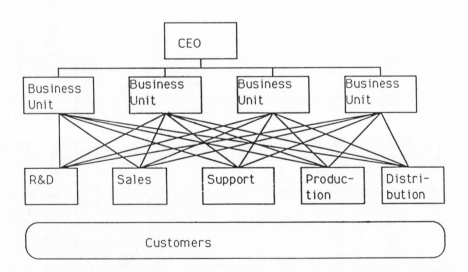

Figure 10.2

A typical nonprofit hierarchy is diagrammed in figure 10.3. There are two new features in the simple structure. First, the "customers," those who are to benefit from the services, "surround" the organization. They come from the same general pool as do the volunteers, in most cases, and as do the paid staff. Second, the board members also come from that pool, and, as mentioned above, are probably tied to it by legitimate self-interests. Hence, everyone involved in the enterprise is close to the product or service and close to the ultimate beneficiary. Communication among the board, executive director, paid staff, volunteers, and customers is simple and ongoing. Elaborate face-to-face meetings or executive visits are not required, nor are newsletters or house organs. Everyone collaborates on the basic nature of the business.

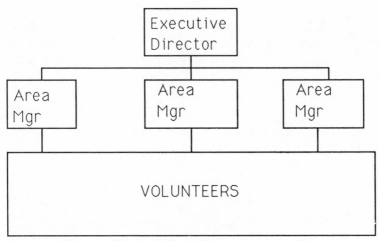

Figure 10.3

In terms of strategy implementation, which of the preceding diagrams presents the easiest structure in which to implement change? Figure 10.4 represents the bane of organization change. Decision making is multilevel; communication is easily distorted; and worst of all, a "thermal layer" is usually present. That thermal layer, which is shaded in the diagram, represents the ability of midlevel managers with vested interests in the status quo to effectively block any attempts at strategic change through their ability to:

- Control information and resources
- Determine local priorities
- Control local rewards and punishments
- Serve as exemplars
- Influence the "grapevine" and rumors
- Confuse issues (tell superiors one thing, subordinates another)
- Refuse to implement new practices

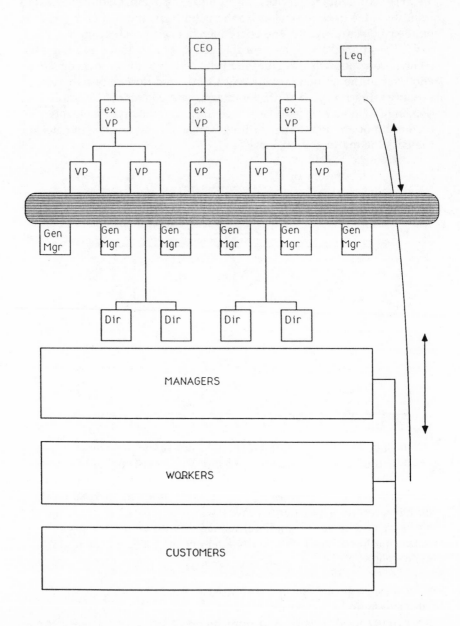

Figure 10.4

In the figure 10.4 type of hierarchy, an exceptionally strong senior management team must work exceedingly hard to overcome the thermal layer—and usually make some unpopular and difficult choices while doing so. Even with the attempts at direct links with customers and workers, an entrenched middle management can usually mortally damage strategic change with minimal effort (or noneffort).

The matrix hierarchy has different but significant problems as well. Strategy implementation requires clarity and continual reinforcement, as established in earlier chapters. Yet the nature of most matrix organizations, with deliberate ambiguities, multiple reporting relationships, and competing priorities, often obscures clarity and negates reinforcement. Our work with one matrix client brought forth this response from key middle managers: "It is premature to talk about our new strategic direction until we can understand our present one. We can't lead our people to a new vision when they haven't understood the old one." This meeting then focused on senior management literally drawing the present organization chart on a board so that everyone in the room could attempt to agree on what the existing organization structure and reporting relationships looked like!

Now envision the implementation of change in the nonprofit hierarchy. The "winds of change" are probably quite rapidly felt by everyone involved, since the entire structure is involved in its constituent area. Volunteers tend to understand the need for change because they are focused on the clear goal of the organization and their self-interest lies in delivering the organization's services in the most effective manner, not in preserving the status quo. When the soccer league determines that it will henceforth be coeducational, the United Way alters its relationship with the agencies it supports, the PTA determines that its future fund-raising should be oriented toward a capital fund, or the local temple decides to use its facilities as a forum for political groups, the organization and its paid and nonpaid staff are jointly aware of the need for change and acutely involved in making change happen. Attempts to delay or undermine change become readily apparent, and protesters are either persuaded or moved aside.

Of course, it's simplistic and irrational to expect that large and sophisticated organizations can convert to the simpler organizations of the nonprofits. But it's not unreasonable to expect that *any* organization, despite its size and mission, can learn from the advantages of short lines of communication, involvement of the board and the customer in active participation in the organization, and the need to take resolute action against those who would impede change to gain a personal advantage. In fact, we've deliberately oversimplified the relationships in this chapter in order to reinforce one central point: The implementation of strategy is not within the private preserve of traditional business and, in fact, may be best learned from nontraditional sources. Excellent strategies are often poorly implemented—making them look like poor strategies—because the nature, philosophy, and very structure of the organization mitigate against strategic change. That is especially true when individual short-term interests are in a position to subvert and damage organizational long-term interests. For their very survival, nonprofit organizations could not afford to let that happen. Now, for their very survival, traditional for-profit organizations may be in the same position.

Finally, there is less difference between the two than most people—and most managers—may realize. The nonprofits certainly haven't had the exclusive rights to providing beneficial services to mankind, nor have they been alone in their intent to make a constructive contribution to the environment in which they operate. It never has been a we vs. them proposition, and current trends would seem to indicate that the collaboration between for-profits and nonprofits will be greater than ever in the future.

The very title of this chapter, "Do Good and Good Will Follow," is an aphorism attributed to George Merck, who holds a near iconlike status at Merck & Co. This highly profitable, extremely successful, and widely admired organization truly believes that if it does well for its physician and patient customers, that appropriate profit will follow. And it has.

11

Strategy Under Siege: Implementation During Times of Crisis

Strategy implementation is simple in times of calm. One could even make the point that a strategy isn't needed in normal times or, if it is, can be implemented without interference. Of course, no one knows what "normal" is any more, and strategies have always been needed precisely because the one sure thing in life is that there *will* be change.

As I write this, the newscasters are speculating on today's market performance, since this is the First Monday after Friday, October 13, 1989, when the market dropped nearly 200 points. However, this hasn't presented quite the shock it might have, because the market has gained *over 1,000 points* since black Friday, October 1987, when the drop was over 500 points. Five years ago a market swing of 25 points made the front pages; now 40-point swings are reported in a hackneyed manner with the observation that "trading was moderate."

In times of accelerating change, it's sometimes tough to determine exactly what constitutes crisis. So perhaps we'd better define our terms, because there clearly are conditions that can derail the most carefully constructed strategy implementation.

"Crisis" for our purposes means "a crucial situation the results of which present critical consequences for the organization." Periods of organizational crises are potential turning points on which hinge the organization's near-term performance and, perhaps, long-term fate. The consequences can include:

- Financial performance
- Employee morale
- Image
- Credibility and trust
- Safety
- Competitiveness
- Market share
- Innovation and creativity
- Internal stability
- Ability to attract talent
- Expansion
- Technology

The criteria for a crisis situation include:

- The impact is at least business unit-wide, and usually organization-wide.
- Top management (and usually the board) must take direct action.
- The media and public are aware of the crisis and are following the outcome.
- Governmental or other regulatory bodies are usually involved.
- There is a threat to the organization's basic business.
- Significant legal action is generally threatened and/or required.

Here are six examples of crisis:

1. Audi had been besieged with chronic complaints about "spontaneous acceleration" of its top-of-the-line model, the 5000 sedan. There were some deaths and many reported injuries. In the United States, the issue became a *cause célèbre* of automotive safety groups, perhaps the largest-scale movement in the industry since the exploding gas tanks of the Ford Pinto two decades earlier. The charges were covered extensively in the press, from local newspapers to network shows such as *60 Minutes*. Audi steadfastly maintained its lack of culpability, and subsequent, independent investigations (see earlier notes) supported the company's position. Nevertheless, Audi's posture with the public—and its present and potential customers—caused tremendous damage and virtually destroyed all resale value of the model in question—even cars in perfect condition. Audi suggested that the drivers (purchasers of its top model!) were at fault. The company's sales and repute suffered grievously, and several years will be required for the consumer to put the issue aside.

2. Union Carbide experienced a horrible accident at its plant in Bhopal, India. The resultant deaths and injuries made headlines around the world. Subsequent investigations indicate that the catastrophe was probably caused deliberately by a disgruntled local employee. But Carbide's early waffling and *perceived* greater concern for financial and image considerations than for human suffering caused devastating damage to the company's repute—exactly the opposite of management's intent. When CEO Robert Kennedy traveled to Bhopal, after what many considered an inexcusable delay, the Indian government threatened arrest and he was, briefly, officially detained. Today, Bhopal is still synonymous with industrial tragedy, and only the intercession of the Chernobyl nuclear accident dimmed the public's memory. (It is interesting to consider the crises that have continually threatened Gorbachev's attempts to implement his strategy for the Soviet Union: Chernobyl, ethnic unrest, Afghanistan, democratization in Eastern Europe, shortages of staples, massive industrial strikes, and so on.)

3. What has entered the general lexicon as The Tylenol Crisis has also become Johnson & Johnson's and CEO Jim Burke's shining hours. Several instances of product tampering resulting in deaths galvanized the press and public within 24 hours. Immediately, however, J&J went public. Although even preliminary investigation pointed to localized criminal

activity and not product defect or factory sabotage, Burke personally went before the press and public and announced his organization's acceptance of its moral obligations. *All* Tylenol was recalled, at tremendous cost to both the bottom line and market share. The product was subsequently rereleased in tamperproof packaging (and, in fact, a new industry was born from that need), and ultimately even capsules were eliminated in favor of safer caplets (which are solid and can't be opened). Burke's accessibility and candor and his company's willingness to subordinate finances and ego to the public trust created a present-day faith in the company and its products that has entered the business school textbooks.

4. Kraft Foods, long the sponsor of high-quality television productions and a central figure in American consumer purchasing, offered a contest in which the grand prize winner would receive a van worth about $17,000 (see earlier notes). Because of an error made by the marketing firm (or printer or distributor, depending on whose finger is being pointed at whom), there were hundreds of van winners instead of just one. Kraft's immediate reaction was to void the contest. After hearing the outrage of the winners and the public in general, Kraft offered a modest cash award to all winners—plus inclusion in a special drawing to determine who *really* would win the van. Many lawsuits are still pending at this writing. And Kraft, ultimately dependent on the good name it has established for quality and trust as it places food on American tables, has received a tremendous black eye, not to mention venomous satire from all directions. Assuming that Kraft could obtain 200 vans at virtually dealer cost, and/or that many winners would just as soon accept a fair cash settlement, I estimate that Kraft could have honored all winners for about $2.5 million. And that, of course, would not only fit well within its advertising budget if used as a promotion but also acknowledge that Kraft's name and integrity are more important than taking refuge in a printer's error.

5. The Exxon Valdez will probably still be an issue with environmentalists and stand-up comics at the end of the century. Unlike J&J's Burke, Exxon CEO Lawrence Rawl couldn't even be *located* after the second day of the crisis. Exxon made several critical errors, such as relying too heavily on its existing communications with the locale, which turned out to be totally inadequate, and directing early press inquiries to a woefully information-starved two-person public relations office. But most damaging was the company's failure to accept responsibility and rapidly go public. The results were that Exxon fed the flames of the worst rumors and failed to capitalize on potentially mitigating circumstances (for example, the Coast Guard maintained that the Valdez's captain maneuvered very skillfully to avoid even more extensive damage after he found himself grounded). Exxon even failed to redeem itself by committing unqualifiedly to the cleanup effort, and was arguing with state and federal agencies about the quality of the effort and its future involvement after the winter halted current activities. The organization clearly decided to circle the wagons and let everyone take their best shots.

6. For over 2 years, Texaco management was engaged in lawsuits surrounding the Getty-Penzoil affair and takeover attempts by outside investors, most notably Carl Icahn. CEO James Kinnear, at this writing apparently past these events, is now trying to instill a new sense of innovation and excitement within the organization. Both his words—in every speech he makes—and his actions—initiating programs in innovation throughout the company—have served to reinforce his vision. By his own admission, during the trying times of lawsuit upon lawsuit, he and his top people were 100 percent involved in dealing with those crises and not involved in running the company. In our evaluation, Texaco was drifting, with middle management trying to simply protect current conditions and self-interest prevailing over organizational interest. Implementing a strategy that relies heavily on innovation and risktaking can be an insurmountable challenge following such a period of risk-averse behavior in what was, to begin with, an old-line autocratic organization.

There are scores of such crises to use as examples—from Three Mile Island to health problems caused by tampons to the sale of adulterated juice for babies overseas. No matter what the particular example, what can we learn about strategy and its implementation during times of crisis? Here are some guidelines that can serve to keep the rudder steady during real or perceived crises. And, like the sprinkler system or the fire extinguisher, these actions can be tested to see if they are in place and ready to be utilized at any time, *even though you hope you never have to resort to them.* This may be seen as a checklist of contingent actions.

1. Maintain normal implementation responsibilities (i.e., reviews, rewards, and so on).
2. Maintain some high-level visibility in the implementation process. Don't allow all executives to suspend their activities, and provide for at least some CEO involvement.
3. Respond to the crisis consistently with basic beliefs and key strategic inputs. The most significant aspect of all about Jim Burke is that he espoused and reinforced values and ethics long before the Tylenol scare made those beliefs and values so public.
4. Create a crisis management team that meets regularly to discuss potential problems and update its envisioned action. Designate responsibilities and accountabilities well in advance.
5. Anticipate and acknowledge that there will be threats to both the strategic vision and the organization's ability to implement that vision. Constantly canvass employees about what could go wrong and examine how you would respond, individually and organizationally. Every medical office I know of is able to respond to an emergency and still handle its patient load in some manner.

Have you ever observed a football team that falls behind early, loses its collective composure (read: the coach loses control), and abandons its game plan, with the result that even greater havoc follows? Or a pitcher

who, giving up a home run early, loses confidence in his traditional assortment of patient pitches and tries to force the fast ball through every time?
Or the golfer who tries more and more desperate shots after early bogies?
The goal is to stay on the same general strategic track, albeit with minor
course corrections, and not abandon one's route altogether. (This assumes,
of course, that the original direction was intelligently arrived at.) *Few crises
merit a reexamination of organizational strategy.* Crisis, on the contrary, is
generally a failure of implementation, yet, facing crisis, organizations tend
to change strategy rather than correct the implementation error.

Take a look at the six examples cited above. One could make the case that
every one was an implementation problem. Under scrutiny, only Texaco
might be classified as a basic strategic error, although one could just as
easily applaud the acquisition strategy while condemning the particular
alternative. (Subsequent court cases, decided after the Penzoil settlement,
support Texaco's position but don't apply retroactively. Consequently, even
the implementation might not have been as flawed as thought.) The key
is to use a crisis to further strengthen implementation and not to allow
the crisis to weaken implementation or, worse, subvert strategic direction.

As figures 11.1 to 11.3 illustrate, there are three possible postures to take
in regard to strategy implementation and crisis.

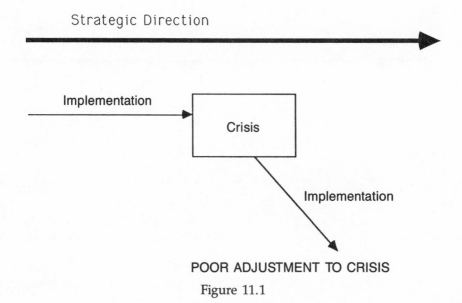

POOR ADJUSTMENT TO CRISIS

Figure 11.1

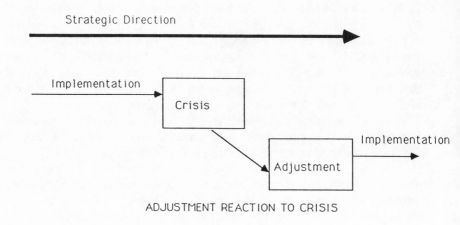

ADJUSTMENT REACTION TO CRISIS

Figure 11.2

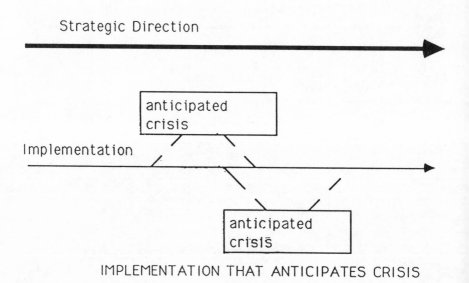

IMPLEMENTATION THAT ANTICIPATES CRISIS

Figure 11.3

1. The organization doesn't prepare for or anticipate crisis, with the result that advertently or inadvertently, the implementation is deflected from the strategic direction. The explosion of the space shuttle *Challenger*, for all the attention given to safety by NASA, left the organization in tatters with a fundamentally different strategy after the tragedy. Rather than a monthly, commonplace event, shuttle launches have reverted to being highly publicized research and military missions that once again are raising questions about the efficacy of a manned space strategy. (If the initial trip to the moon had ended in disaster, would we have abandoned all further attempts? Probably not. The public was much more sensitized to the danger and possibility of loss of life and safety considerations had, belatedly, become a paramount implementation issue.)

2. The organization doesn't anticipate crisis well, but it does adjust well when crisis occurs, with the conscious objective of maintaining an implementation thrust consistent with strategic vision. That is, the organization may be taken by surprise, but it is not derailed by the situation. Three Mile Island was an unexpected (though not inconceivable) disaster. Yet after all the accusations and hearings, Pennsylvania's General Public Utilities continues to provide nuclear power, Three Mile Island continues partial operation, and Bechtel has been cleaning up the damaged reactor. Debates about the safety of nuclear power aside (some authorities contend that the disaster itself proves that the industry can handle even the worst calamity, while others claim we were just a hair away from meltdown[1]). GPU made a substantial but apparently successful adjustment in retaining focus in the midst of one of the most horrible of recent crises. Texaco is struggling to regain its focus, as is Union Carbide.

3. Crisis is anticipated and, although not "taken in stride," is dealt with within the apparatus of the organization. J&J handled Tylenol consistently with its stance on values and ethics and, one would assume, consistently with the planning any pharmaceutical company engages in to anticipate product failure for any reason.

Another way to view crisis within strategic implementation is in the manner of occurrence and resolution shown in figure 11.4. Note that the key in this scenario is to resolve the crisis while heading back in the same direction as ongoing implementation demands, even if temporarily diverted. So even if taken by surprise and not having anticipated the crisis—and this will sometimes happen even to the most careful among us—the resolution process must leave you in the same general direction as when the crisis began to affect the implementation.

---

[1]Chernobyl lends itself to neither argument, because it is a type of reactor not used for commercial generation in the United States and is used at only one, old weapons facility here.

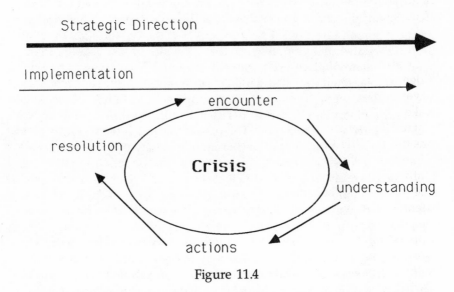

Figure 11.4

How can management anticipate crisis which, by its very nature, would seem to be unanticipatable? After all, if one could predict a crisis and prepare accordingly, it would hardly be a crisis. The San Francisco earthquake of October 1989 was a devastating event. Billions in property was lost; thousands were displaced; and over 50 people perished. Yet if it weren't for the collapse of the double-decked Nimitz Freeway (I-880), the death toll would have been fewer than ten. Subsequent investigation revealed that the Nimitz was known to be vulnerable to quake damage, had received some repairs in 1977, and was scheduled for more—postponed because of lack of money—at the time the structure failed. The fire and life loss in the Marina District was expected by the experts because the area is built on fill, which is the worst base in terms of resisting tremors. The quake struck on Tuesday, October 17, and by Monday, October 23, the city had returned to a virtually normal existence. Commuters proceeded to work, even with the Bay Bridge out of commission, by utilizing a toll-free (during rush hours) Golden Gate Bridge, ferries pressed into service, car pools, and the Bay Area Rapid Transit System. Not one modern, high-rise building sustained any damage worth mentioning, and the vast majority of San Franciscans went on about their lives. Emergency relief agencies, government disaster relief, and the philanthropy of the general public provided assistance for those worst affected.

San Francisco was prepared for crisis. Despite the notorious American indifference to any safety measure, from wearing seat belts to listening to the airline safety procedures prior to takeoff, the city's strict building codes, emergency preparedness planning, and past experience with lesser quakes made a huge difference. After all, the quake struck during rush hour and on the night of the third world series game, the first at Candlestick Park. The timing couldn't have been worse.

The Japanese are even more prepared, having experienced far worse quakes in modern times and with tightly packed populations and congested major cities, being far more vulnerable. Every Japanese citizen knows what his or her role in an earthquake is; every school child is drilled; and every bridge and building must meet the toughest codes on earth. Inevitably, Tokyo, San Francisco, and Los Angeles will experience even stronger quakes. But so will Memphis, Louisville, and perhaps New York (there is a fault line much greater, though less active than the San Andreas that runs through the Appalachians). What might happen to the latter cities?

If anyone can prepare for earthquake, war, death, or dread disease, is it difficult to imagine a business condition so dire that it defies anticipation? Amazingly, not many organizations take the time to think about potential crisis when they establish and implement their strategies. Someone might ask "What could go wrong with this strategy?" or "What might happen to interfere with our plans?" but those are quite different questions eliciting different responses. Management should be asking about *anything* that might gravely affect the business in the future, irrespective of whether or not the event is directly linked to the proposed strategy. In doing so, an evaluation should be made as to:

1. The *seriousness* of the event if it occurs.
2. The *probability* of the event occurring at all.

The combination of these two factors will provide a Crisis Quotient reflecting the overall threat that the event poses. Future crises have causes—the triggers that bring them into existence—and effects—the manifestations that adversely influence the enterprise. Probabilities refer to the likelihood of the crisis occuring—*in other words, the likelihood that a given cause will create the crisis condition.* Seriousness refers to the effects if, indeed, the crisis occurs—*i.e., to what degree is the result of the event going to affect us?* Yet when we consider crisis, what do most managers think in terms of?

Here's a quick test. Your CEO has convened the top management team and said, "We are here to consider a potential crisis for our organization. That crisis would be a fire in our major production facility, which produces 85 percent of our product. What actions do you recommend?" Indicate your responses here:

_____

_____

_____

_____

_____

_____

_____

_____

_____

_____

Compare your responses to the two lists below:

List 1
1. Have comprehensive insurance policies.
2. Create additional manufacturing facilities to spread the production.
3. Install state-of-the-art firefighting equipment.
4. Provide for on-site firefighters.
5. Create alliances with other firms to share production in emergencies.
6. Stockpile goods for use if production is interrupted.
7. Plans for emergency evacuation of personnel.
8. Fireproof areas in which essential materials, patents, and so on, are stored.
9. Draw up contingency plans for massive cutbacks during the rebuilding effort.
10. Procedures in place to appeal to government for emergency aid.

List 2
1. Hire full-time fire marshalls to patrol facilities.
2. Train entire staff in fire prevention techniques.
3. Segregate all stored flammable materials.
4. Adopt electrical and gas codes to exceed government recommendations.
5. Allow no smoking on the site.
6. Have a 24-hour security and emergency patrol.
7. Pay a bonus to every worker tied into plant safety and cleanliness.
8. Have quarterly meetings on fire safety for all staff.
9. Request tough inspections by local firefighters.
10. Review causes of all plant fires, and check for similar conditions locally.

Which list does yours most resemble? Or is it a combination of the two? List 1 is totally concerned with *effects*. It focuses on what is to be done *after* a fire occurs. That is the common mode for most managers, in that they generally think of effects and how to combat them. It's easier to think about effects because they can come from experience and are directly linked to events.

The second list deals exclusively with causes and their prevention. Causes aren't always so easy to link to events and, when they are, they tend to be the readily apparent ones. Everyone is generally aware that careless smoking can cause a fire, but who's responsible for checking the flammability of a new material that a vendor begins supplying?

In anticipating crises, it's important to consider both the cause and the effects of the event, because probability can be evaluated (and reduced) only by understanding cause, and seriousness can be assessed (and mitigated) only by comprehending effects.

To effectively anticipate a crisis and plan for it within the strategy implementation process, three sets of questions should be asked:

The event:

- What future events present a danger to our organization and its goals?
- What might happen internally to endanger our performance?
- What might happen externally to endanger our performance?
- What trends might evolve into business-threatening events?
- What instabilities would threaten us?
- What are the worst economic scenarios for our organization?
- What might threaten the most vulnerable aspects of our operation?
- What innovations or obsolescence would endanger our status?
- Whose loss might imperil us?
- What natural disasters might imperil us?

The causes:

- Under what conditions would this event happen?
- What would cause this event?
- How could this take place?
- What changes would lead to this?
- What distinguishing factors would have to be present?
- Would something have to fail for this event to be triggered?
- Is there a trigger mechanism?
- Why would this happen?
- Is this more likely to happen at some times than at others?
- Is this more likely to happen in some places than in others?
- What combination of factors would be responsible for this?

The effects:

- What would this mean to us?
- What is the worst that could happen?
- What are the market implications?
- What are the people implications?
- What are the financial implications?
- How much of the operation would suffer?
- What would be the duration of the effects?
- What are the short- and long-term competitive implications?
- What would recovery require?
- How much would it hurt?

By asking and answering these questions, we can establish:

1. What the events are that might endanger us
2. What the causes of those events are likely to be
3. What the seriousness of the event's occurrence is likely to mean

If we assign a measure—of any calibration—we can establish the crisis quotient. For example, after asking the cause questions we may determine that the event is at least a 50/50 possibility, so we'll assess it a 0.5P. And, in studying the seriousness questions, we determine that the effects would be highly damaging, knocking out 90 percent of our operation. We'll assign it a rating of 0.9S.

If, for our purposes, a 1.0P means that an event is guaranteed to occur (100 percent likelihood) and a 1.0S means that it is guaranteed to kill us (100 percent devastating), then our assessment of 0.5P and 0.9S represents a very serious crisis: It has a 50 percent chance of occurring and, if it does occur, it will nearly wipe us out. (This is the equivalent of betting nearly everything you own on either black or red on a single spin of the roulette wheel.)

Fortunately, we're only half done. The reason for separating cause from effects and probability from seriousness is that we are now in a position to prescribe *actions* which can become a part of our strategy implementation. In our example above, list 1 was aimed completely at the effects and list 2 completely at the causes. We want, in reality, to establish a healthy blend. Organizations have fire insurance and fire extinguishers as well as fire prevention programs and no-smoking areas. Ships incorporate the latest innovations in hull design and fire prevention, but they still carry lifeboats.

After assessing the potential crisis *and* assigning actions to try to eliminate the causes (prevent the event) and mitigate the effects (adapt to the event), we are left with a residual crisis quotient. It is this value that represents the true liability of the potential crisis, because ideally it reflects the remaining probability and seriousness *after* you have attempted to deal with each within the resources, abilities, and talents available to you at the moment. If the residual crisis quotient is high, you have only three choices:

1. Intensify your investigation, until reasonable actions can be determined to lower the residual crisis quotient.
2. Abandon or radically change the strategy implementation to reduce vulnerability to the events that are projected.
3. Accept the risk.

An example of situation 1 occurred when DuPont first developed its wonder material, Kevlar. Despite its tremendous versatility and potential, Kevlar provided a tremendous liability in that it contained potential carcinogens. DuPont, with an investment of $300 million, found a way to eliminate (reduce probability to 0) the problem. Situation 2 is represented by most moving firms, which absolutely refuse to transport flammable or dangerous materials in their vans. Despite the competitiveness of the market and the accent on service, the movers can't accept the risk and liability of a disaster during the transport of goods. Situation 3 was, literally, the *Titanic*. Because the builders were convinced that the preventive actions alone—the construction of the hull—were sufficient to prevent disaster, the mitigating actions—lifeboats—were woefully inadequate. People Express seemed to similarly roll the dice when it acquired Frontier Airlines. In general, situation 3 is the all-too-frequent resort of undercapitalized organizations, which can't afford to engage in the proper sets of actions. Unfortunately, it is also the inadvertent resort of "underconceptualized" organizations, which don't bother, through sloth, to consider the unthinkable.

Anticipating crises, as J&J did and Union Carbide didn't, can be systematized in the fashion of figure 11.5. Your strategy should never be in the position of being under siege if you organize your strategic thinking and implementation along the lines depicted in the figure. A siege mentality arises when an organization (and its management) is surprised by events and reacts defensively and inappropriately. Audi clearly felt besieged and acted like it: It was "us" against "them," except the "them" happened to be customers and prospects! J&J reacted as though "We knew such a thing might happen, although we certainly hoped it wouldn't, and we did everything we could to prevent it. Now, let's take action based on our joint interests."

Anticipating crisis need not be an ongoing endeavor, nor should it be a subject at every strategy implementation session. But it does merit a periodic review, and it demands review whenever strategy is changed. In fact, "crisis review" should take place under these conditions:

1. Your strategy is changing.
2. Your implementation is changing.
3. Crisis has struck elsewhere (and there are things to learn).
4. Environmental conditions take a radical turn.
5. Government regulations change severely (e.g., deregulation).
6. Economic and/or political conditions change severely.
7. Your key management changes personnel.
8. There is a technological breakthrough.
9. There is a radical change in public perception.

The last one on the list is as fickle as a spoiled child. Procter & Gamble suffered through accusations of "satanic" symbols on its products, for example, and I don't know anyone who will buy a used Ford Pinto. Braniff Airlines, recently in Chapter 11 for the second time, viewed condition 5 as a wonderful opportunity to expand without considering the crisis that overexpansion combined with increased competition from larger carriers would engender.

Crises usually provoke emotional responses. By anticipating them, however, an organization can safeguard its strategy from knee-jerk reactions by thoughtfully analyzing them under nonthreatening conditions. Ultimately, they can even be reduced to a quantifiable dimension for discussion

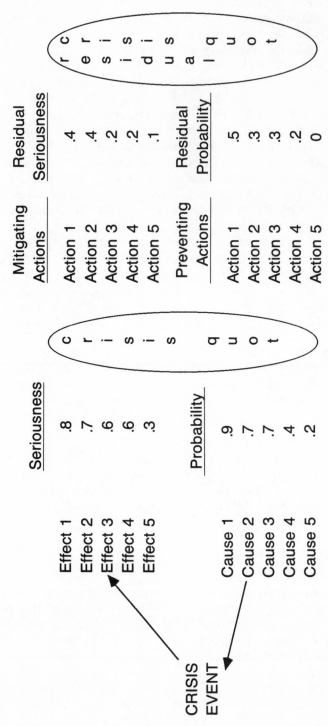

Mitigating Actions	Residual Seriousness
Action 1	.4
Action 2	.4
Action 3	.2
Action 4	.2
Action 5	.1

Preventing Actions	Residual Probability
Action 1	.5
Action 2	.3
Action 3	.3
Action 4	.2
Action 5	0

	Seriousness
Effect 1	.8
Effect 2	.7
Effect 3	.6
Effect 4	.6
Effect 5	.3

	Probability
Cause 1	.9
Cause 2	.7
Cause 3	.7
Cause 4	.4
Cause 5	.2

CRISIS EVENT

Figure 11.5

and analysis. Consider the scale of figure 11.6 for the residual values
arrived at above.

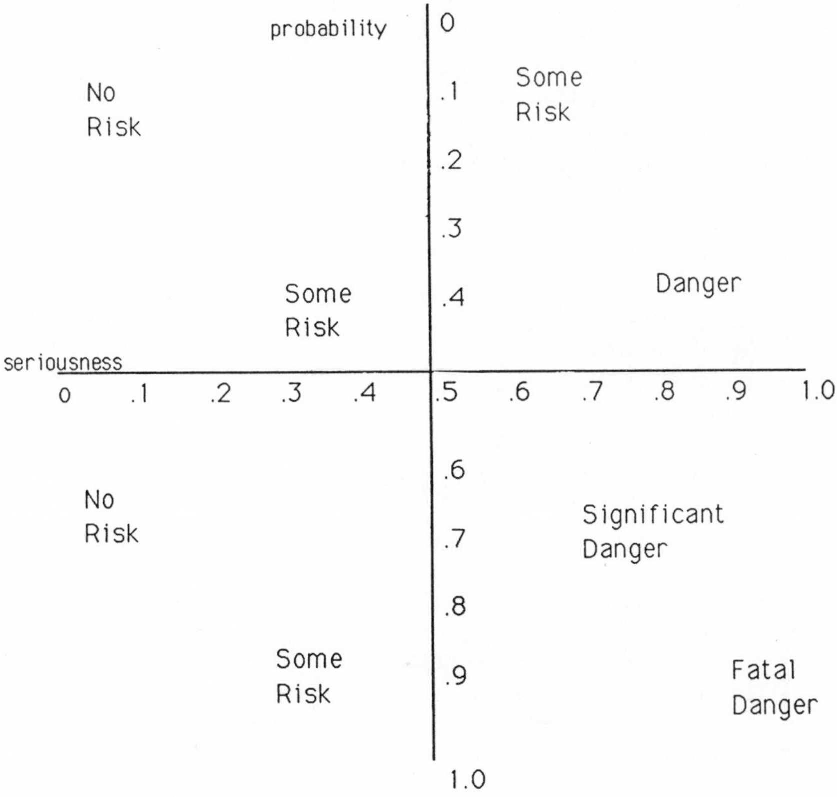

Figure 11.6

In the upper-right quadrant, for example, are the potential crises which
have high seriousness but fairly low probability. Remember, these are
residual numbers that reflect the outcome *after* all available and reasonable
actions have been taken. In general, no organization should choose to ex-
pose itself to anything in the bottom-right quadrant, and many choose to
avoid any situation which places them to the right of the vertical line at
all. (Note that these assessments are made on the basis of the governable;
i.e., nuclear war and 9.0 earthquakes are not considered.[2]) By using this

---

[2]Incredibly enough, when I began my career at Prudential Insurance in the late 60s I learned
of the company's plans from the late 50s to store triplicate copies of all transactions in abandoned mine shafts, with the intent on resurfacing and conducting business after the nuclear
holocaust. More recently, we've heard of plans from both the IRS and the postal service
to return to operations after nuclear attack!

or any similar systems of quantification, a management team can begin to intelligently prepare for crises and accommodate them as much as reasonably possible within implementation plans.

Crises are not, generally, the radically unexpected events falling on the organization like a ton of bricks. Most often, they originate in fairly familiar ground that you simply hadn't expected to tread. A few people did predict the stock market crash and, in any event, it had happened before. Airline deregulation took place with all the speed of a leisurely turtle. Aside from terrorist acts and totally unexpected product failure—or new diseases, such as AIDS—calamity isn't as sudden as it used to be. Here are examples of "expected" crises cited in a survey[3] of Fortune 500 executives:

- Industrial accidents
- Environmental problems
- Union problems or strikes
- Product recalls
- Investor relations
- Hostile takeovers
- Proxy fights
- Rumors and media leaks
- Government regulatory problems
- Acts of terrorism
- Embezzlement

Of actual crises reported by these respondents:

- 72 percent escalated in intensity
- 72 percent were subject to close media scrutiny
- 32 percent were subject to close government scrutiny
- 55 percent interfered with normal business operations
- 52 percent damaged the organization's bottom line
- 35 percent damaged the company's public image
- 14 percent of the 70 percent of reporting CEOs who were in place during the crises felt that their personal reputations had been damaged

Crises are usually brought on by management's own errors of commission or omission, and they are almost always exacerbated by those factors even if the origins are external. The Tylenol crisis is a glowing exception in that it was externally induced and management immediately contained and dampened it, but it is cited so frequently precisely because it *is* an exception. Bhopal was external, and it was then made worse by management actions, as was the Valdez disaster (at this writing Exxon is actually engaging in world-class audacity by suing the state of Alaska for cleanup

---

[3]*Crisis Management: Planning for the Inevitable*, by Steven Fink, AMACOM, New York, 1986.

costs, on the basis of the state's early refusal to allow use of chemical oil dispersants), as was Kraft's contest, as was President Reagan's trip to the Bitberg, Germany, cemetery which contained Nazi war dead. Braniff management incorrectly interpreted deregulation's impact on its airline's prospects, and American automakers refused to consider foreign competition until it was too late.

The implications for strategy implementation are clear. Successful implementation must include the provision for crisis contingencies, both the anticipated and the unanticipated crises. The questions posed earlier in this chapter are a good starting point. Anticipation of and reaction to a crisis must be accomplished within the scope of the strategic plan, meaning that discrete resources and people should be allocated and dedicated against that contingency. A crisis control team is no less important to have in place—with support and opportunities to practice—than is a fire control team. If all of top management is subsumed by crisis, the strategy will be also.

The final reason for taking such tangible steps is to preserve the quality of decision making. Crisis induces stress, and excess stress deleteriously affects decision making. This means that either top management gives short shrift to operating decisions within their purview or it ignores them, allowing alternatives to be chosen by default. That rudderless-ship syndrome can exist for prolonged periods, as it did at Texaco during the Getty and Icahn crises. There is a danger that it exists today within major airlines subject to hostile takeover and/or militant union action, which is why the federal government is taking a harsher approach toward safety and inspection.

By anticipating and planning for crisis within the strategic plan, decision making can be protected and the organization's ability to implement its future can be maintained. The difference isn't in simply losing ground; it's in losing direction altogether. Virtually every organization faces crisis at some point. Some organizations allow the crisis to change their direction, and they wind up in a port they hadn't prepared to enter. Others are able to maintain their headings, albeit a bit more slowly, and eventually reach their chosen destinations.

12

"Your Mission, Jim, If You Decide to Accept It..." Mission Statements vs. Mission Impossible

Strategy implementation revolves closely around mission statement. In fact, the mission statement, often an obscure and esoteric peroration on good to humankind, can serve as *the* driving force behind successful implementation. Organizations are much stronger when every employee can answer these questions easily:

- What business are we in?
- Who is our customer or user?
- What is our direction?
- What are our core products, services, and relationships?
- What changes are we deliberately making toward what end?
- What are we going to look like tomorrow?

These are simple but vital questions. Specific answers enable employees right down to the clerical level to act in a manner consistent with the organization's direction. (And, if they are not acting that way, supervisors are able to point out the discrepancy quickly and accurately: "I know you're trying to take care of as many people as possible, but our mission is to create a long-term relationship through personal care. Handle fewer people with more empathy.")

Try to envision an organization taking its daily cue from platitudes such as "We want to be a leader in our field" or "We seek to provide a positive environment" or "Our actions speak louder than words." Hershey is not in the business of "turning chocolate into edibles" and Bayer is not in the business of "making drugs." Vision must be interpreted in terms of goals so specific and worthy that employees can build their values around them. In fact, clear mission statements are required if the organization is to:

- Connect its core beliefs with the daily operating beliefs of employees
- Create the communication base that results in shared and clear goals
- Justify its strategy implementation alternatives
- Monitor and evaluate activities in view of that strategy

- Exploit the power of its resources by encouraging employee suggestions
- Evaluate prudent innovative risks
- Treat the customer in a manner commensurate with the direction

"Corporate culture" is a big phrase these days. But the establishment or modification of an organization's culture is not a semantic endeavor. Culture *reflects* beliefs, values, and direction. It is philosophical, not physical. Once established, the culture then guides decision making, particularly decision making that is intrinsic to strategy implementation. Thus, the culture becomes a self-fulfilling prophesy. "We make our houses, then they make us."

Mission statements may be broad, but they shouldn't be generic. They can be appropriate for the annual report, but they should reside in the memory of employees without recourse to three-ring binders, signs in the cafeteria, or quarterly management meetings. They *should* be reinforced, of course, but they should be able to endure without constant reinforcement (for example, through periods of crisis, as discussed in the preceding chapter). Now for the test. Write your organization's mission statement(s) below:

_____

_____

_____

_____

_____

On the assumption you've been able to articulate something, you might want to ask some colleagues or subordinates to write their impressions and then compare the results. Mission statements shouldn't be "in the same ball park." They should be in the same seat. Too often they're at different events.

A good mission statement explains why your organization is unique. It should encompass why you are different from competitors. In general, the test of a mission statement is whether it can be indiscriminately applied to other organizations. If it can be, it's probably either overly generic, and therefore useless in guiding strategy implementation, or it's the result of insufficient thought, which may well be applicable to the rest of the strategic process, as well. Here is a qualities checklist for clear and useful mission statements:

1. Is the statement for the longer term—sustainable for an indefinite period?
2. Does the statement distinguish your organization from others?
3. Does the statement specify some boundaries or scope?
4. Does the statement clearly stipulate image and/or customer/user interface?

5. Is the statement conducive to establishing values that guide behavior?
6. Are the products, services, and relationships reflected in the statement in some way?

How many of those questions are asked when a mission is being formulated? And how many missions are checked against them? The questions aren't lengthy or complex, but they are effective criteria for determining whether you are creating a mission statement that will assist, ignore, or deter effective strategy implementation. Ironically, they become more and more ignored as management becomes larger and more sophisticated.

Think of the lone-wolf entrepreneur who is beginning an airport shuttle service with a rented van. He or she has a vision of what the business is supposed to be doing, who it serves, why it has an advantage over the existing competition, and what key elements will support—and determine —not only its growth but its very existence. Steven Jobs knew his mission when starting Apple, and he was eminently successful at communicating it. Fred Smith did the same at Federal Express. It's not uncommon to hear Federal Express people tell of a pilot who restarted two flamed-out jet engines in midair and then calmly continued to the Memphis hub (rather than make an emergency landing) because the pilot's sense of mission was preeminent. (I have a theory that strong, clearly articulated and easily communicated mission statements generally create loyal work forces immune to the inroads of unions. Federal Express was militantly unionfree until the Flying Tiger acquisition caused problems.[1] Delta has always been the least unionized of the major airlines, and it is generally regarded as providing the best service. When people buy into the mission, their goals merge with organization goals, and "us" replaces "them and us." Most motivation approaches seem to focus on finding what motivates the individual rather than attempting the logical approach of creating a stake for the individual in the organization's goals.)

Perhaps large organizations might be best served by looking at themselves as if they were small ones, beginning ones, entrepreneurial ones, and asking the same questions that the van owner or Jobs or Smith asked. Mission statements evolve, of course, especially with the changing strategies of growing companies. But they shouldn't be revolutionary. Many organizations have allowed growth to become an enemy rather than an ally because the growth nudged them away from their original mission. People Express Airline is an illustrative case of growth overwhelming the original mission. People's mission statement surely would have included "reasonable fares to allow anyone the option of flying." Early, phenomenal growth brought increased flights, an appeal to the business traveler—who is more demanding about service and amenities—and, eventually, the acquisition of a conventional carrier, Frontier. The result was the demise of both. (Point of interest: People Express was not unionized; Frontier was.)

---

[1]See "Federal Express Corp.'s Fliers Reject Affiliation with Air Line Pilots Union," by Peter Waldman, *The Wall Street Journal*, Oct. 27, 1989, page A5. "Pilots of Federal Express Corp. voted to reject affiliation. . .giving a resounding victory to the company's founder and chairman, Frederick W. Smith."

So, although mission statements may change to reflect changing times, they should retain the philosophic core that set the organization apart from the competition from the beginning. Perhaps one of the reasons for the difficulty that AT&T had in competing in the deregulated world was that it had no such philosophy from the beginning. When you're the only game in town, you tend to be a broad thinker but not a deep one. It's no accident today that utilities, moving companies, airlines, and banks are all adopting mission statements that reflect their individuality in a competitive environment. "You have a friend at Chase Manhattan" was merely a clever advertising campaign that wasn't (in my experience) actually reflected in the treatment of customers. Treatment at Chase was no better and no worse than at any other major bank. But today, legions of private bankers are doing their best to make certain targeted customers fully aware that the red carpet is out. Last year, for the first time in my experience, a banker who is not a client of our firm but wanted us as *his* client took me to lunch.

Here's one authority's suggestion for what the components of the mission statement are, irrespective of changing times or changing fortunes:[2]

> As the business grows, the need may arise to redefine the company mission, but, if and when it does, the revised mission statement will reflect the same set of elements as did the original. It will state: the basic type of product or service to be offered; the primary markets or customer groups whose need will be served; the technology to be used in the production or delivery of the product or service; the fundamental concern for survival through growth and profitability; the managerial philosophy of the firm; the public image that is sought; and the firm's self-concept—that is, the image of the firm that should be held by those affiliated with it.

Pearce's formula is highly specific and, in fact, may be too limiting for some organizations. However, his final point is an important distinction: The mission should include self-concept, not merely public concept. This will guide not only incentive, feedback, performance measures, and the like but also hiring practices, succession planning, and identification of high-potential people—precisely the people who should be able to fulfill the organization's vision. We've worked with many organizations whose public images are vastly different from their internal ones. "We'll do anything to please the customer," assured one frustrated worker, "including step on the employees." United pleads with us to "fly the friendly skies" while flight attendants audibly bicker and complain about management's treatment of them.

Even when mission statements are lengthy, by nature of the business, a shortened version must be disseminated for employee guidance. In fact, I've never encountered a mission statement that couldn't be reflected in less than 50 words. Some examples:

---

[2]"The Company Mission as a Strategic Tool," by John A. Pearce, II, cited in *The Strategist*, published by Decision Processes International, Vol. 1, No. 2, Oct. 1989, page 11.

- Department store chain: We are a retailer serving the upscale female consumer with distinctive, high-quality merchandise in an environment of undisturbed personal attention.
- Trucking company: We will transport any legitimate customer goods within the continental United States in the most cost-effective manner possible.
- Insurance company: We are in the business of providing financial security to individuals and small businesses through a network of independent agents whom we will closely support.
- Chemical manufacturer: We manufacture the highest quality emulsions for use in the professional photography and medical x-ray fields.
- Hobby shop: We acquire and sell hard-to-find games and hobbies for the aficionado who has a passionate interest, and price our services based on the value of our products and unique service.
- State motor vehicle agency: We help people to obtain licenses and registration papers in accordance with the law and promote safe driving habits.
- Appliance manufacturer: We produce toasters, irons, and coffee makers for the mass market and discount retailers, providing the lowest cost product possible while meeting all product safety and underwriter's minimum requirements.
- Film and camera manufacturer: We provide our users with the ability to create memories of the important moments of their lives.
- Overnight delivery service: We will guarantee that any package we accept will get to its chosen destination by a promised time the next day, without qualification, exception, or error.

Perhaps the most famous mission statement of all is from a government institution. It simply and eloquently states: "Neither rain nor snow nor gloom of night shall stay the mail carrier from the swift completion of his appointed rounds." Of course, the postal service has been accused of not living up to the mission statement, and there are two schools of thought on the subject. One holds that the postal service is a lumbering bureaucracy that proceeds at its own pace no matter what and is more concerned about employees' well-being than the public's (it has one of the country's largest and most militant unions). The other is that the mission statement is pretty well met, since the great preponderance of all mail arrives where it is supposed to when it is supposed to, and the cost of a stamp in the United States remains one of the great bargains in the industrialized world.

Sometimes a mission can be *too* all-consuming. Domino's Pizza has been known for its commitment to "deliver the order within 30 minutes, or it's free." Over the past 2 years, concerns have been raised about the safety record of Domino drivers, and the question whether or not the mission overwhelmed basic safety considerations has been debated. As a result, Domino's put its mission into perspective by intensifying driver safety training and changing its guarantee to a $3 rebate if the delivery is late.

(Although it abandoned the advertising slogan, Federal Express has never had to back off its "absolutely guaranteed to get there the next day" promise.)

Sometimes missions can be *over*simplified. For example, one early states-man was fond of pointing out that the government has only two missions: to protect the coasts and to deliver the mail. Yet Rider has been effective with "We rent trucks." The mission statement has to be appropriate to the conditions and environment of the organization and its market. That's management's primary duty in creating, supporting, and fulfilling the mission statement. Strategy implementation should be embraced by it, not operating in isolation or, worse, opposition to it.

Some aspects of a mission statement are assumed and inherent. For example, every organization seeks to survive, to reward its shareholders and/or stakeholders. (Theoretically, an organization engaged in finding a cure for cancer would seek to go out of business. Yet any organization takes on a momentum and *raison d'être* of its own. For example, the March of Dimes quickly went on to other fund-raising activities once a cure for its original cause, polio, was found.) In most organizations, profit and return on invest-ment (or equity or sales or assets) will be a part of the mission statement. Here is a mission statement from Hewlett-Packard, one of our clients:

> Objective: To achieve sufficient profit to finance our company growth and to provide the resources we need to achieve our other corporate objectives. In our economic system, the profit we generate from our operations is the ultimate source of the funds we need to prosper and grow. It is the one ab-solutely essential measure of our corporate performance over the long term. Only if we continue to meet our profit objective can we achieve our other corporate objectives.

Survival requires profitability and, in most cases, some type of growth. Hewlett-Packard goes on to say growth be limited "only by our profits and our ability to develop and produce technical products that satisfy real customers needs." When you talk to H-P people in the hall or at a meeting, they are all crystal clear on the kinds of products they provide, their customers, and the role of profit and growth within that context. Although quotas and sales performance are important, they are tempered by the clients, products, and quality missions of the organization.

What about the other side of that coin? Do clearly worded and communi-cated mission statements tend to *inhibit* strategy implementation by delimiting options and discouraging innovation beyond certain bounds? Is there room for too many interpretations or even an excuse *not* to adhere to some of the requirements for strategy implementation?

Mission statements are flexible in that they can specify conditions under which the organization will depart from certain norms and requirements. For example, "We will make acquisitions outside our basic business if those acquisitions represent opportunities to significantly increase the invest-ment we are able to make in our core business, and if the acquisition is compatible with our core business and self-concept." Or, "These are our priorities for growth:

1. Increase existing products and services in existing markets.
2. Introduce new products and services in existing markets.
3. Introduce existing products and services into new markets.

We will undertake these efforts in this priority and will not move to the next step until profitability and self-sufficiency are established in the prior step. We will not undertake to provide new products and services in new markets under any conditions."

The mission statement may be seen as the leading edge of the organization's culture—a concise explanation of what the organization stands for and where it is heading. It is a relatively simple tool, really—just a few sentences or less that sum up the organization's values and goals and allow strategy to be implemented within those parameters. Yet relatively few organizations bother to take the time to develop them, and many more accept the platitudes and hackneyed phrasing of the bland. There are three basic tests for a successful and accurate mission statement:

1. It represents general consensus. There is little debate or argument about it from any quarter.
2. It generates enthusiastic support, not forced commitment. There is emotion behind it. Adhering to the mission is important, and violating the mission statement immediately raises cultural sanctions.
3. It can be used inside and outside the company with consistency and clarity.

General Consensus

Employees at all hierarchical levels must buy into the values and goals expressed in the mission statement. Every time you hear postal workers complaining about having to work certain shifts, deliver special delivery mail, or brag about finishing a route at noon and hiding for the rest of the day, you are observing an organization with a lack of buy-in. (Please don't send me letters. I know that many postal workers are conscientious and are committed to good service, but I also used to work in the post office and watched people beat the system as a daily challenge.) I've been in a utility company that placed a high emphasis on its mission of top-quality customer service only to find customer service representatives giving short shrift to callers. "If management cares so much about customer service," one employee asked, "then why are we the lowest-paid and worst-treated unit in the company?"

On the other hand, the American Express customer service representative who arranged for a replacement card to be shipped out via overnight courier after a short phone conversation has, indeed, bought into "membership has its privileges." Every organization will (and should) have its share of debate and conflict. But these debates and conflicts should revolve around how *better* to meet the mission statement that everyone has agreed on, not on whether the mission statement is appropriate or, worse, how to circumvent it. Part of Merck & Co.'s mission is to act with the highest degree of ethics and integrity. In a survey conducted for the entire U.S. field force, *only one respondent in a thousand indicated disagreement with that statement.* There's considerable discussion about *how* to resolve the many ethical challenges the organization faces, but virtually no one at any level disagrees with the mission.[3] The debate may be about alternatives to reach the goal, but it should not be about the goals themselves.

Enthusiastic Support

Not long ago our office postage scale died. We called Pitney Bowes, the supplier, and were advised by a client service person that the scale was nonrepairable because of its construction, was not covered by a service contract because we had purchased it rather than rented it, and was for all intents and purposes, worthless. We talked to the local manager, and he, with tact and care, explained the same thing. We called customer relations in headquarters, and a senior manager, with even more tact and greater care, supported the prior position. So we sent a letter to the president of Pitney Bowes. Three days later the local manager called to say he was delivering a new scale at no charge and hoped we would be happy with that resolution.

The president, of course, not only understood the mission of superior service, he enthusiastically supported it. His subordinates—three of them at various levels—understood the policy and thought that their careful and polite explanations were sufficient. (The scale costs about $125.) If you think about it, you can probably place restaurants in which you've dined and had problems into two categories: Those in which the waiter immediately resolved your problem by bringing a new meal or deleting a charge and those in which the manager had to be summoned. Often this is a case of who has the *authority* to take remedial action, but that, too, is an indication of whether the organization is permitting its people to support its position enthusiastically or is advertently restraining them through delimiting policies and procedures.

Comprehensive Use

I've never heard of an instance in which an organization's mission statement couldn't be shared with customers, and it's incomprehensible to imagine one that can't be shared with employees (assuming the organization is involved in a legitimate business). In fact, the more the public is aware of the mission statement, the more the organization and its people will be forced to live up to it. I recall a Federal Express supervisor calling me to explain that a package had been inadvertently left off its intended flight. "We can," she said, "go to the trouble of sending it on a commercial, direct flight [not through their hub] and have it picked up by courier if it's urgent. Or we can send it by the traditional means and it will get

---

[3]"Ethics and Values Survey" conducted by Summit Consulting Group, Inc., June–July 1989.

there on the second day." My office manager responded, "But we use Federal Express precisely because you guarantee overnight delivery. Why would you even think of asking us if we want it there a day late?" The supervisor replied with a "No problem—it'll get there tomorrow." And that was that. The more public the statement, the more the public can hold the organization's feet to the fire.

Many organizations hide their mission statements from their employees and their customers. And then they wonder why their strategy isn't implemented.

Shared expectations—as consolidated and symbolized by the mission statement—are affected by elements such as the degree of employee participation, the role of management as exemplars, feedback loops, and reward and reinforcement. These elements have been discussed in prior chapters, and they apply directly to the formulation, communication, and acceptance of the mission statement. The danger of not deliberately realizing this sequence is that employees will infer a mission statement in any case. They will pick up cues from the environment, and not only will their perceptions dictate what they think the mission statement is but their ensuing actions may dictate what it actually becomes. Consequently, we may say that the process of formulating a mission statement progresses irrespective of whether the organization chooses to consciously control and influence it! When the organization does not influence the process, and management actions cannot be perceived as a coherent force or direction, it's quite common to hear:

"In this place, it's every man for himself."

"Whatever you do, protect yourself."

"Don't take any risks."

"Pass on customer problems to someone else—you can't win."

"Don't volunteer."

And the mission statements, by default, become:

"We are here to conduct our business with a minimum amount of disruption. Innovation and risk taking will be punished, and should be avoided. Don't settle customer complaints, pass them on so you can't get blamed."

Sound outlandish? Have you ever tried to reconcile a problem with virtually any government agency or get the telephone company to fix a problem rapidly? Bureaucracies don't spontaneously spring to life. They are not configurations normally found in nature, nor are they evolved designs of efficiency. Bureaucracies are the cumulative result of powerless people whose mission includes ultimate safety, avoidance of risk, refusal of responsibility and accountability, and a philosophy of "it's not my job." No one in an organization that features high commitment to explicit missions statements ever says, "It's not my job," do they? They say "Let me see how we can get this done," or "I'll get the person who can help you right now."

Charles O'Reilly, of the University of California,[4] cites four steps that a manager can take to attempt to mold and support consensus:

- Identify strategic objectives, then specify the short-term objectives and critical actions they require.
- Analyze the organization's existing norms and values by focusing on what people feel is expected of them (by peers and bosses) and what actually gets rewarded. What does it take to get ahead? What stories are routinely told? Who are the people who exemplify the group? Look for norms that are widely shared and felt.
- Once the norms have been identified, search for norms that may hinder accomplishment of critical tasks, norms that would help but are not now present, and conflicts between what is needed and what is currently rewarded.
- Once the conflicts are identified, design programs to start shaping or developing the desired norms.

Social influence systems are operating in every organization. It's management's responsibility to understand them and to determine whether they are in concert with the mission statement or not.

Mission statements made public "force" an organization to conform with its strategic vision; that is, implementation will be guided by external as well as internal forces in a manner consistent with the organization's direction. For example, Cross Pens manufactures high-quality, professional writing instruments. When pens are given for gifts, the Cross brand is regarded as a sign of very high quality and, consequently, thoughtfulness in the gift. The company has a lifetime guarantee that it scrupulously honors, even when its pens have been subjected to nontraditional challenges, such as supporting the weight of a 2-ton vehicle or serving as diversion for an 85-pound German shepherd.

If Cross were to market a 98-cent disposable pen, it would encounter problems from the public, with both its new product and its old one. (Recall that in an earlier chapter we cited Caterpillar Tractor's problems in the asphalt business, when customers expected Cat quality but didn't want to pay for it.) Bally makes fine leather goods, BMW fine automobiles, and Head fine skis. The marketplace expects nothing less. Mission statements should embrace public perceptions whenever the perceptions are intrinsic to the success of the strategy (and they usually are). The result is that marketplace forces will assist in adherence to the mission statement and will provide unmistakable signals to management whenever the mission is being violated.

Eastern Airlines got the message. Postbankruptcy Eastern, in the midst of a continuing and bitter strike, gradually rebuilt its schedule around on-time performance and passenger service, two elements that were generally

---

[4]"Corporations, Culture and Commitment: Motivation and Social Control in Organizations," by Charles O'Reilly, *California Management Review*, Summer 1989, pages 9–25. Cited in *Behavioral Sciences Newsletter*, Oct. 23, 1989, Book XVIII, Vol. 20, pages 2–3.

missing from Eastern's operations in the preceding decade during both good times and bad. The employees clearly bought into the mission—pilots, ground personnel, and cabin attendants were lavish in their appreciation for my business, stressed their concern with getting the flight off on time, and reminded me of "another on-time arrival." Eastern media ads cited Eastern's top ranking for punctuality. At this writing, Eastern Airlines has a work force and performance record as fine as those of any domestic carrier. Prior to its resurgence, I did everything I could to avoid flying it (and that included one fortunate 6-year stretch in a career of constant travel).

Having arrived at this point, and taking the guidelines provided in this chapter thus far, let's try our opening exercise again, but in a slightly different vein. Write below what you believe your organization's mission statement *should be:*

_____

_____

_____

_____

_____

How well does it answer these questions:
- What business are we in?
- Who is our customer or user?
- What is our direction?
- What are our core products, services, and relationships?
- What changes are we deliberately making toward what end?
- What are we going to look like tomorrow?

How effectively does it accomplish these ends:
- Connect core beliefs with the daily operating beliefs of employees.
- Create the communication base that results in shared and clear goals.
- Justify strategy implementation alternatives.
- Monitor and evaluate activities in view of that strategy.
- Exploit the power of varied resources by encouraging employee suggestions.
- Evaluate prudent innovative risks.
- Treat the customer in a manner commensurate with the direction.

How completely does it meet the criteria in this qualities checklist for clear and useful mission statements?
1. Is the statement for the longer term, i.e., sustainable for an indefinite period?
2. Does it distinguish your organization from others?
3. Does it specify some boundaries or scope?
4. Does it clearly stipulate image and/or customer/user interface?
5. Is it conducive to establishing values that guide behavior?
6. Are the products, services, and relationships reflected in some way?

How well will it achieve these three keys?

1. It represents general consensus. There is little debate or argument about them from any quarter.
2. It generates enthusiastic support, not forced commitment. There is emotion behind it. Adhering to the mission is important, and violating the mission statement immediately raises cultural sanctions.
3. It can be used inside and outside the company with consistency and clarity.

The absence of mission statements that are deliberately created, consciously communicated, and conscientiously reinforced by management will create a real mission impossible. As dramatic as their exploits are, no one wants to have to bring in commandos and explosives experts to ensure the success of strategy implementation. The mission statement cuts through the heart of the operation, keeping everyone on track as implementation progresses.

The mission statement keeps the organization on track, especially when implementation may be rocky or interrupted. It is consistent with strategic vision, but it is oriented toward the realities of day-to-day operations. It links what employees at all levels are doing today and what the organization wants to look like tomorrow. It is the common challenge that, when asked of everyone, "Will you accept it?" the common response is "Absolutely!"

This is how effective supporters are created and nurtured. Let's now turn to what is required of the effective leader.

13

I Like to Lead When I Dance: Leadership and Strategy Implementation

I once heard Bill Ouchi, creator of Theory Z management, tell the ultimate leadership story at an executive conference. He cited Moses, attempting to lead his people out of Egypt and out of the slavery imposed by the Pharaoh.

Lost, hungry, and confronted with the Red Sea, Moses received word that the Pharaoh had changed his mind and had dispatched his army to recapture the Hebrews. Moses looked at the Red Sea and realized that boats would be the salvation. So he found Abraham along the bank and proposed his idea.

"You see, Abraham, with boats we could get our people across the sea before the Pharaoh's troops arrive."

"Moses," said Abraham, "I'm a philosopher. I can discuss with you the metaphysical aspects of being lost and hungry in the desert, but I can't help you with boats."

Moses now came upon Joshua and repeated his idea about boats.

"Moses," proclaimed Joshua, "I'm a general. We will make our stand here and throw ourselves at the wheels of the Pharaoh's chariots! It will be glorious."

Moses now felt somewhat desperate for boats, and he found Jonah, who was Moses's PR man. Jonah wasn't helpful, however.

"Moses," explained Jonah, "I'm the public relations guy with this outfit, and I don't know anything about boats."

"That's it," exclaimed Moses. "If no one chooses to help build boats, I'll simply throw up my arms, part the Red Sea, and we'll escape across its bottom to freedom!"

"Now you're talking," shouted Jonah. "I can't help you with boats, but you do that and I *will* get you ten pages in the Bible!"

Leadership comes in every shape and flavor. There are those who proclaim a "perfect" leadership style that all of us should aspire to, which will be effective in any situation. Approaches such as the management grid have advocated a 9.9, or high attention to both task and people, as its favored style. Then there are contingency models, such as those advocated by Fred Fiedler, which focus on the interactions between leadership style

227

and the situation and the effects of power and influence. Hersey and Blanchard have been proponents of situational leadership with stress on the maturity, abilities, and motivation of those being led. Victor Vroom has been among the leaders of normative models, which emphasize a range of behaviors that are available to the leader and depend on such issues as quality, commitment, and time available.[1]

We also have the business-person-as-guru syndrome. We can learn—through books, tapes, or seminar attendance—how Lee Iacocca views management, what Augustine's laws are, how to swim with sharks and, generally, how to emulate the business superstars. The problem with these approaches is that, although they would seem to have to be the most pragmatic and least academic, they are usually intense rationalizations. That is, a successful business person retrospectively looks at his or her business history and constructs those elements—or that philosophy—which he or she believes created the success. This is akin to George Bush citing his life-long belief in "a thousand points of light" as the key to his cumulative success and people attending points-of-light seminars to try to learn the skills! (Actually, it sounds like a reasonable pursuit while practicing fire-walking.)

At one point in my career I was president of a company owned by the millionaire philanthropist, W. Clement Stone. Stone made his fortune in insurance sales as a younger man, deliberately or fortuitously, found some financial people who were able to leverage his outstanding results into a considerable fortune. As he reflected on his success later in life, he became convinced that his positive mental attitude, PMA, was actually responsible for his success. In fact, that PMA was the *result* of his financial independence and the freedom, philanthropy, and life-long learning it supported. But Stone insisted on launching companies, publications, and seminars based on his PMA philosophy, not one of which ever made a dime while I observed them, and not one of which provided an ounce of hard skills to transfer to would-be participants.

Leadership is mostly art with a soupçon of science. Although Bennis[2] and others claim it is a learnable skill, I would interpret their data to mean that leadership is an understandable activity, which is something quite apart from a learnable skill. I can understand how Larry Bird maneuvers to successfully make a jump shot, but it's no learnable skill as far as I'm concerned. Similarly, most executives and managers can understand what Iacocca did at Chrysler (or Bill Gates at Microsoft or Ed Colodny at USAir),

---

[1]See any of the following: "Group Development and Situational Leadership: A Model for Changing Groups," by K. H. Blanchard et al., *Training and Development Journal*, June 1986, pages 46–50; *A Theory of Leadership Effectiveness*, by F. E. Fiedler, McGraw-Hill, New York, 1967; *The Managerial Grid*, by Robert R. Blake and Jane S. Mouton, Gulf Publishing, Houston, 1964; *Leadership and Decision Making*, by Victor H. Vroom and Philip W. Yetton, University of Pittsburgh Press, Pittsburgh, 1973; *Organizations: Behavior, Structure, Processes*, 6th ed., by James L. Gibson et al., BPI/Irwin, Homewood, Ill., 1988.
[2]*Leaders: The Strategies for Taking Charge*, by Warren Bennis and Burt Nanus, Harper & Row, New York, 1985.

but most could never replicate it. Zaleznik, a pole away from Bennis, contends that leaders are born, not made, and there's not much more to talk about.[3]

We are going to focus on a specific facet of leadership: leading the implementation of a strategic vision. There are two aspects of such leadership, push and pull:

1. The pulling role is that of exemplar and front-stage person. This is not necessarily the infantry officer personally leading the troops over the top, instead it usually is the steady, always accessible, continually visible executive or manager who exemplifies the role and values involved in the strategic direction. The management of values may be the single most important element in this role.

2. The pushing role is that of supporter, cultural change agent, and backstage person. This is the generally invisible effort to modify and influence the reward, feedback, compensation, and other systemic procedures so that they support the strategy and the efforts of the people engaged in its implementation.

The effective leader of strategic change should be actively involved in both roles—visibly demonstrating the direction while quietly ensuring that the organization's momentum supports it. It's the difference between the front wheel of the bike, which sets direction, and the rear wheel, which provides the real power. As you can readily imagine, all the power in the world from the rear wheel will be useless or worse if the front wheel isn't headed in the intended direction. And the most refined and accurate direction will do little good if there is no power to take you in that direction.

There are two equally troublesome extremes: to be pointed in the right direction with no headway, and to be traveling at a ferocious pace in the wrong direction. There is also the fire engine direction, symbolized by the hook and ladder. If you recall those vehicles, they require a driver—a tillerman—in the rear, to steer the back wheels while the conventional driver steers the front wheels. Many organizations unwittingly assume this configuration, which occurs when the same leader doesn't take responsibility for both direction and support. The main body of the organization may take on a will of its own. Not only will it fail to negotiate sharp turns and changes in the course, but even straight and level movement will become tricky and filled with risk.

So the leadership of strategy implementation is a dual role, and it is one that requires technique, finesse, and generous use of intuition and emotion. This leadership should be an effective bridge that connects the current organization with its future:

> "Demonstrating to subordinates a well-thought-out business strategy...means communicating connections between current accomplishments, available resources and goal attainment. It means, for example, proposing plans for

---

[3]*The Managerial Mystique: Restoring Leadership to Business,* by Abraham Zaleznik, Harper & Row, New York, 1989.

product development, financing, advertising, etc. with clear descriptions of who is responsible for what. That may require broadening job descriptions, creating new teams, hiring new experts."[4]

Here are ten traits for front-wheel and rear-wheel leadership. The more of these you can master, the more likely you are to stay on the bike. And, like riding a bike, once mastered, these traits are seldom lost despite the environment, conditions, or people involved.

Front Wheel or Direction Traits

1. *Serve as an exemplar.* I pointed out earlier that people believe what they *see* and not what they hear or read. The strategic leader must be an unerring example of how people are to act in implementing strategy. That doesn't mean never making an error; instead it means never deviating from the established direction despite short-term pressures or seemingly contradictory self-interests.

Example: If the strategy dictates that customer service is to be a key emphasis area and all managers are to be evaluated on the basis of their customer responsiveness, the leader should spend time in customer service on the phones, sit in on (or run) customer focus groups, and carefully rate his or her subordinates against the criteria. Such actions give everyone a clear vision of how they are to act. The executive who cites an overloaded schedule as an excuse not to visit customer service or who rates subordinates on different terms because "they have special responsibilities that make customer service evaluation impossible" is exemplifying either how unimportant the goals are or how uncommitted he or she is to them. Lack of commitment is very common. Often it is encapsulated in a coterie of managers winking at each other after a policy pronouncement: It was for the troops but not for them.

2. *Manage values.* Linked closely to the role of exemplar is that of managing values, arguably one of the most important jobs any manager performs, strategic change notwithstanding. To manage values means to visibly reward the values, beliefs, and behaviors that support the strategic direction and to frustrate, discourage, and, yes, punish those who detract from it. Values are internal, but their management is purely external and requires constant vigilance.

Example: In an organization placing emphasis on answering on the same day every piece of customer correspondence that is received prior to 2 P.M., a division manager finds that his people often must spend an hour or so past quitting time to clean things up. He notes that another division, clearly visible across the hall, quits at precisely 5:00 every day, even though some customer correspondence that should have been answered hasn't been. The manager does three things:

---

[4]"Question: What Is Leadership?" by Dr. Leonard Sayles, *Boardroom Reports*, Aug. 1, 1989, page 10.

a. He investigates changes in his systems that will allow the goal to be met within the normal workday or, failing that, will investigate whether the goal is reasonable (has anyone ever met it?).
b. He arranges for compensatory time off, or whatever benefits are permitted him to bestow, for the people forced to put in extra hours.
c. He seeks to influence his neighboring division manager to adhere to the goals or, failing that, seeks remediation with their common superior.

In other words, the manager seeks to discourage the behavior that violates the values, reward the behavior that supports the values, and enable people to conform to the values within normal work routines. If extraordinary efforts are continually required to adhere to values, something is wrong with either the values or the system. (Not, as is often assumed, the people.)

3. *Serve as a buffer and protector.* Despite everyone's best efforts, there will be attempts to interfere with strategy implementation—sometimes caused by internal pressures for short-term results, sometimes caused by external pressures from customers, agents, suppliers, and so on. These potential disruptions should be shunted off to the leader (or to a mechanism he or she provides) for resolution. It's difficult to implement change, and it can be nearly impossible to do so when a critical mass builds up to resist it or interfere with it. Leaders protect their people not from deserved feedback, but from disruptions to their work.

Example: Customers of the local post office complain incessantly—and justifiably—about long lines at the windows. The postmaster instructs his window clerks to move as rapidly as possible, to explain unavoidable delays, and to always be cordial. However, the postmaster fails to provide for any mechanism to deal with the heavily time-consuming rare transactions. Consequently, when someone comes in to apply for a passport, open a new post office box, or send a registered letter to Asia, no amount of rapid movement, explanation, or cordiality can assuage outraged customers who spend 15 minutes in line to buy stamps. The postmaster should have complaints routed directly to him, have a special clerk available to be called (from other duties) for passports, and have registry material in the lobby to be completed in advance by the customer. In most bureaucratic settings, the employees have no buffer, meaning that their work routine—and their temperament—are constantly subject to the exception, the irregularity, and the complaint.

4. *Educate and communicate.* Leadership requires that *all* employees be educated about the nature and direction of the business in clear, simple, and pragmatic terms. Questions and debates should be encouraged and formally structured to allow for the greatest possible degree of interchange. The difference between healthy and unhealthy skepticism is usually whether the criticism is voiced or withheld. When people are comfortable asking questions and questionning policy, it is dialogue; when they are uncomfortable, it is grumbling.

Example: Human resouces departments and all other units with responsibility for training should be required to detail for management *precisely* how the strategic direction will be tied into *every single training and education program in existence or being planned.* Education on the job is simply inadequate if it neglects to consider the goals and direction of the enterprise. Virtually by dint of its existence, a charitable organization will educate its volunteers in its mission and goals so that they are more effective in their jobs. Similarly, every organization should not only create such education but also relate it to the individual's specific responsibilities. The leader must do this for his or her reports and ensure that subordinates have done it for their reports, and so on. "Poor communication" and "communication breakdowns" aren't generally caused by overt acts of sabotage. They are more commonly the result of default—a lack of leadership in this area.

5. *Innovate and take risks.* The leader must encourage change agents and accommodate new ideas. An effective strategy demands it. Consequently, the leader must establish an environment in which the freedom to fail is a reality, not a metaphor. The leader, however, has to provide the specific tools and pathways that will enable people to actually be innovative, especially in traditionally risk-averse environments. That requires a process for objectively evaluating risk, for nonjudgmental generation of new ideas, for assessing contribution to strategic direction, and for influencing and persuading those in other areas.

Example: "Idea meetings" often devolve into subjective guesswork, exercises in volume control, or reversions to hackneyed methods of problem solving because participants do not share a process or methodology for creating positive change. (Schumpter's definition of innovation is "creative destruction.") An effective leader will beg, borrow, steal, or invest such methodology (many models exist) that enforce its use in the organization. Time should be dedicated to these pursuits—if the key people are spending 10 hours a week on solving problems, shouldn't they be spending at least an equivalent amount of time on anticipating and preparing for the future? Leaders control time allocation by establishing priorities. There really is no such response as "I don't have time to do that." What that really means is "That issue is not a high enough priority, according to my emphasis areas, to merit taking time from something else to spend on it." Why is it you had the time to attend your good friend's party, but not your obnoxious cousin's? Time allocation is a conscious choice influenced strongly by clear leadership.

6. *Provide perspective.* Strategic issues and organizational direction tend to take on Herculean proportions. Some people act as though nothing else were as important, and others concede that there's nothing they can do to influence so weighty an endeavor. Strategic change must be implemented within the practical confines of the existing business. I know of no organization that decided to implement change by closing up for

a year so it could make a clean start.[5] Sometimes employees feel torn between the tried and true (and existing customer obligations) and the new wave. The leader must accommodate the best of the present while helping people prepare for the future.

Example: A favorite, intimate restaurant of ours changed management. On our first visit under the new regime, a waitress told me to order my drink straight up with ice on the side or I wouldn't get as much as I used to. She also warned that the shrimp were smaller. When I spoke to the manager I learned that the drink volume was exactly the same, although the shape of the glasses had been changed, and the smaller shrimp were provided because the taste was thought to be better and the restaurant was providing six instead of four. The manager condescendingly told us that the employees were threatened by the management change and that they would soon be "back to normal." After all, I "knew what waitresses could be like" didn't I? Well, I also know what inept leadership is like, thank you very much, and it entails not explaining change, providing rationale, and anticipating problems. The manager allowed a relatively simple management change and minor service changes to be blown way out of proportion. The leader failed or, more properly put, the manager failed to be a leader.

7. *Regulate velocity.* This is different from sheer power. It's more a question of speed and control. You can't turn the front wheel of the bike too sharply at too high a speed or you're likely to be bloodied. Some areas of strategic change are amenable to the damn-the-torpedoes approach, and some require a more sensitive hand on the gears and wheel. Effective strategy implementation is not a headlong rush up a hill. It's usually a steady but careful climb.

Example: Airlines have been in the strongest position when they have differentiated among their customers and offered various discounts and perquisites to market segments: frequent flyers, students, senior citizens, vacationers to a given destination, and members of allied hotel clubs. The velocity and direction of the strategy is carefully controlled under these circumstances. But compare that to all-out price wars, or the triple-mileage offers that damaged most balance sheets, and you can see organizations moving too fast and turning the wheel too sharply all at the same time. There were no leaders; there were only reckless followers in the executive suite. (At one point, the personnel of United Airlines, which was then engaged in a bitter turf war with Continental Airlines at Denver's Stapleton Airport, were wearing buttons with a picture of a Continental jet pierced by a huge screw. United management called it elán, but most of us had little difficulty picturing ourselves in the place of the Continental jet. With admirable restraint—and leadership—Continental chose a higher road.)

---

[5]Although Sears did close for a week in order to implement its new strategy of "one low price," I think this had more to do with attempting to manage public perception than with a pragmatic need to change price tags.

8. *Admit error.* The best organizations I've ever seen aren't those that never make mistakes. And the best leaders aren't those who are never wrong. You see, if you're never wrong, only one of three conditions can prevail:

- You've been wrong and don't realize it because you're either isolated from the event or people are reluctant to inform you.
- You've never been wrong because you've never taken on anything but supersafe, superconservative issues that have ironclad guarantees.
- You're lying to others and/or yourself.

We learn most dramatically and most thoroughly through our setbacks, not our victories. The best organizations and the best management teams are those that are continually trying to understand what went wrong and why. They look for *cause*, not for *blame*. Of course, no one is satisfied with a constant string of failures, and learning hasn't occurred if the same mistake is made repeatedly.

Example: The finest customer service people I've seen never waste time debating with a customer whether the airline or the manufacturer or the insurer was actually at fault. They say something like "I'm terribly sorry we didn't meet your expectations. What can we do to improve the situation?" It's tough to remain irritable when someone's trying to help you. On the other hand, I've actually had an Aetna claims adjustor (you'll remember Aetna from an earlier chapter—they were engaged in trying to keep customers away from their leadership) tell me belligerently, "You seem to be in a big hurry, and I've got a lot of work to do," when I inquired about a claim that he hadn't done one piece of work on in 2 weeks. Excellent strategic leaders say, "I blew it. I should've listened to you to begin with. I'm sorry for the extra work I've caused—let me make it up to your staff." Poor leaders say, "It wasn't my fault. You shouldn't have gotten us into this mess to begin with." Or the greatest leader cop-out ever told: "My hands are tied. It's the policy from upstairs."

9. *Use a telescope, not a microscope.* Lead for the long term. Spending inordinate amounts of time on late expense reports, incomplete sales forecasts, amounts of time spent out of the office, and so on, isn't leadership and isn't even good management. Napoleon and Richard III notwithstanding, battles aren't won or lost by buttons being shined or horseshoe nails being lost. They are won or lost depending on whether the army is headed in the right direction and arrives at the right place. Confederate General Bedford Forrest said, "Get there firstest with the mostest." I once observed a media vice president squander the potential contribution of his star trainer and program designer because the latter couldn't get her expense reports in on time. Rather than provide help to get it accomplished, the detail work became a battleground that ruined the relationship and demeaned both. It was incumbent on that manager to lead—to change and improve the situation—not to enter into combat over minor matters. (If you think paperwork is not a minor matter, you've already read too much of this book without understanding it.)

Example: Leaders consistantly orient issues toward the goal of the enterprise. When a decision is to be made, they ask, "What will the various alternatives mean for us in terms of achieving our mission?" They help subordinates to look to the destination, not look over their shoulders to what was done before. The postal service follows the lead of Federal Express. American car manufacturers have been following the lead of the Germans and Japanese. Similarly, subordinates will follow the lead of the people who seem to have their eyes on a clear, but distant future.

10. *Take charge.* Ultimately, in some way, shape, or form, leaders are identifiable because they take charge. They set the direction of the front wheel: they steer. This may be formal or informal, on small issues or large, but we've all experienced it. Taking charge occurs when the room quiets to listen to one person when no one else had been able to command attention. It occurs when people think, "That was an incredible summary of what I thought was a complex issue; now it's clear." It occurs when people simply "feel" that they are finally moving in the right direction. Alexander Haig's famous—and constitutionally incorrect—"I am in charge here" when President Reagan was shot is the clear signal of a retired general that someone has to be in charge and make it visible. "Chains of command" are meant to relay orders, but "lines of succession" are intended to provide for the continuity of leadership. *Anyone* can take charge if he or she has the vision, the volition, and the voice.

Example: The real take-charge people are to be found where the rubber meets the road. In my utility clients, I find low-level people taking charge every day. They determine how best to respond to customer problems, they interact with other utilities, city officials, police, and others in construction, emergencies, and other collaboration. These aren't traits taught in company courses or learned from instruction manuals. They are realities of daily business that are imbued and reinforced by the need to get things done. Interestingly, I've found that people who actually have to meet and face customers are more likely to take active leadership roles in solving their problems than employees whose only interface is by phone or mail. After all, leaders must lead other people. It's easy to see that your job is helping people if a person needing help is in front of you. Otherwise, it's all too easy to regard your job as "dealing with mail complaints" or "talking to customers over the phone." Sorry, the job is to *help* people. The job is to take charge—*to lead*.

Rear Wheel or Support Traits

1. *Align systems and procedures.* One of my favorite signs sighted on an employee's desk was, "There's no damn reason for it—it's just our policy." Part of the backstage work of leaders is to ensure that the organization isn't working at cross-purposes with its people and its strategic vision. If you want to become more of a risk-taking company as a part of your strategy, and policy continues to dictate that there be three levels of

approval on every field office request, you're simply not going to get out of the starting blocks. I remember an American Express manager telling me that it would be quite difficult to rapidly retrieve a copy of a bill I needed. When I reminded him that "membership has its privileges" and I wasn't above reminding his boss of that, he quickly found a way to circumvent his own system. Leaders have to ensure that the proverbial back room is supporting the folks on the street in concert with the direction of the organization. This is often tough, because there is a legion of back-room managers whose vested interest is to maintain and perpetuate the status quo.

Example: For a long time the Bureau of Prisons of the Department of Justice was a client of ours. Over a period of years the organization infallibly paid our invoices within 30 days, impressive for any organization and downright astounding for the government. But officials explained to me, "We want [prison industries] to compete with private enterprise, so we have to set the example, and interact with vendors and suppliers and customers in a competitive manner." So far, so good. Suddenly, however, the Bureau began paying in 6 weeks, sometimes more. The reason floored me. The government, in its infinite wisdom, decided that *every* agency should pay vendors within 30 days and passed legislation to enforce such payment. Unfortunately, the legislation was worded in such a way that payment was *forbidden to be made prior to 30 days*. And, as far as I know, that flawed legislation still prevails. Someone had a good idea, but there was no effective back-room leadership. The support failed to match the direction set by the front wheel.

2. *Subordinate ego.* Many feel that the demands of leadership are justified by the psychic and emotional rewards. However, those ego needs often become the goal when, in fact, they should be merely salutary effects of reaching the real goal: the organization's strategic vision. It is often more effective *not* to stand out in a crowd, particularly if the take-charge need isn't required. Reward and positive feedback must be shared, and the only person who can effectively distribute it in quality and quantity is the leader. That may mean assuming a subordinate role while your people stand in the spotlight, even if "they couldn't have done it without you." The most effective rear-wheel leaders I've seen are those who achieve their mission without expecting kudos or thanks. It's the difference between the drama adviser who gets the local production launched with a minimum of self-congratulation and the adviser who primps and prepares carefully for the "spontaneous" display of the cast's gratitude at the end of the show. Did you ever notice, when they shout "Author, author!" at the end of a show, that some can't be found and others are already on the stage? The same holds true when the company president figuratively yells "Author!"

Example: I love to get letters from organizations that are signed "Joan Thomas, processing clerk," or "Jim Davis, dispatcher." These are organizations in which leadership is encouraged to take a back seat. There's no reason why a manager has to sign every letter, especially if it's the subordinate who's dealing with the customer. I recently was asked by *USA Today* to make a presentation to a committee of 25 people to assess whether my firm could assist their organization in an employee survey. The committee was a cross section of the organization, including secretaries and clerical help. They were professional, totally committed, and as tough—and fair—a group of evaluators as I've worked with. The group established the criteria, found the alternatives, and made the final decision. Now there's an organization that knows how to subordinate ego and simply allow leadership to happen.

3. *Develop people.* This is different from educating people, or training them, because education and training are geared toward the present and generally require visible, front-wheel direction. Development refers to the future, toward the preparation that is required for a person to continue to grow and improve consistent with the direction of the organization. It sometimes requires a deft touch by the leader because it is best accomplished in one-on-one feedback, mentoring, and on-the-job support. You don't send people to an off-site program to be developed. Rather, you help them develop by reviewing the decisions they've made on a promotion, suggesting how a difficult assignment might be handled, counseling them on sensitivity to customer concerns, and generally having an open door when a sounding board is required. Leaders who can develop people are *approachable* leaders, people with whom others feel comfortable and secure. This is a rear-wheel trait that not all leaders possess—often their very strength of personality preempts this role. Yet this development role can determine whether your organization is developing future steam locomotive firemen or jet pilots. You might do a spectacular job at nurturing the former, but then again, there are no more steam locomotives.

Example: Contemporary organizations talk in terms of training and development but treat those endeavors with a common alternative, usually classroom training. (As we mentioned earlier, even the word "training" is repugnant. True leaders should think in terms of education.) Development is a softer and more sensitive requirement demanding more finesse and personal attention. We develop for the future as we evolve in our jobs and careers. The leader must be sensitive to that growth and help to guide it in the appropriate strategic direction. The worst organizations I've seen in this regard are those that select people based on "10 years of experience" or some similar quantitative measure. Ten years of experience in a job usually means that an individual has been performing in the same manner for 10 years, has been trained to do so, and is probably repeating a single year of development 10 times over. Are those the kinds of people you want to promote, reward, and have take your leadership positions? In fact, are those the people you want in your organization in any capacity?

4. *Do your homework.* Leaders have to help their people in this progression. We are besieged today with data. At best, employees are trained to

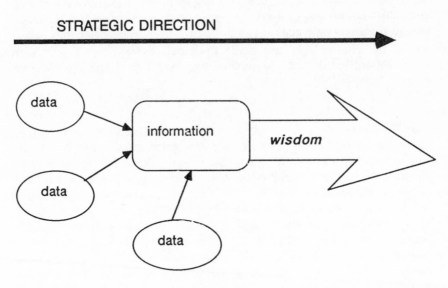

Figure 13.1

interpret the data so that it is useful information (figure 13.1). But information isn't enough. When we learn from the information—that is, we educate ourselves—so that we can improve and evolve, we've created a body of knowledge. And it's at that point that many leaders sit back and begin the self-congratulation. However, the ultimate goal is to use that knowledge to move the organization and its people toward the strategic goal, and we define that use of knowledge as *wisdom*. And one can make a case today that we have tons of data and a lot of information (as in "information explosion"). One can even say that our knowledge is increasing. But we have precious little wisdom. Data are all around us; information is on every computer screen; knowledge is recorded in reports and analyses and guidelines. *Wisdom* is in the ineffable role of the true, backstage leader. It's common to hear "He knows a lot," or "She's very knowledgeable." But how often do you hear, "What a wise decision"?

Example: Leaders "do their homework" by evaluating current knowledge and information with an eye toward the strategic vision. They must afford themselves the luxury—and necessity—of simply thinking issues through. This is often solitary work, and it is certainly never performed on stage. But it is one of the most crucial of all the rear-wheel traits, because it is pure leadership—turning information into organizational wisdom. The ability of people to shop through the mails has been with us for a century or better. The venerable Sears Catalog appears to be the *ne plus ultra* of the technique. It took a *Sharper Image* to apply the knowledge to span a modern industry. It took Jobs and Wozniak in their garage to change the shape of computing. And it takes leaders doing their homework—trying to create wisdom out of a chaos of information—to lead organizations toward their strategic goals.

5. *Listen carefully.* I am continually surprised at how many organizations ask our help in developing effective listening skills and how often "listening" shows up in polls as a key and underutilized managerial trait. I finally discovered something: Managers are passive listeners, whereas leaders tend to be active listeners. That is, leaders concentrate on listening and give it 100 percent effort. In so doing, they are able to "hear what is unsaid" and determine their actions accordingly. "Management by wandering around" has become one of those wonderful, allegorical, and totally vacuous phrases of our time. Most managers I've observed "wandering" see only what they choose to see and hear only what they choose to hear. They could have done just as effective a job in their offices while not lousing up everyone else's productivity. That's because wandering around has been construed to be an overt leadership activity—a front-wheel trait in our terms—when that very posture *precludes* the ability to listen (because you're too busy making yourself *seen*). Leaders listen to the people, the particulars, and the pulse of the organization. It's often perceived as very unleaderlike behavior, but it's an absolutely essential rear-wheel driving force.

Example: I once worked for a marketing director who went on—over the space of 2 years—to become president of the consulting firm for which we worked. No one could quite understand the speed of his progression, since he was a slow-moving, infinitely patient type who seemed to waste endless hours and days talking to people—or, rather, encouraging them to talk. People who didn't understand him said he was "political." (He may well have been, but it was irrelevant to this particular technique.) He listened as no person I had yet experienced listened. He exhibited a genuine interest in others' opinions and analyses, and he would "passively" sit for hours while he listened. He seldom read or otherwise diverted himself if he could talk to someone, even to strangers on long airplane trips around the world. What I eventually realized was that he was engaged in highly active behavior: On the one hand he was turning information into wisdom about the firm and its direction, and on the other, he was establishing relationships that encouraged people to come to him with still more information. And he was open to everything—good, bad, and indifferent. His detractors called him a "sponge" with an infinite capacity to absorb bad news. I came to see him as a formidable leader whose most highly developed trait was his ability to listen actively.

6. *Do the dirty work.* It's almost mystical how managers who steadfastly refuse to delegate become enlightened when a dirty job comes along. "Here's a good one for you, Smith. We have to lay off the underwriting department. Let's see what you're made of." Dirty work can be much more subtle—and usually is—than firing people or enforcing discipline. It often comprises the meetings you'd rather not attend, the trips you'd prefer to pass on, the reports you can't bear to read, and the evaluations you don't have energy to do. These accomplishments—or their absence—are seldom noticed by others. They are not the stuff of serving as an exemplar in many cases, and they can often be avoided with some passable attempt at rationalization. But they are the underpinning that keeps organizations functioning, and it's the leader's job to ensure that they get done.

Example: I once came across a group of excellent customer service people who were suffering from the "blues." This is a technical, consulting term that means morale is low and the client hasn't a clue as to why. All of the traditional factors were positive: They were well paid and perceived that they were; working conditions were comfortable; freedom was exceptional; and everyone liked the boss. Was it something in the water? It took almost a week to find the problem: No one had received a performance review in nearly two years. (By the way, this is *very* common in professional firms: lawyers, stock brokers, accountants, and so on.) Oh, everyone was paid well, and there were no complaints about performance, and it was one big "family." But the formal feedback *including, perhaps most essentially, development suggestions for how even better performance could be achieved,* was absent. It was absent because the department head abhorred having to provide feedback, didn't want feedback himself, and considered himself the luckiest person in the world because "his unit didn't require feedback since it was performing so well." This was a dirty job that he was relieved didn't have to be done. We all have our definitions of dirty jobs—at least, I've found no common *Dirty Jobs Manual* lying around. Leaders get them done. Personally.

7. *Exercise patience.* "Managers are paid to take action" is among the worst in the business rubrics. It is stuff and nonsense. If managers were paid to take action, the Keystone Kops should have been among the highest-paid management team of all time. They were *always* in action. Sorry, managers are paid to get results, and that endeavor often necessitates *inaction.* Eisenhower didn't say "Ignore the weather, we must invade Europe and we only have a limited window in which to do so." He waited. Good leaders keep their eye on the goal and have the ability to actively utilize patience as a technique to reach that goal. Poor leaders keep their eyes on the activities, and they are constantly urging more and more activity—irrespective of the effect on the goal—in order to justify their existence. An early mentor told me, "I don't judge a person by how much time he spends on the road or how much time he's in the office. I judge him by how well he meets the objectives we agreed on." It's tough to stand on stage as a leader and announce, "I'm going to be patient, and I'm proud

of it." (Remember "benign neglect" and Walter Mondale?) That's why patience is a rear-wheel trait.

Example: My firm has been called, by people who know us, "the world's worst marketing organization," albeit with some affection. We never actively solicit business. We make no cold calls. What we do is, stay in touch. We send articles, books, and just plain notes to contacts, clients, and prospects several times a year. We'll stop if someone asks us to, but no one has ever asked. We try to send items of information that we think are useful in managing organizations and in leading people. And, of course, sooner or later we're asked to do some work. It's not unusual for the informal relationship to last for 5 years or more before the formal one begins. But that's all right. We're patient. We judge ourselves by the kinds of clients we acquire—GE and Mercedes-Benz, and *The New York Times*— and the percentage of our business that originates with existing clients— over 80 percent—which signifies to us a constructive, successful relationship. We never measure ourselves by the numbers of proposals sent, or the number of new clients acquired or, heaven forfend, the number of sales calls made (which, for us, is always 0). Similarly, leaders need to exhibit patience and not be lulled into a false security of "doing something." Nine times out of ten, that something will be inimical to the strategic direction of the enterprise. It might feel good, but when you wind up at the wrong destination, it will have been long forgotten.

8. *Manage the boss.* Every leader is someone else's follower. Even the CEO has the board to contend with. The weak managers are the ones who say, "It's not me, it's the boss." The true leaders are the ones who say to the boss, "Look, we've got to change this if we are to achieve our goals." One executive once defined "subordinate" to me as "someone who provides me with creative alternatives to solve problems and to achieve our mission." Some people would say that there are exceptions to this position and that an overly rigorous boss or company policy precludes the wielding of influence from below. But I've found that the best leaders are those who, without fanfare or public notice, effectively influence and persuade their superiors on a regular basis. Surprisingly, the key element in accomplishing this is not in a mastery of the content of the issue or in lining up political allies (though that seldom hurts). Rather, it's in identifying the main receptors of the boss and approaching him or her along the best-traveled route. In other words, if the boss is a people person, go to lunch. If the boss is a numbers cruncher, prepare a detailed report. If the boss is a mover and shaker, keep it brief and explain what your suggestion will result in. There are no guarantees, but it's important to travel the path of least resistance.

Example: In 1989 a United DC-10 lost virtually all control when its tail engine disintegrated in midair, destroying all hydraulic lines. In the cockpit, the pilot, first and second officers, and another pilot who happened to be on the aircraft managed to crash-land the plane by using only variances in power to the two remaining engines. It was reported afterward that the crew functioned as a team, constantly supplying the captain with information and alternatives and the captain asking for options and recommendations. Similarly, when a United 747 had a huge hole ripped in its fuselage, the flight crew performed in the same manner and landed the plane safely, with no additional loss of life, in Hawaii. Airlines have actively educated captains to elicit such help in a crisis and subordinates to provide it whether or not they are asked. Several years ago an Eastern jet crashed because it ran out of fuel, without the captain realizing it, while another problem was being addressed. Neither of the other officers in the cockpit brought the fuel situation to the captain's attention because they thought he must be aware of it and it wasn't their place to do so, anyway.

9. *Be your own customer.* We mentioned earlier that executives should shop their own stores to see how customers are treated and how well their people are equipped to deal with daily issues. Similarly, leaders should practice a key rear-wheel trait: Don't accept what you're told, what you read, or what's supposed to be. Experience what your customers experience. If your customers are other internal people, spend a day in their environments to see how your area responds to their needs. What is the level of cooperation? What do these customers say about your area? If the customer is external, use the phone lines, the stores, the services, and the products that the customer utilizes. What kind of relationships are formed? How does the experience compare with your managers' perceptions (based on what they've told you)? What information that can be acquired can lead to improvements? One simple power source for the bicycle is contemporary, accurate experience based on what the customers are receiving.

Example: Sam Walton of Walmart is famous for the morale he generates in his stores and for his intimate knowledge of his operations. He is constantly on the move visiting stores and talking to people. True, he is recognized and known, but he has become adept at sampling his products and services from a customer's viewpoint. Similarly, the Marriott hotel chain has an aggressive policy of sampling guests' treatment. A questionnaire is usually included in the bill and is always prominent in the room. Any time I've filled one out, I've received a personal response first from Frank Marriott and then from the general manager of the hotel in question (presumably with the latter also copying the former). The responses are detailed and sincere. The Marriott chain uses this device—and clearly gives it a very high priority in terms of executive attention—to monitor how guests perceive they are treated, which is far more important than how the hotel staff feels they are treating guests.

10. *Surrender leadership.* One should never abdicate leadership, because that generally leaves a vacuum and also destroys the leader's credibility ever after. But there are frequent occasions when it should be surrendered. By that I mean that no one truly functions 100 percent of the time as a leader. There are times when the leader is someone else's follower, as noted above. There are times when the leader is a sole contributor, working on

reports or creating new alternatives alone. There are times when the leader is a peer, cooperating with colleagues. In fact, the leader actually has many roles, of which leadership is only one. In figure 13.2, note that the

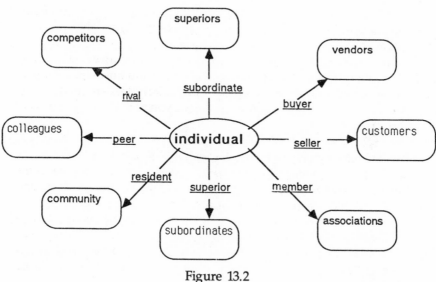

Figure 13.2

relationship with subordinates is called "superior," not "leader." That's because the organizational hierarchy can install you as someone's superior, but it can't make you a leader. Similarly, any of the other roles, whether member or resident or even subordinate, can entail leadership. As you can see, we are seldom called upon to be leaders 100 percent of the time, 24 hours a day, or even for most of a workday. So, by "surrendering leadership," I mean to consciously get out of the role. A leader's attitude won't gain you any ground among peers, and it won't even help if it's the *sole* role you choose to assume with subordinates. Your rear-wheel power will come from the perspective of the variety of real roles you play and from the relaxation that comes from not having to shoulder the burdens of the world on a continuous basis.

Example: I am often confronted with client executives who cite poor performance in their areas and a wealth of "yes, buts" to demonstrate why any alternative to solve the situation will just make it worse. They can make a Hobson's choice into an art form. "My people won't cooperate with each other. If I insist, they'll resent me and won't be sincere about it anyway. If I try to lead a group discussion, they'll be polite and feel it's just another psychology session. If I ask my boss for advice, he'll think

I'm weak." And so on, and on, and on. *The primary problem in a situation in which the leader feels trapped is that he or she insists on being the guru.* People must be forced to take responsibility for their actions, and they will never be able to do so if the leader decided on all the actions and takes responsibility for them. (Remember, the manager's job isn't *action*, it's *results*.) Consequently, I usually suggest a radical solution: Explain the situation to the troops; ask them to sit down and come up with a solution; and leave. If they can't develop their own solution, then you'll dictate one, but only after they've had their chance. Guess what? In most cases, the solution is not only generated but it's usually a better-quality one than the leader could have come up with because (1) it comes from the people closest to the problem and (2) it is owned by the people who must implement it. Leadership should be surrendered as a leader's tactic in certain situations, and those situations are much more common than most people suspect. This is the ultimate rear-wheel power.

Those are the ten front-wheel and rear-wheel traits that make for a leader who is able to stay on the bike. They provide for sensitive steering and velocity. One is front-stage and apparent, the other is backstage and subtle.

It's vital to bear in mind that *leadership is a role that we all move in and out of.* It is not a permanent, fixed position, nor is it one necessarily dependent on organization charts or hierarchies. Therefore, my position is that we *all* need leadership skills to some degree because we're all coaching a child's team, or helping colleagues, or being active in the community, or being outraged at poor treatment. The best followers have to be aware of what excellent leadership entails if they are to respond in an optimal manner. In terms of strategic vision, we all serve as leaders at one time or another, and the more our jobs are "officially" responsible for implementing that vision, the more important our leadership skills become.

Here are my nominations to the hall of fame and the hall of shame of leadership. Some you might recognize and some not, but they are all real instances which I've directly observed. The criteria for entry into either hall are simple: Behaviors of a key manager that either led the way in achieving strategic goals or lead the way in subverting them. We'll start with the horror stories so we can end on a positive note.

Leadership Hall of Shame

1. The insurance company senior vice president of human resources who was seeking an effective listening program in order to help his people be more sensitive to field and customer communications over the phone. He insisted that the program be "self-contained" in the classroom and that the skills be transferred irrespective of a lack of reinforcement and management support back on the job. When it was explained why such an approach was folly—the job environment, not the isolated

classroom, is the key modifier of behavior—he cut off the dialogue, shook his head violently from side to side, and repeated three times, "I don't agree, I don't agree, I don't agree!" And this man was responsible for the education and development of his company's work force.

2. The president of a major cosmetics company who was personally involved in the search for new, key management talent to help meet a dynamic new vision for the company. During the interview process, she opened and read her mail, accepted phone calls, and disregarded most of the candidates' responses to her questions. I watched several excellent candidates rapidly head for the door and several excellent managers roll their eyes and shake their heads in disbelief.

3. The CEO of a major textile manufacturer who berated his top executives in front of colleagues and in front of outsiders. This is a multiple entry in the hall of shame, since not only was he undermining any possibility of management synergy and harmony in achieving corporate goals but his people scrambled back to their areas and treated subordinates in the same manner as the role model. There wasn't a backbone in the room.

4. The president of a New England cellular phone organization, engaged in a fierce competitive battle, whose people were rude on the phone and sent threatening, obnoxious letters to customers on the slightest pretense. He refused to return customers' phone calls or respond to letters, and he generally set that poor example for anyone who cared to watch. His company steadily lost market share.

5. The president and top officers of a West Coast utility which brought in a technique popularly known as Kroning named after its leading advocate, Charles Krone. Based on the teachings of an Armenian mystic, the approach uses bizarre jargon and convoluted phrases ("There is an inability for participating parties to reach mutually harmonious relatedness over job-specific end products," meaning: "We don't get much done at meetings."[6] Many employees felt that this was "new age" brainwashing, and they objected on religious and ethical grounds. The Public Utilities Commission discovered that *$40 million* had been spent on this effort and decreed that $25 million of it would have to be charged to the stockholders, not the rate-payers. The president took early retirement and the executive vice president, and heir apparent, was transferred.

6. The president of a midwest financial services company who wanted to revitalize and change the direction of his organization's relationships with clients. He convened his four top officers to arrive at a consensus on what had to be done to implement that vision and then proceeded to drive his views home despite what anyone else suggested. Typical retort to an opposing view: "Well, Joe, I appreciate your viewpoint, but I have to tell you that if that's the way you feel after 12 years with the organization I have to wonder where you've been spending your time."

---

[6] See "Let the Manager Beware: The Dangers of Mystical Management Advice," by Alan Weiss, *Success Magazine,* Oct. 1988, page 96.

7. The president of a major automaker, which has been lagging, who acquires a major organization with an outspoken, independent, and very successful leader. It's first viewed as an attempt to break through some of the hardened arteries and bring a rejuvenated strategy to fruition. Instead, the president rapidly sinks into an ego battle, bristles at the suggestion of past mistakes, and ends up paying a fortune to be rid of his rejuvenator. The board sits idly by and allows it to happen; the president is still there; and the automaker still has its woes. Its most highly proclaimed new entry for the 90s, based on unprecedented cross-functional cooperation and simultaneous plant creation and auto design, appears to be a poorly conceived and ill-fated product.

8. A midwest consulting firm with a blue-chip client list, about $40 million in billings, and a highly talented, creative work force, is led by the founder and a coterie of top officers who spend much of their time engaged in internal, political turf warfare. More and more managers grow weary or disillusioned and leave, and the firm continues more on name than on performance. During the last year of impressive growth it goes public at $13 a share. Within 6 months it is selling at $2.50, there are mass layoffs and defections, the founder is shunted aside, an outsider (who doesn't know the industry) is brought in as president, and investors are howling.

9. A UK high-tech manufacturer is trying to instill more innovation among its ranks. The two founders and top officers arrange for comprehensive education and development activities for midlevel management, an unprecedented move. The managers respond excellently and develop over 120 ideas for products and procedures, including some which they document as generating millions of pounds in savings and/or revenues. At a formal day of presentations, after 2 weeks of preparation among the managers, the founders sit silently while the managing director, the superior of all the managers in the room, ridicules and criticizes every presentation with comments such as, "If that's such a good idea, why isn't anyone else doing it?" and "You must be fools to think that can be marketed." The session breaks up with management morale lower than ever. A year later, the company is sold under adverse conditions.

10. An airline gate agent is closing out a flight at the jetway door 5 minutes prior to departure. A man arrives with his ticket but with a piece of luggage too big to carry on board. The agent tells him he'll have to return to the ticket counter to have it checked or stand in line at the nearby customer service desk (behind 15 people with later flights). He protests, but he gets in line. Finally, a supervisor finds him there, gives him a claim check, and tells him to simply carry the bag to the aircraft door, where it will be taken outside, something which the gate agent could easily have done to begin with. The man takes his bag, cursing, and states that he'll never fly the airline again if he can help it.

Leadership Hall of Fame

1. Lee Iacocca—forget the books and propaganda—led the way not only in restoring Chrysler to fiscal health but in reclaiming the trust of the consumer. He made both tactical decisions—provide longer-term warranties, personally be the spokesman—and strategic decisions—sell that profitable tank division ("We're an auto company, not a defense contractor"), reintroduce the convertible, initiate the minivan—that set the tone for the "new Chrysler." He became the embodiment for the kind of quality, straight talk, and sincerity that brought the company back into prospective buyers' hearts and minds. He became, according to polls, one of the most trusted people in America, and I believe that he instilled those qualities in his organization. He was able to make the tough decisions as well, whether in dealing with the unions or in paring down management, because his strategic vision for the organization was always clear in his mind.

2. Walter Alston, manager of the Los Angeles (neè Brooklyn) Dodgers for 23 years. Working on a series of one-year contracts—all that owner Walter O'Mally would allow—Alston persevered for over two decades, winning four world series. He successfully led conventional, hard-working superior players like Gil Hodges, once-in-a-lifetime talents like Sandy Koufax, and tempermental superstars like Don Drysdale through 150-game seasons while utilizing the existing talent to meld a team that, once in Los Angeles, went on to lead the leagues in attendance through good times and bad. Alston's own baseball career comprised one, solitary at-bat in the majors, during which he struck out. He is one of the finest examples of the axiom that you don't have to have been a superstar to successfully manage superstars, and you don't have to have been a top salesperson to know how to lead salespeople. His tone was quiet and reserved. He simply kept his eye on the goal and reached it more often than not.

3. One seldom thinks of a defeated politician as an effective leadership, but former mayor Ed Koch of New York was one of the best. Especially in his heyday, he was able to resolve the city's financial crisis—which many say couldn't be resolved short of default—and revive a sense of pride and accomplishment in the city. He worked with intransigent unions, chronic shortages of resources, and an ever-vigilant opposition ready to rouse the natives. Yet he melded the various interest groups, boroughs, and races into a working amalgam. Most significantly, he did it by forging alliances and affecting compromises leading through a mine field of special interests and political patronism. During one election he ran on both parties' tickets, virtually unopposed, and until 1989 there was never even a hint of scandal or inappropriate behavior suggested.

4. James Burke of Johnson & Johnson, for the reasons cited earlier, not only concerning his outstanding performance during the Tylenol crisis but for the ongoing management and reinforcement of values that he engendered. Burke's actions stand as one of the clearest examples of how

the employees of his organization should act. His continuing rear-wheel strengths became visible front-wheel leadership when needed. Not only has the public received a signal lesson in how an organization can behave responsibly and conscientiously, but one has to believe that every employee of Johnson & Johnson retains the vision of those shining moments when faced with the daily exigencies and demands of their jobs. This was leadership at its best: accountability, honesty, clarity, and forthright action.

5. Bill Gates of Microsoft has created an environment that accommodates both scientific curiosity and overriding customer service. That duality has prevailed despite size, growth, competition, and the complex changes of an unpredictable industry. At the same time that Microsoft can introduce what is probably *the* state-of-the-art word processing software, Word 4.0, it can also set new standards for accessible, helpful customer service and support. Gates seems to have the knack for "staying out of the way of good people," and perhaps he is the master at rear-wheel leadership. His axiom about "putting good people in a room and occasionally throwing in some raw meat" is an oversimplification of his recognition that, to achieve strategic goals, leadership involves the confidence to allow for freedom and experimentation in the work place.

6. The human resources function at Walt Disney. There is no finer example of employees being painted into the picture and holding a stake in the outcome of their actions. Street sweepers don't see their jobs as cleaning streets; they are performers and, as such, are part of the show. Small wonder the streets are so clean if even the "menial" jobholders can identify with their contributions to the overall results. Unfailing courtesy, thoroughness, and consistency are never lucky and are seldom fortuitous. They are the result of deliberate leadership from management that includes tireless vigilance, attention to detail, and view from the customers' perceptive. There is no higher morale than at Disney properties, and their human resource people deserve hall-of-fame status for their continuing leading-edge approaches in helping people to identify with and achieve strategic goals.

7. Fred Smith and the employees of Federal Express. I don't remember any single organization in which so many different interfaces yield exemplary service and the willingness to go the extra mile. If the pickup driver is delayed, a local dispatcher calls to ensure that you don't worry *before you even have cause to worry*. Supplies are provided immediately. Supervisors are accessible. The entire organization seems filled with the urgency created by a single, clear strategic goal: Customers' packages will be unerringly delivered the next day, courteously and accurately, no matter what. No detail is too small: "You can take the final copy of the routing slip before I get here," advises the driver one day. "That way I don't have to leave you anything and your records will be complete." An automated system takes my call and provides a confirmation within 60 seconds. The crisp, clean leadership here—exemplified by *all* employees—is so outstanding that I sat down to think of some weaknesses. I came up with one: Federal

Express does not provide return envelopes for their bills. (If Smith reads this book, they just might begin to.)

8. The Marriott family. Marriott hotels are the most consistent, high-quality properties of any mass-market chain. The owners have taken a personal interest in service that is almost legendary: They are said to read *every* customer feedback form that is submitted and demand answers from local management when problems are cited. Not surprisingly, response to guests from all Marriott people is fast and effective. Marriott has sent a clear message to its people: We will gain long-term commitment through unqualified service and responsiveness. No other hotel chain—and few other organizations of any type—are so consistent in this pursuit. Training is also a zealous pursuit. The organization's vision is achieved because the components for strategy implementation are so scrupulously observed.

9. Elizabeth Dole, current Secretary of Labor and former Secretary of Transportation. While serving in the transportation post, she was delivering a speech down the hall from a presentation I was making in Mobile, Alabama. During a break, she was told that there were four Coast Guard junior officers in my group (the Coast Guard is part of the Department of Transportation). She made a point to personally stop by—privately, with no fanfare—to chat with the officers and ask how things were going. They were sincerely thrilled by the attention, and her aides told me that she tried always, within the limitations of a hectic schedule, to exert such personal leadership.

10. John F. Kennedy, but for a very singular reason. And for that, you'll have to read the final chapter.

14

The Future of Organizations: Come, Look into My Eyes

In 1958, to much surprise and consternation in the West, the Soviet Union launched Sputnik, the first orbiting man-made satellite. Two years later, John F. Kennedy stated that the United States would place a human being on the moon within the decade, a vision considered by many "experts" to be so much rhetoric and persiflage.[1] In 1969, the Eagle landed, creating the greatest "small step for man" in history and sending us soaring back to 1492 to generate even a crude analogy.

I know of no finer example of a strategic vision being faithfully pursued and implemented, particularly in the face of all that's slow, cumbersome, and ornery within public administration. How *dare* any organization fail to implement its strategy—its vision—when Kennedy's *vision* (he was assassinated in 1963) could lead an entire, pluralistic nation to the moon?

The future of organizations—and of our society and of our lives—is dependent upon our achieving our visions, be they of an environmentally sound relationship with the planet, a strife-free world, or a productive existence. As this chapter is being written, the Berlin Wall is being dismantled. Hungary, Czechoslovakia, East Germany, Poland, and Bulgaria have announced open borders, massive changes in their leadership, and the promises of more freedom. The Soviets are not protesting and, in fact, are busily addressing themselves to improving domestic conditions while candidly broadcasting current conditions on unprecedentedly blunt and accurate media.

It's not unusual for the stock market to gyrate by 40 points in a day or 100 in a week. Ford has purchased Jaguar; Braniff has filed for Chapter 11 for a second time; the Japanese have introduced two new luxury cars— Lexus and Infiniti—and:

- United Airlines continues as a takeover candidate.
- Abortion has been the key issue in New York City's mayoral race and the gubernatorial races in Virginia and New Jersey.
- The U.S. navy has "shut down" for 2 days to review safety procedures in light of a spate of recent accidents and deaths.

---

[1]By way of comparison, JFK's goal was akin to someone watching early gliders and proclaiming that powered flight was on the horizon, a feat the Wright brothers achieved some centuries after model gliders were first flown.

- The two most significant television stars are a black, male, former stand-up comic who exemplifies middle-class virtues and an obese, white, female, former stand-up comic who exemplifies blue-collar values.

Otherwise everything is pretty normal.

The future of organizations lies in the ability to establish pictures of themselves in the future and to remain true to that vision. The first is relatively easy. The second is called implementation. As change accelerates, it doesn't threaten the formulation of strategy—the visioning—but it certainly creates potholes on the road that leads to it.

What crystal ball do we use; which fortune-teller do we consult; what scapulimancy do we perform to divine how to sustain ourselves during the travails? I've tried to demonstrate in the preceding pages that there are no magic potions; there are only simple, basic management techniques that keep the machine oiled—that enable the rear-wheels to continually support the direction chosen by the front wheel. For example, successful strategies—that is, those that are successfully implemented—view change as an ally, not an antagonist. Management exemplifies and manages the values underlying the strategic direction. Ownership and constant two-way communication must be encouraged, enforced, and enhanced.

Yet the probability is that you've heard many of these admonitions before (though, we suspect, not within a model for strategy implementation as presented here). Why are these seemingly simple tenets so difficult to implement? Why do we need videos of "paradigm shifts" and seminars on "leadership for the 90s" and books that offer instant results? (One client, when I asked why he chose our services, stated what I think is a maxim for modern management: "One-minute approaches are fine as long as you're not looking for anything more than 60 seconds of results." Would you trust an attorney who has *The One-Minute Guide to Torts* on the shelf or the surgeon who you catch browsing through *Sixty Seconds toward Better Oncology?*)

And therein lies the proverbial rub. Over the past decade, there has been a ferocious preoccupation with productivity in the West, most particularly in the United States. We have bemoaned the fact that the Japanese coopted us by using Charles Deming, an *American*, of all people, as their guru of quality and productivity. We have engaged in managerial self-flagelation, rending our business suits and appealing to our own gods, be they Drucker or Iacocca or Reagan, while attempting to determine just why we abandoned the pursuit of quality, productivity, and the *American way*. But the problem of modern management is not one of straying. It is not one of quality or productivity. *It is the problem of stupid management.*

Do you remember how we reacted to Japanese products of the 50s and 60s? We said "junk." We laughed at them. We always had a respect for quality, and we always knew how to discern it. No, the American consumer and the American manager were not and are not people to be easily lulled into a quality coma. Nor does a nation of people who can put a man on the moon, a personal computer on every desk, and a phone in every car suffer productivity lapses gladly.

The American people know quality when they have it and productivity when they experience it. But no one is quite sure what good management is, because we're unwilling to try to measure it. Consider these unsurpassed calamities:

- The massive failure of savings and loan institutions because of bad loans, corrupt officers, and inattentive regulators.
- The explosion of the space shuttle *Challenger* because of poor design, inadequate quality control, and an unrealistic NASA strategy.
- Toxic dump sites polluting the environment because of a disregard for future impact, lack of social consciousness of the dumpers, and insufficient understanding of the problem.
- Chronic government trade imbalances and huge debt because of U.S. protection of weak industries and laissez-faire toward strong ones, while the Japanese allow weak industries to die and support strong ones.
- Stock fraud and manipulation of historic proportion that are due to greed.

Are these problems that stem from quality and/or productivity issues or has management—both private and public sector—simply been asleep at the switch, to be kind, or been an active abettor of the decline, to be harsh (and, I believe, accurate)? It's time for management to have its feet held to the fire, and the wing tips of executives should be the first to feel the heat.

The most difficult kind of hard work is *thinking*. The very reason why I have suggested models and processes in this book—and provided some rudimentary checklists and aids—is that they are of help in instantiation: making the abstract thinking process real and pragmatic. The reason for the reliance on the shortcuts and crutches I've decided above is that they *replace* the act of thinking. Simply by throwing money at a problem (which is a commodity in eminently greater supply than clear thinking), management is often able to fool its constituency and, worse, itself, into believing that effective action is being taken. Buy a course or a guru and your thinking days are over, because someone else is now taking care of business. But wait a minute. If the lawyers and accountants and consultants are doing all the thinking and making all the decisions, why are we paying senior management? Do we need six-figure salaries and stock options just to obtain people whose job it is to obtain *other* people?

The future of organizations is terrifyingly simple to determine by using figure 14.1, where FO=future of the organization, QM=quality of management, QE=quality of employees, AU=amount of uncertainty, CT=competitive threat.

Let's use a scale of 10 (high) to 1 (low). If you were to rate your current management team as an 8, better than most but not at the very top, your employees also as 8, the amount of future uncertainty in your business

$$FO = \frac{QM \times QE}{AU \times CT}$$

Figure 14.1

as moderate, 5, and competitive threat as moderate, 5, then your organizational future would appear to be as in figure 14.2:

$$FO = \frac{8 \times 8}{5 \times 5} = 2.56$$

Figure 14.2

The future is "positive" in the sense that you've generated a positive number. But what are your competitors' numbers? What are you doing to improve your numbers? What's happening in the environment to threaten your numbers? We don't pretend that this is a scientific test, but executives to whom we suggested it find it can be a haunting refrain. Interestingly, *we find that many executives tend to underemphasize the amount of uncertainty and competitive threat while they overemphasize the quality of management and employees.* You see, the top factors are dependent variables: the quality of management will help determine the quality of employees. Consequently, a high QM and low QE are more unlikely than a low QM and high QE. The latter could accidentally develop; in my opinion it did at Braniff and International Harvester and General Motors. But I can't easily cite an example of strong leadership resulting in a successful operation without first creating strong employees. Leaders get results through people (that's what "empowerment" really means), and sometimes people get results despite poor leadership, but seldom, if ever, do leaders get results without followers.

The optimal, and I believe unobtainable, FO quotient in our equation would be 100, which would occur if both management and employees were perfect (10×10) and uncertainty and competitive threat were nil (1×1). On both pragmatic and mathematic grounds, we are going to disallow a 0 in any category. The closer an organization comes to 100, the stronger and clearer its future. The closer it comes to 0 or, send for the triage team, the larger the negative number, the greater the impending disaster. However, don't be lulled into thinking that the higher the number, the better you are than others.

Some industries and organizations will traditionally have higher AU and CT factors—pharmaceuticals and high tech, for example, more so than soft drinks and detergents, one would think. (Although reflecting on radical changes in areas like health care or leisure makes one wonder if anyone has it easy in those areas.) Competitive threat is probably the most difficult of any of the factors to affect, although ongoing insight and knowledge—the difficult *thinking* processes—of present and future competition can help. The sewing machine and pattern industries, for example, no longer compete merely with each other—Singer vs. Brother, Simplicity vs. McCall's—but with all those leisure time activities vying for time from the modern, employed woman.

The other three factors are directly influenced by the strategic process, *more so by implementation than by formulation.* Our contention throughout this book has been that establishing a strategy is not like sculpting the *Pietà.* It is a conceptual process that has the benefit of many validated models augmented by the organization's own experiences. It is the implementation of strategy that is difficult because there have been no models and because experience has been muddied by short-term pressures and perceived crises.

The future of an organization is not dependent on the fortune teller and her crystal ball or on the Great Kreskin who says, "Come, look into my eyes." It *is* dependent on the mental toughness of management to create and manage an implementation system that is designed to fulfill strategic goals, because most of the equation, figure 14.3, is influenced by the quality of implementation:

$$FO = \left(\frac{QM \times QE}{AU \times CT} \right) \longleftarrow \text{influenced by strategy implementation}$$

Figure 14.3

The future isn't in our eyes or in our stars, it is in ourselves.

Our little equation is meant only to give you a means to begin to evaluate your relative implementation strengths and progress. Perhaps you have a better system or can invent one. Our encouragement is that you have *some* system that is—*shudder*—quantifiable and reducible to comparative numbers. Too many of us feel good about ourselves, good about our management, and on top of things as long as we have a strategy in place. But the strategy itself is inadequate, because it "only" establishes the goal; the route is a function of the implementation plan. So, to complete our definitions, FO=future of the organization, as determined by the strategic vision.

There are no sure things in life, so 100 (and that entire neighborhood) is unattainable. But negative numbers are attainable, as are distressingly low positive ones. Our rule of thumb is a modification of the conventional one: 7 is a passing grade or, perhaps, a surviving grade. If you are continually at that degree of positive position in achieving your strategic vision and are continually evaluating the components of the equation, the chances are that you're headed in the right direction with the support to get you there. The more you're at 5, the more iffy are your chances of strategic success (despite short-term, tactical victories). If your number is under 5, you'll have a hard time convincing me why you shouldn't drop this book right now—*this instant*—and start taking some actions, because three-quarters of the equation is within management influence if management has the volition to do something about it.

In the event you haven't just dropped the book and sounded the Klaxons, we're going to provide you with some criteria to help assess your current position. These ought to be amended and altered to fit your circumstances, but we find that they constitute a sound, generic approach to understanding your current position.

QM: Quality of Management

10: Management actively and explicitly establishes and participates in strategy implementation as a daily responsibility. Managers at all levels make decisions and question actions in view of the organization's strategic goals. Innovation is encouraged, and the freedom to fail is a reality. Managers consistently exemplify the values commensurate with the strategic goals and reward and support people in concert with those goals. There is open and candid communication. Leadership is based not on hierarchical position but on trust, risk taking, and involvement. Decision making is pushed downward. There is not one weak link among senior management members. Among middle management, the emphasis is on finding cause, not blame, and on exploiting opportunity, not protecting self-interests.

7: Management at all levels is consistently positive and constructive. There are certain issues (e.g., crises or labor negotiations or relocations) that may temporarily derail strategy implementation, but day-to-day decisions are consistent with strategic intent. Any weak links are compensated for by the preponderance of solid management. "We vs. them" thinking is absent in relations between management and workers, and participation and involvement are actually practiced and are not mere buzzwords. Senior management is highly visible and frequently interacts with people at all levels.

4: Management is uneven. There are pockets of very good people and pockets of inadequate people. Political wars and turf battles are daily events. Managers try to aid their departures or units at the expense of their counterparts. Hierarchical and seniority criteria dictate relationships and protocol. Senior management is distant and considers itself above the fray. Blame, rather than cause, is pursued when things go awry. The organization's values and vision are secondary or even tertiary to one's own self-interests and departmental interests. Management has allowed—and even encouraged—many parts of the organization to secede from the whole.

1: Management is in disarray. No one actively seeks responsibility or authority; it's "every man for himself." Managers are energetically looking for other jobs. Substantial time is stolen from the organization because managers simply don't work or moonlight. Equipment, supplies, and money may be stolen. Controls and oversight procedures stop working because the managers responsible for them have no interest in making them work. Intellectual corruption is high: managers openly criticize superiors and peers and form alliances with employees. Focus on product, service, and relationships falls to the minimal levels necessary to generate weekly paychecks. Senior management is concerned about its own escape from the morass.

QE: Quality of Employees

10: Employees are totally in step and in synch with the organization's goals, mission, and plans to achieve them. They feel free to critique what they see and hear, knowing that their feedback will reach responsive management. Conflict and confrontation usually revolve around better ways to get the job done. Decisions about overtime, tough assignments, and unpleasant tasks are generally made by the employees themselves. There is no we-them attitude. There is little turnover caused by people leaving for better jobs, and there are many applicants waiting for the available openings. Any employee could recite the organization's key values and describe its direction, as well as his or her role in achieving it. There is a common pride in the work itself, and virtually 100 percent of employee energy is invested in the products, services, relationships, and customers in one way or another.

7: Employee attitudes are generally good. People work in a manner commensurate with the organization's values and strategic direction, although they may not be able to articulate easily that they are doing so. They will tend to be innovative and creative in their work and in their approach to problems and challenges, but they will realize that there is a point at which matters must be referred upward. There will be some complaining and some indifferent attitudes toward work, but they will be balanced and overcome by the attitudes of the vast majority of workers. There may be some variance in the quality of the work based on tenure or department or nature of the tasks. Most people will find credibility in management decisions, and most can see themselves with the organization for the long term. Customers are treated well, despite an occasional "bad day."

4: The quality of work is highly situational. There are pockets of people who take pride in their work and perform well, but even they will admit that they do so "in spite of management." In most instances, it's a question of "what's in it for me?" Workers will probably not understand the values and strategic thrust of the company, and they will be highly skeptical of any attempt by management to convey or explain those elements. Large amounts of time will be wasted in idle talk and speculation. Most people will take advantage of an opportunity to put one over on management, and organizational objectives will be lost in the shuffle. Customer complaints will be on the rise, and attitudes will be to do what is minimally necessary to keep customers quiet.

1: Anarchy prevails. There are widespread absenteeism, thievery, and even sabotage. No one expects to stay for the long term, so the short term is seen as an opportunity to "get what you can." Alliances are made with management to foster such self-interest, always at the expense of someone else. A minimal amount is done to keep paychecks coming. There is total disrespect for management, and employees may deliberately subvert even legitimate organizational interests. Anyone who is qualified is looking for a better situation.

AU: Amount of Uncertainty

10: Virtually nothing is known about the future. The emphasis has been so strong, for so long, on short-term performance and firefighting that events seem to constantly sweep the organization off its feet. The government may pass legislation that the organization hadn't anticipated; technology may leapfrog current states of the art; customers and users may violently shift buying patterns or allegiances; competitors may take wholly new approaches to marketing. The organization has no tool or techniques in place to evaluate trends, and no senior manager is responsible for long-range forecasting or planning (or if one is responsible, nothing of import is ever generated). The organization is continually reactive, anxiously awaiting each new morning to see what obstacles and threats the environment produces. It considers itself successful when it has reacted well to current threats and has not suffered too much damage.

7: The organization is more uncertain than not about its future and its environment. It has learned some lessons from the past and uses some simple tools to help it determine what may lie ahead. However, the tools that do exist, internally or externally, are usually either unheeded by senior management or misinterpreted. The organization is basically reactive in nature and spends a considerable amount of time analyzing competitive actions, under the guise of competitive analysis, when it is actually scrambling to try to catch up. The organization may perform well in times of calm and stability, but it is consistently thrown from the horse whenever a change takes place, since virtually every change is unanticipated.

4: The future is consistently analyzed and evaluated. The organization utilizes internal tools, such as environmental scans, focus groups and surveys, and external tools, such as subscriptions to trend newsletters and participation in public hearings, to try to forecast its future. It can be sidetracked in this endeavor by short-term pressures and will sometimes sugar-coat the future by choosing the most favorable interpretation of events as the most likely one. But on the whole it is careful in its data gathering and gives significant attention to alternative futures. When changes do occur, the organization is better prepared then most, and it can often turn the change into opportunity because it was prepared for the particular eventuality.

1: This organization is future wise. It has in place mechanisms that enable it to keep its finger as close as possible to the pulse of its business and relationships. It has established a network of customers, suppliers, intermediaries, and others (i.e., congressmen, university professors, consultants) which it accesses on a regular basis to gather information about prospective events. Having done so, it uses its best management talent to synthesize the findings from disparate sources into knowledge about its unique direction and vision. It consistently recognizes trends (as compared to fads) and puts contingent plans into place to exploit them if they do develop. It doesn't just hear opportunity knocking; it continually hears the knock before others *and* is in a position to take advantage of it before others. Change is viewed as opportunity, not threat, and other organizations look to this one as the leader in adaptation and flexibility. This organization is bold and unafraid.

CT: Competitive Threat

10: This organization is in an industry in which competitive threat is endemically high. Low-margin organizations, such as supermarkets and retailers, fit this profile. It also includes organizations whose products or services are subject to peer pressures and in-crowd fluctuations, such as alcoholic beverages and clothing. They may be those that involve look-alike products in which a sudden differentiation creates uniqueness, as in the perceived value of oats in cereals or cholesterol in any number of foods. And they may be those in which sudden technological or scientific breakthroughs can predominate—pharmaceuticals or film in competition with each other or video rentals in competition with traditional movie theaters. (Note that, since this one category of competitive threat is not subject to strategy implementation abilities, there are no value judgments about where an organization fits. That is, some organizations are in worse competitive threat situations than others unavoidably, and that factor will always be higher in our equation. Note also that this rating can easily change over time as competitive pressures ease or intensify.)

7: This organization is on a healthy competitive battlefield. It is the printing franchise competing with other such franchises or the farm equipment manufacturer or the interstate bank. No unique customer loyalty is intrinsic to the business, and customers may switch allegiances no matter what the organization does or doesn't do. Competitive action is an important consideration in its strategic plans, and it must monitor the competition closely. It is probably best able to develop a particular clientele or buyer through the quality of its *relationships*, since its products and services are not sufficiently differentiated to accomplish that alone. Since those relationships must be constantly maintained and are a focus of competitive actions as well, the competitive battle tends to be ongoing and consistent.

4: Competition to the extent that it exists at all, tends to follow this organization. However, the name of the organization, its repute, and its relationships dictate its market position. Years ago, the metaphor that people used to portray excellence was, "It's the Cadillac of our line." Today, if someone used that example, the response might well be, "Well thanks anyway, but I'm looking for the Mercedes." These are organizations that have created significant *relationships* and have a "value-added" aspect that transcends actual worth. A Cross pen is the traditional symbol of an expensive, tasteful writing tool (the recent resurgence of high-tone fountain pens notwithstanding). Cross provides a lifetime guarantee, no questions asked. Most people set out to buy a Cross, not to buy a good pen with the intent of comparing Cross to Schaeffer or some other brand. (Ballpoint pens have withstood the assaults of rolling-ball markers and the resurgence of the fountain pen. Only some new technology, supplanting the ballpoint, would threaten Cross's position, assuming its quality standards and relationships don't change.) Rolex enjoys a comparable position in watches (although its competition is of a different sort: rip-offs), as does Hoffritz in cutlery, Boeing in aircraft, and Disney among theme parks.

1: This category is becoming more and more of an impossibility. It was best represented by the preregulation phone company and the postal service of 20 years ago. It may still apply to certain utilities. The Hunt Brothers tried to become part of it in the futile effort to corner the world's silver market. Some local enterprises might be in this position: the only hardware store in town, the only Ferrari dealer in the state, the sole Lithuanian restaurant in the area, the only hospital performing a given procedure on the West Coast. Yet even here, the local gas station is opening minimarts to compete with the hardware store, the Lithuanian restaurant is competing with other ethnic restaurants, and as for Ferraris and expensive hospital procedures, people tend to travel far and wide to satisfy themselves as prices escalate. (Anyone who can afford a Ferrari can afford to fly to New York—or to Italy—to get one. However, the repair and servicing would be competition-free, at least during the warranty period.)

What is the factor for the future organization? Is it better or worse than it was a year ago? Use the above criteria, and enter your results in figure 14.4.

$$FO = \frac{QM \times QE}{AU \times CT} \qquad FO = \frac{(\ ) \times (\ )}{(\ ) \times (\ )}$$

Figure 14.4

One could make the case that the single most pervasive event affecting the future of organizations is the supplanting of the importance of land, labor, and capital—the three historic sources of wealth and power—by information, a renewable resource.[2] As George Gilder so eloquently states the case:

> Wealth comes not to the rulers of slave labor but to the liberators of human creativity, not to the conquerors of land but to the emancipators of the mind. . . . The power of entrepreneurs using dispersed information technology grows far faster than the power of large institutions that attempt to bring information technology to heel. Rather than pushing decisions up through the hierarchy, the power of microelectronics pulls them remorselessly down to the individual. . . the world economy has clearly emerged as an intellectual system driven by knowledge.[3]

Information may be power, but there's information and information. In fact, there's a lot of information, but precious little of Mr. Gilder's knowledge, and the computer revolution generates information—or even more primitively, data—but not knowledge. Expert systems and artificial intelligence notwithstanding, knowledge, like Dorothy's scarecrow friend, requires a brain. Modern organizations are surrounded by data, aflood with data, immersed in data. Very little of it is relevant to any particular issue at hand. In fact, the critical need today, in marked departure from times past, is not to find scarce and invaluable data but rather to be able to expeditiously flush away the superfluous and retain the relevant. We suffer from too many data, a kind of organizational sensory overload. Paleontologists, historians, archaeologists—they may search for the rare missing piece of the puzzle. But managers already have the pieces. Their challenge is to separate them from everything else so that the pieces make a coherent whole.

By assembling data into related and supporting units, we're able to amass information. And that was thought to be good enough. But information is what's recorded in countless memoranda, policy statements, and ubiquitous three-ring binders. It's there and it's accurate, but it's useless unless it's applied at the right time to the right issue by the right people. Aha! This brings us to knowledge, as diagrammed in figure 14.5.

Knowledge is acquired information in usable, utilitarian form. Consequently, knowledge is usually in our heads, or at least at our fingertips. Knowledge is the ability to bridge the gap from the abstract to the tangible, to apply theory—information—to create a result. The auto mechanic has a datum when you tell him your car makes a pinging noise. He gets more data as you describe the conditions under which it occurs and how

---

[2]This is still a source of astonishment to many and the basis for current revelatory literature, but hardly a new prediction. See both *The Revolution around Us: Human Resource Development in the 80s*, by Alan Weiss, Princeton Research Monograph, Princeton, N.J., 1983, and *Microcosm: The Quantum Revolution in Economics and Technology*, by George Gilder, Simon and Schuster, New York, 1989.

[3]"The World's Next Source of Wealth," by George Gilder, *Fortune*, Aug. 28, 1989, pages 116, 120.

USING DATA TO ACHIEVE GOALS

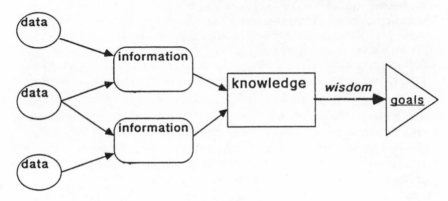

Figure 14.5

it does or doesn't affect the car's performance. He develops information from the data that tells him the noise occurs only at speeds over 50 miles per hour (you never hear it in the city, you do hear it on the highway—those are data). Then he applies his knowledge—a combination of experience and learning—which tells him that the only thing which varies with speed that can cause a noise from the passenger door are the window and door fittings.

Then the mechanic fixes the molding with a screwdriver and doesn't charge you anything, because his overriding business goal is not to make a $5 repair, but to have you as a steady customer, especially since you have your choice of auto repair services to patronize.

You see, even knowledge isn't enough. Wisdom is the application of knowledge toward the end goals of the enterprise—toward the vision of the business. A doctor records symptoms and complaints—data—and formulates patterns—information. He combines this information with his own regarding indications and remedies and, with this knowledge, prescribes treatment. However, the outstanding doctors look to the longer term: What does the treatment imply, given the patient's overall health picture, age, occupation, and so on?

Where do these examples come from? Look around you. Who is successful and who isn't? My eye doctor wouldn't prescribe contact lenses for me until he made sure I understood the increased trouble I'd have reading with them as I progressed into my 40s, and he deliberately didn't use the strongest possible prescription for distance so as to maintain the best reading results. (He knows that my job and avocations involve a great deal of reading during times when I'd also have to be wearing the contacts.) I acquired my auto mechanic when I tried to have a bulb replaced in an expensive foreign car and no one wanted to take the time to do it (or even look up the part number) without an appointment. He took 10 minutes to replace it at no charge. Then he showed me around the shop while pointing out its advantages (pickup and delivery, the latest diagnostics, the ability to handle any foreign car). He didn't even know I had an even more exotic car at home! To date, I've spent tens of thousands at his shop. It's easy to say that he was smart to do the original job for free. I like to think that he's a very wise man. He didn't stop with knowledge or with a good deed. He took action to meet longer-term business goals, and that takes wisdom.

So, too, does wisdom have to be applied by managers in their business environments. It's one thing to take a survey or establish focus groups or talk to employees and customers. That gets you data (as does management by wandering around.) It's another to compile the data into information and yet another to build it into knowledge. The sequence can look like this:

Data	Information	Knowledge	Wisdom
Customer complaints	The customer service department is experiencing problems that require remedial action.	We have changed supervisors in that unit three times during the last year, and we must provide for more stability and continuity.	In the future, our succession planning must be coordinated with the needs of line units.
Morale problems			
Late reports			

The future of organizations will be dependent on the wisdom of line management to consistently apply knowledge to organizational issues in concert with the strategic vision of the organization. When people remark, "That was a wise move," they mean it in the sense of its contribution to the overall scheme of things. In the shorter term it may have been a smart move, an enlightened move, or even a brilliant move, but "wise" must meet the test of time. That is why we've differentiated between the training and education of managers and of all employees. People can be trained to deal with data and use information, but they have to be educated to apply information knowledgeably. They need an understanding of contexts broader than those of their immediate responsibilities. That can be had only by interaction with senior management. You see, the future of organizations is not in George Gilder's microcosm or in the technology of superconductivity in new markets in Eastern Europe after the fall of the Iron Curtain. The future of organizations is in the people within organizations.

Formulating strategy is not, in and of itself, an extraordinarily difficult task. In fact, I've been in many strategic sessions in which the participants were asked to map out alternative futures for the organization and did so with admirable zeal and ability. It seemed—and I'd be willing to bet—that several of the strategies could have been adopted. (The notion that there is one unique strategy ideally suited for an organization is somewhat akin to the mythic belief that for each of us there is one ideal person we are meant to marry and that we somehow find these persons—often next door, amazingly—in a world of four billion people. Perhaps that's why the divorce rate is so high—and why the failure of strategies is so high.) The tough part is the implementation, no matter what high road has been decided on. And the sad fact is that in most cases, implementation doesn't succeed. Oh, it might get closer in some instances than in others, but if success is measured by realizing the future that the formulation process has created, then implementation fails more than it succeeds.

The irony, of course, is that the failure to implement is not the fault of the *implementors* as they are conventionally recognized. The great preponderance of middle management and the rest of the organization would be all too happy to work toward implementing a strategy if they were given the proper leadership to do so. But people are distrusting their leadership more and more, and small wonder that they are. Strategy is being successfully formulated, but there is no leadership for its implementation.

There is an analogy that I've never been able to rid myself of. It's like a recurring nightmare, although it's a true—and, at first glance, unrelated—story. Many years ago, Notre Dame was playing Michigan for the mythical national collegiate football championship. It had been determined by the sportswriters, or polls, or tarot cards—whatever strange mechanisms that choose "champions" in a competition in which most top teams never play each other—that the winner of this final game of the season would reign as national champs. However, because of the comparative records, schedules, and phases of the moon, a tie would mean that Notre Dame would be the champ. Michigan needed a win, Notre Dame a win or a tie.

As the fates dictate these things, the game was tied with 2 minutes left to play. Notre Dame's defense held Michigan, which had to punt. And then the nightmare began. In possession of the ball with 2 minutes left—an eternity in football, which has more ways to stop a clock than television has commercials—Notre Dame coach Ara Parshegian instructed his team to "sit on the ball." That's right, with 2 minutes left, they ran a series of conservative plays to run out the clock to preserve a tie! Now, as you might expect, the Michigan fans were pretty upset. But of even more interest, the Notre Dame fans didn't seem too happy, either. The players themselves showed signs of frustration.

Parshegian said later that "his boys had worked too hard all year to be denied the national championship" in the event a final drive produced a turnover that led to a Michigan score. In other words, he didn't trust his players enough to believe that they wouldn't make an error if they tried to win the game (or if they did make an error, they couldn't recover from it). So he "won" a national "championship" by "achieving" a tie. Join me, if you will, in considering the kind of message that was sent to his team and to those aspiring to play for Notre Dame someday. Playing your best to win doesn't count, but playing the odds to preserve an unofficial status does. Don't trust yourself to play hard and intelligently to achieve your goal without qualification and without reservation, because you might just blow it, even if it's only a game.

What of that team's seniors, about to go out into the world to face much tougher opponents, sooner or later, than Michigan's defense? Is the valuable lesson they learned from their college athletic field to always play it safe? Is timidity the better part of valor? After all, Parshegian was hailed as an excellent coach, and he went on to be a television sportscaster and commentator. Isn't life really about protecting and conserving and playing it safe—and ignoring the critics who call for bold action as reckless adventures?

I've never understood Parshegian's ghastly decision or the university's quiet acceptance of it, either in terms of a love of the game or in terms of a philosophic position. The nightmare aspect is that it seems to permeate senior management's intent to preserve and protect. Strategies themselves can be bold and dashing, because they exist only on paper and in people's minds. When they begin to become tangible—the implementation process—the boldness and dash tend to disappear as management is called upon to commit their energy, time, and resources.

How visible is this to the inhabitants of organizations? Well, a recent article contains this nugget: "People below the acme of the corporate pyramid trust those on top just about as far as they can throw a Gulfstream IV [executive jet] with shower."[4]

A survey by the Hay Group[5] found that employees are feeling increasingly unlistened to and uncommunicated with and are responding in kind. It identifies a "fraternity of skeptics" that forms below vice presidential level and is sparked by increasing inconsistencies between what management says and what management does. "We respect innovation and creativity" doesn't carry a lot of credibility weight when employees who do take risks and suffer setbacks are summarily fired. Yet the kind of communication that employees are seeking is damningly simple, and pertinent to our topic: "When the Hay Group asked what kind of information workers wanted more of from top management, the troops checked 'reliable information on where the company is headed' and 'how my job fits into the total.' "[6]

Unless senior management makes a determined effort to involve the total employee work force in the nature and direction of the business, that fraternity of skeptics will grow into an army of cynics. The strategy implementation process gives management the ideal tool with which to achieve this involvement, and it has a dual benefit:

---

[4]"The Trust Gap," by Alan Farnham, *Fortune,* Dec. 4, 1989, page 56.
[5]Ibid., page 58.
[6]Ibid., page 58.

1. Employees are kept intimately involved with the business and with senior management's intentions.
2. Employees become an integral part of the process to implement the strategy and achieve the future vision of the company.

The tool is there, and the need is there. Yet top management consistently alienates the very people it needs to recruit as allies. That's why we've stated with such assurance that, life cycles and Japanese competition and complex technology aside, the reason for most business failure is simply stupid management. And that stupidity is tolerated much too long by the board and by the stockholders (and, usually, by the employees, who have more recourse than they generally believe).

The future of organizations will be bleak if this involvement is not stimulated and nurtured, because the alternative is a growing number of managers, technicians, and professionals joining the ranks of the historically most alienated group of workers of all—the hourly employees. This is hardly far-fetched. Airline pilots—highly trained and educated, often making a six-figure income—have formed militant blue-collar unions that have been in terrible conflict with management at United, Eastern, Continental, and other carriers. This is akin to the research staff at IBM or the legal department at AT&T or the general managers at Procter & Gamble walking out the door in a labor dispute. What's that, you say, professionals don't act that way? Tell that to the Eastern pilot who's lost his house or the Eastern shareholder who's lost his shirt.

And consider the position of teachers in the United States. I can't readily think of a professional group that has so deliberately adopted such a militant, hourly mentality toward management—in this case, usually the school's administration, boards, and/or municipal officials. The result is a public education morass that might require two generations of unprecedented cooperation to escape. By anyone's standards, our public school education is inferior to most of its counterparts in the industrialized West (and, often, beyond), our inner-city schools are unmitigated disasters that barely keep kids off the streets, and our teachers are underpaid and underappreciated. The average American probably invests much greater care in assessing the choice of a doctor for family health, a lawyer for family legal affairs, or an accountant for family financial matters than he or she does a teacher for family education. We'll trust our kids' future to people more easily than we'd trust this year's tax returns or the sales of our homes.

Don't misunderstand; the teachers and their unions have not created the problem, but they have certainly poured the cement on it. It's not our intent here to detail the history of educational inadequacies in this country, but we do want to establish a key parallel. *Once a breakdown in communication and involvement occurs, the more disaffected that employees* at all levels *become, the more difficult subsequent communication becomes, despite the best of intentions.* Trust is not a renewable resource. It can be used up. At this writing, Eastern pilots are crossing picket lines to return to jobs that they can only hope still await them, the air traffic controllers original union (PATCO) is only a memory of a bluff that shouldn't have been called, and "illegal" teachers' strikes still spring up like wildflowers in the spring. The organizations—Eastern Airlines, the air traffic control system, the schools—are the worse for it, as are the participants. *It doesn't even matter who was originally "wrong." Everyone loses.*

The same holds true for organizations. Once communication stops—or is suspect—it takes an inordinate amount of energy to turn things around again. Trust may be the most difficult privilege to reclaim in the world. And we've seen countless organizations in which trust is gone, communication is worthless, and the sincerest moves by management are scoffed at. Strategy could no more be successfully implemented in such environments than a snowball could survive on a street corner in San Antonio. Conditions simply prohibit it.

The future of organizations will be a grim one if there are only two classes of people in them: the ruling elite and the disaffected masses (i.e., everyone who isn't a member of the ruling elite). Have you ever heard a senior manager make an untoward remark about his or her superiors? Or a vice president demean the actions of the CEO in public? Those are not rare occurrences, and although they may occasionally be the result of a bad day or personal feud, they are often the venting of a disaffected individual, no matter what the title.

The rosiest future for organizations will occur when and if senior managers remain in touch with employees at all levels. That will enable them to understand motivating influences, current needs, and future desires. I'm convinced that many executives still harbor the belief that most employees are concerned first and foremost about job security, but my observations and our work would indicate that such issues as communications, consistent leadership, involvement, empowerment, and self-esteem are more important. In yet another example of somewhat misplaced priorities, organizations large and small will audit their finances, review their patents and copyrights, and even assess the physical well-being of their people. But they tend to invest precious little in evaluating the psychological temperature of their employees: expectations, needs, and perceptions. (As long as you help people stay fit with health clubs and preventive medicine, you're doing nothing more than you'd do for any asset: making sure that it stays in peak operating condition, just as you would a postage meter or a lathe. But once you ask for feedback, you're creating an interactive process that is much more difficult to control.) Inevitably, when we are asked to conduct internal surveys for organizations, someone will nervously state, "Surely, you're not going to ask him *that!*" And when we respond, "If you want to find out about *this,* then you must ask them *that,*" there's a debate that includes, "Then perhaps we don't want to know about *this.*"

Lest you feel we're painting some great togetherness for future organizations, no one believes that organizations should be happy families that never quarrel or disagree. Far from it, because confrontation and conflict create some of the best sources of new ideas, innovation, and progress for any enterprise. And one can always point to autocracies and dictatorships that are doing very well, thank you very much. (Periodically, *Fortune* publishes a perverse piece about "America's toughest bosses," as though anyone really cares. Many of these reputed SOBs are running highly successful businesses.) The question is, however, how much better can *any* organization do if it isn't encumbered and slowed by the friction of class warfare?

The bottom line is irrelevant, because I'm not talking about the difference between making a profit and not making one or between reaching our goals or not reaching them. I'm talking about the ability of any organization to perform better in the absence of class conflict than in the presence of it. And I've refrained from pontificating about the ethical implications or the erosion of values. The pragmatics speak for themselves. Organizations in which senior management has insulated itself from everyone else will not be able to implement their strategies and, therefore, realize their futures. Senior people won't receive the information or cooperation that they need, and that is the end of that particular equation.

There are signs of such potential caste systems that can be observed and evaluated in the present. (And this would be a key component of the Quality of Management—QM—factor we used above.) An elitist, class-conscious management retains all valuable perks in good times and bad and inflicts pain on subordinates when times are bad and budgets must be cut. Lip service without action is another dead giveaway. ("Every employee survey says that communication is lousy, and they always publish the feedback and thank us for our candor, as if that takes care of the issue.") There is open bickering among a variety of hierarchical levels below the elite class.

The opposite of this is "walking the talk." Open-door policies seldom result in endless streams of employees usurping all of senior management's waking hours. Just knowing that the offer is real and that some colleagues have occasionally used the open door is generally enough to prove one's intent. The act of communicating is, after all, fairly simple. The volition to do so is the hard part. In a survey conducted by the consulting firm of Foster Higgins it was found that although "97 percent of the CEOs it surveyed believe communicating with employees has a positive impact on job satisfaction, and 79 percent think it benefits the bottom line, only 22 percent actually do it weekly or more often."[7]

Organizations that get the full measure of devotion from their people are those that give their people respect and attention. It's not a question of health clubs, or gyms, or sales contests, or protected parking spaces, although those are nice gestures which certainly don't hurt. The future of organizations will depend upon management's capacity to work with their own people, to communicate, and to listen. That is hardly the stuff

---

[7]Ibid., page 70.

of post-doctorate study in behavior, or even of current MBA rituals. It is the stuff of common sense and caring. We have enough "numbers people" to fill the Federal Reserve vaults. What we need is "people people." I don't find it amusing or superficial or gimmicky, for example, when the CEO of Hyatt Hotels works as a doorman or the officers of Southwest Airlines work as ticket agents or the management of McDonald's flips hamburgers. That is the best way I know to stay in touch with people, to experience what they experience, and to test strategy implementation plans in the environment in which they will have to take root. (Would so many miners have died of black lung disease, so many meat cutters have suffered from carpal tunnel syndrome, so many people in a variety of occupations have endured what they have if the top people ever spent time in the trenches? Indeed, would the Wall Street swindles and manipulations have reached the level they have if a CEO had said once or twice, "Let's see what's really going on"?)

Even the military has come to understand that sheer weight of numbers and weaponry isn't always enough, that God is not always on the side of the heaviest battalions, despite Voltaire's admonition to the contrary. Defense Intelligence Agency analysts have had trouble understanding, after evaluating recent conflicts such as the Iraq-Iran war "that sometimes the outcome of a battle depends upon intangibles like morale more than it does upon weapons and firepower."[8]

The future of organizations depends upon the synergistic involvement of all people in the enterprise. The ability to implement strategy is first and foremost a *leadership* function that senior management must fulfill. Formulating the strategy is not enough and, in fact, is a worthless expenditure of time and effort if the bridge to implementation is not created. The organization as a whole must be responsible for implementation led by a management that is open and responsible and that exemplifies the implementation itself.

I'd like to conclude with a live example of how this process can proceed. I asked a client to develop a vision statement, that is, how the organization should look as a result of implementing current strategy (which is known and understood). The top people in the unit—which is responsible for management education and development for a large financial institution—put together this vision:

- To care if we make our clients' lives easier, their expenses smaller, and their profits bigger.
- To be credible in the eyes of our clients.
- To commit to excellence as a department in developing programs and services.
- To appreciate and acknowledge individual contributions in our quest for excellence.

---

[8]"Civil War's Fields Are Intelligence Classrooms," by Bernard E. Trainor, *The New York Times*, Nov. 19, 1989, page 37.

- To be willing to communicate openly and honestly without fear of consequence.
- To understand and support the mission and strategy of the bank.
- To promote creativity in the context of cost-effectiveness and productivity.
- To maximize the professional and personal growth of each other and our clients.
- To value and respect each other for our personal beliefs and professional strengths.

What is your advice to these senior managers? Is this a good vision statement? Does it constitute the basis for the employees' effectively implementing a strategy, no matter what that strategy happens to be? What are its strengths and weaknesses? How does it compare to your efforts in encouraging people to see the future of the organization and their role in it?

In our joint discussions and open debate, we concluded that the statements were an admixture of beliefs, values, vision, hopes, and intentions. We formulated some basic rules for creating the vision statement:

1. It had to describe *what* the unit would be doing (strategy) as well as *how* it would be doing it (tactics) so that everyone could understand his or her role in those two dimensions.
2. It had to result in tangible performance, in terms of products, services, and/or relationships for the unit's internal customers.
3. It had to provide a measure against which anyone could compare current practices, at any given time, and assess progress and performance.
4. It had to have everyone's buy-in and commitment.

After we tested the statements against these criteria, and after a wonderful, sometimes heated, debate, we emerged with this modified list:

We are an organization that:

- Improves our clients' business performance through targeted management education and consulting interventions.
- Consistently develops interventions in anticipation of client need through ongoing interactions with the client.
- Encourages, rewards, and exploits individual initiative and innovation.
- Exemplifies the best of the leadership, communication, and related skills that we develop for our clients by practicing them among ourselves and assessing our use of them.
- Supports and helps attain the bank's mission by orienting our interventions toward achieving specific, tangible business goals as detailed in the strategy statement.

That isn't a "perfect" vision statement; it is merely one that everyone involved felt described the organization they wanted to be a part of in the future. There are still some ambiguities and uncertainties, but the statements accurately reflect what people expect and are seeking to work toward. Most important, it is a *joint* effort. Senior managers might have created a "better" fit with the organization's strategy, and they certainly could have accomplished it with less time and bother. But the statements are those of the group, and every employee has contributed his or her views. Management's job isn't to create some perfect fit, but to create a fit that *works* to support the strategy's implementation while respecting employees' positions and expectations.

Our position from the outset has been that strategy formulation is a natural focal point for senior management attention. It is worldly, long-range, and exalted, and it seems to justify the involvement of the big-bucks folks. It is also esoteric and abstract, and it has refuges—the matrices and models that academicians and consultants can provide for management to hide among, a kind of dungeons-and-dragons game for executives. That is the easy stuff. The real mettle of executives is tested when it's time to make strategy happen, otherwise known as implementation. And there are no convoluted models, no magic potions to ensure successful strategy implementation, because it must be done in the very real world of employees and competitors and crises and change. That is where the rubber hits the road. That is where push comes to shove. And that is where gold is often turned into lead.

The key to successful strategy implementation is in top management taking the leading role in *becoming* implementors themselves and thereby setting the standard for all employees to become implementors. I've tried to suggest various skills, behaviors, and techniques that can aid in that endeavor. None is guaranteed, because it is one of those areas in which management is much more art than science. Consequently, the manager is called upon to be not a technician, but a leader.

The greatest irony of all, perhaps, is that applying the organization's talents and resources toward effective strategy implementation is such a win-win situation. The organization's top management needs to stay in touch with its people if it is to acquire the intelligence necessary to plot a correct course for the future. In so doing, it can automatically involve people in the strategy implementation process. And in doing that, it creates a dynamic in which employees are much more likely to feel involved, to be listened to, and to contribute in such a way as to maximize the chances that the strategy will be realized.

A CEO in the retail industry once complained to me that his vision wasn't really accepted by his people and that the organization seemed to set its own course, despite his best efforts.

"Have you tried communicating with people, expressing your frustration and your intent," I asked.

"I publish an article in every issue of the house organ," he explained, "and we put out periodic updates in management memos."

"Yes, but have you personally talked to employees?"

"You mean like address them at the annual report on the industry?"

"I mean like talk to them in the halls, or invite them to sit in on meetings, or convene focus groups, or sit in the cafeteria."

"My God, what would my executives think?! If I talked directly to their people, I'd threaten the hell out of them!"

"I take it that they don't just talk to anyone either?"

"What you're suggesting isn't done here, and couldn't be done here."

What I was suggesting, of course, *wouldn't* be done there because the person who was really threatened was the CEO. After all, he hadn't worked hard for all those years to be placed in a position in which he was called upon to be *responsive*. Yet wasn't that the very thing he was complaining about—his people weren't responsive to his vision?

The future of our organizations is dependent upon our ability to implement our strategies—to achieve our visions of the future. And that is dependent upon our ability to utilize the single greatest resource that any organization possesses: the talents and abilities of its people. The ancient alchemists tried to turn lead into gold by mixing exotic components and intoning ritual incantations. The modern manager has succeeded in turning gold into lead by ignoring the most valuable of the organization's components and relying on ritual phrases.

There is gold in all of our organizations, in our ability to define our own destinies and our own contributions to our environment. The mining is a lot easier when all of the organization's people are searching for it together. Even at the rate of one golden pebble at a time, the more people engaged in the pursuit, the greater the reward for everyone concerned. How well are you mobilizing your people to pursue a common future?

Bibliography

There simply is no body of work devoted to the implementation of strategy. The works listed below were chosen because they focus on the preceding task of strategy formulation and/or on the specific talents that managers need to implement strategy successfully. I've opted to be highly selective and present a few good sources, regardless of age. You could do a lot worse than to make this a priority reading list.

Bennis, Warren: *The Unconscious Conspiracy: Why Leaders Can't Lead*, AMACOM, New York, 1976, 176 pp.
  Still Bennis's best work, this provides an excellent discussion of difficulties in implementing the best-laid plans. In this case, Bennis the academic was asked to preside over a major university, which provided him with some unexpected difficulties and the reader with firsthand advice.

Bennis, Warren, and Bert Nanus: *Leaders: The Strategies for Taking Charge*, Harper & Row, New York, 1985, 235 pp.
  This is a solid effort at describing leadership as a learnable skill based on a series of interviews and observations with an eclectic selection. It's an honest attempt to find the competencies underlying leadership through objective observation. The authors' later, updated version of essentially the same work is unnecessary.

Drucker, Peter F.: *Managing in Turbulent Times*, Harper & Row, New York, 1980, 239 pp.
  One of the master's best, this book is a valuable contribution to anticipating and managing change and thereby successfully implementing strategies and plans consistently.

Fink, Steven: *Crisis Management: Planning for the Inevitable*, AMACOM, New York, 1986, 245 pp.
  This is a somewhat dry but comprehensive treatment of what crisis is and how management should prepare for and/or react to it. Its use of actual business crises is helpful, though crises occur so rapidly in real life that some of the illustrations seem tepid by comparison.

Fox, Joseph M.: *Executive Qualities*, Addison-Wesley, Reading, Mass., 1976, 256 pp.
  Using corporate examples, Fox describes the attributes he thinks make for the ideal executive. This is a thought-provoking book that provides the opportunity for tough assessment of whether or not the abilities and talents to successfully implement strategy are present.

Robert, Michel: *The Strategist CEO: How Visionary Executives Build Organizations,* Quorum, Westport, Conn., 1988, 140 pp.

Although using a methodology similar to that of the Tregoe book below, Robert emphasizes the role of the CEO as "chief strategist," based on his personal strategy sessions with major corporations around the world. Again, the emphasis is on the formulation of the strategy—the "business concept"—and not on the implementation.

Robert, Michel, and Alan Weiss: *The Innovation Formula: How Organizations Turn Change into Opportunity,* Harper & Row/Ballinger, New York, 1988, 124 pp.

A work on the specifics of innovation, including the processes used in innovative organizations to stimulate and foster entrepreneurship within management. The techniques are based on the authors' work with hundreds of firms in introducing practical innovative techniques.

Tregoe, Benjamin B., and John W. Zimmerman: *Top Management Strategy: What It Is and How It Works,* Simon and Schuster, New York, 1980, 128 pp.

A classic book on a simple and direct technique of strategy formulation. The authors have helped to set strategy among scores of large and small organizations. It's also instructive in its omission of specifics on implementation and monitoring. Their 1989 work *Vision in Action* (with Ron Smith and Peter Tobia) is a superfluous and unnecessary "follow-up."

Weiss, Alan: *Managing for Peak Performance: A Guide to the Power (and Pitfalls) of Personal Style,* Harper & Row, New York, 1989, 177 pp.

Specific discussions and examples of the behavioral attributes that comprise success in a variety of management settings and how to tell if they are present. The book includes a variety of self-assessment profiles, exercises, and evaluations.

Index

Abdication of leadership, 242–44
Academy of Motion Picture Arts and Sciences, 172
Accountability, 11
Acura (Honda), 10
Advertising: automobile industry, 9–10; soft drink industry, 79. *See also* Publicity
Advice, 187
Aetna, 186
Air traffic controllers, 267
Airline companies, 266; strategic fit, 128–31
Alcoholics Anonymous, 184
Alliance building, 167–81; alternatives to alliances, 178–79; communication, 172–73; constructive alliance, 181; cooperation, 175; durational alliances, 177; exploitation of success, 173; forced alliances, 177; growth and, 179–81; information, assessment, 178–79; management and, 175, 179; poor alliance, 180; problem-solving, 175; products, assessment, 178; publicity, 175–76; relationships, assessment, 178; services, assessment, 178; steps necessary, 171–76; strategy sharing, 172; threat, recognition, 173; trust, 171, 174; voluntary alliances, 177. *See also* Relationships in the marketplace
Alltel, 10
Alston, Walter, 247
American Airlines, 3, 98, 101, 113, 121, 125
American Cancer Society, 184
American Express, 32, 101, 116, 117, 121, 123, 140, 221, 236
American Management Association, 186
American Medical Association, 172, 183
American Philatelic Society, 184
American Press Institute, 152, 172, 177, 184

American Society for the Prevention of Cruelty to Animals (ASPCA), 184
American Telephone & Telegraph (AT&T), 22–23, 218, 266
Amtrak, 176
Apple Computer, 62, 175, 217
Aramony, William, 183
Arkwright Mutual Insurance, 10
Arm & Hammer, 103, 140
Atlantic Electric, 57
AT&T. *See* American Telephone & Telegraph
Attitudes: of employees, 257; as obstacles to strategy, 31; positive mental, 228; strategy and, 12–13
Audi, 20, 22, 198
Autocratic style of leadership, 55
Automobile industry, 3, 168, 235. *See also* specific automobiles

Bakker, Jim and Tammy, 116
Bally, 224
Banc One Corporation, 32
Bank of America, 32
Bay Area Rapid Transit System (San Francisco), 204
Bechtel, 203
Behavior, strategy and, 12–13, 31
Behavior modification, 31–32
Belief systems: core beliefs of organization, 156, 162; obstacles to strategy, 29–32
Bell Labs, 114
Bennis, Warren, 228, 229
Berlin Wall, 251
Bhopal disaster, 20, 198
Bigotry: nonprofit organizations, 188–89
Bitberg, Germany: Reagan's visit to, 213
Blanchard, K. H., 228
Bloomingdale's, 4, 33, 140
BMW, 113, 224
Boeing, 3, 107, 260
Bonwit Teller, 4, 33